W9-BKY-525

One Day in the Life of the English Language

One Day in the Life of the English Language

A Microcosmic Usage Handbook

Frank L. Cioffi

Princeton University Press
Princeton & Oxford

Copyright © 2015 by Princeton University Press

Published by Princeton University Press
41 William Street, Princeton, New Jersey 08540
In the United Kingdom: Princeton University Press
6 Oxford Street, Woodstock, Oxfordshire OX20 1TW

press.princeton.edu

All Rights Reserved

Library of Congress Cataloging-in-Publication Data

Cioffi, Frank L., 1951–
    One day in the life of the English language : a microcosmic
usage handbook / Frank L. Cioffi.
        p. cm
    Includes bibliographical references and index.
    ISBN 978-0-691-16507-3 (hardcover : alk. paper) 1. English
language—Usage—Handbooks, manuals, etc. 2. English language—
Grammar—Handbooks, manuals, etc. 3. English language—
Rhetoric—Handbooks, manuals, etc. I. Title.
    PE1460.C47 2015
    428.2—dc23
        2014024276

British Library Cataloging-in-Publication Data is available

This book has been composed in Sabon Next LT Pro and
ITC Franklin Gothic Std

Printed on acid-free paper. ∞

Printed in the United States of America

10 9 8 7 6 5 4 3 2 1

IN MEMORIAM

_____

Frank Salvatore Cioffi
Teacher, Philosopher, Uncle
(1928–2012)

Contents

Preface

Grammar handbook. The words provoke dismay and revulsion in the hearts of millions. The proverbial ugly duckling of textbooks, the grammar handbook might well be the most dreaded yet least read or consulted book people own.

But this grammar handbook strives to be different. I want you to actually read it—and maybe even to enjoy it. Like other handbooks, it outlines, in an abbreviated form, a standard grammar of formal English. At the same time, it argues that learning and using such a grammar actually matters. The book's six central chapters—covering the parts of speech, punctuation, and diction—briefly present various aspects of sentence morphology and syntax: "morphology" being the forms of words; and "syntax," the place or order of words within sentences. (This sounds like technical language, I know. From now on I'll avoid such lingo as much as possible.)

I want to make grammatical issues vital and immediate by debunking some standard "rules." Is it acceptable to end a sentence with a preposition? Yes. Is it "correct" to use split infinitives? To boldly do so is fine. Start a sentence with a conjunction? Sure. How about a plural pronoun used to refer to a singular entity? Not yet, but soon, soon.

At the same time, I want to reinforce some of the precepts of Standard Written English that still count, that make language, and the language-user—the "you" of this book—more communicative, more effectual. I argue for an ethics to language use: people consciously use language too often to hide what they really mean, or their slovenly use of it hides or distorts their meaning, or for some reason they are ignored when it's vital they be recognized: well, this just mucks things up in general. People get misunderstood, time gets wasted, vital information gets lost. Being more attentive to how we speak, how we write, and how we evaluate others' language use will help us gradually create a culture altogether more honest, ethical, and functional—one in which more people will understand what others mean, or at least one in which it becomes common practice to strive to figure out what they mean. In short, we need to up the ante in our use of language. We need to make precision of expression more important and crucial, more of a desideratum than it is right now.

Big goals? Yes. But I believe that usage matters quite a lot. I offer two main reasons it does, and I will invoke these several times. First, poor or incorrect usage often blocks communication. For example, sometimes writing lacks clarity or specificity, its message so muddled as to be incomprehensible. A significant subset of unclear language even inadvertently invokes what I term an "absurd universe." This kind of language, which usually contains an ambiguity or an unfortunate phrasing, fails to clearly communicate its message because the reader, attempting to parse the sentence and understand its message, finds him-

or herself suddenly thrust into some preposterous alternative universe where things just don't make any sense. This brief, linguistic abduction can be unsettling. The reader soon comes back to our own universe, it's true, but with less confidence in the writer or message conveyed. Here's a classic example: "With a husband and five children, her washing machine was always running." Is this a universe where washing machines are married with children? "Her great loves were cooking her family and her friends" is perhaps even worse: the absence of the commas turns an ordinary sentence into one about cannibalism. Of course most readers know soon enough that it isn't really a sentence about cannibalism. But it is for a brief moment, and in that moment, something is lost.

I'd also avoid sentences that don't evoke the absurd universe but trick the reader into parsing them in one way and then shift contexts so that the initial parsing doesn't make sense. Termed "Garden Path Sentences," these include ones like "The old man the boat" or "The cotton clothing is made from grows in Mississippi" (Dalgish, "Garden"). Expository prose should probably not displace, alienate, or trick its readers, at least not through its sentence construction.

Standard or "correct" usage also matters because its absence or apparent flouting often stigmatizes the speaker or writer, thus undermining the writer's authority or character and diminishing the value of any message. People hear errors or linguistic anomalies and stop listening because they see such imperfect language as indicative of the speaker's (or writer's) unreliability or unimportance as a thinker or as a narrator of events.

In short, correct usage might not have absolute, eternal truth value—English continuously evolves, and expert opinion about it frequently changes—but even if you are not convinced about the ethics of clear language use, you'll probably have to admit that standard usage does have significant practical value insofar as it helps you communicate what you want to communicate.

I try to make this handbook relevant, timely, and maybe less ugly duckling–ish by using example sentences drawn directly from already-published material: "real-world" and actual, these are not merely contrived to illustrate a grammatical precept. I narrow this sampling down to material that was published on a single, typical day (the "One Day" of my title): December 29, 2008. Using newspapers and magazines with this date, I have culled examples both of misusages and of distinctive, complex, correct language, so that with some three hundred example sentences at its core, the book outlines the fundamentals of the way sentences are put together in English at the same time that it provides examples of common pratfalls and confusions. In addition, perhaps adventitiously, the book offers a linguistic, microcosmic "snapshot" of a single day all of its readers have lived through.

Throughout, I also discuss many complexities of Standard Written English that are in dispute (e.g., pronoun gender issues, or the aforementioned kinds of dogmatic "rules" people were taught—many by the beloved-but-flawed *Elements of Style* by Strunk and White). In fact, I stress that linguists hotly debate many issues of usage, style, and "correctness," and that many of these issues also provoke controversy in a wider public arena. Recently, even Weird Al Yankovic jumped into the fray, with a music video called "Word Crimes." It was immediately criticized by— and also drew praise from—a writer for *Slate*, and another for the *Daily Beast*. As I said, these issues stir people up.

Almost all of the example sentences in this book were generated by professional writers and vetted by at least one editor. Thus these sentences, many of which I find inadequate or in need of revision, have already passed editorial scrutiny. Why might that be? It's not just that everyone's working to a tight deadline (though that certainly does figure in). Something else is going on. I'm not sure what. But by examining contemporary language now, in what I label "The Epoch of the Post-Original," a time of significant language change sparked by the Internet, by digital media, and by the increasing globalization of English, I want to initiate, along with you, the reader, a joint exploration of some of the contemporary flashpoints in English language studies. I'm not simply proclaiming about grammar and usage, "This is how it is; learn it," but rather "What does this 'nonstandard' usage suggest?" or "Why is language going in this direction?" and "What is the best usage in a given rhetorical situation?" At the same time, I do come down on the side of tradition and fundamentally advocate for a fairly standard variant of English. So what I am offering here should be continuous if not quite congruent with what you've been taught.

I round out the book with a pair of appendixes—one on how grammar, correctness, and the like have come to be envisioned in the digital age, and the second on how to use this book in a class requiring the writing of essays—followed by a short glossary of technical terms.

I have dedicated this work to the memory of my uncle, Frank Salvatore Cioffi, whose philosophical writings and conversations inspired me, from a very young age, to go into academia and to become a writer. His ideas permeate this work in more ways than I can enumerate. He was always eager to talk about language, usage, grammar, even punctuation. He always had stunning insights that he delivered with precision and clarity. He liked this book, which he referred to—nondisparagingly, I should add—as my "book about commas." He was a teacher, a writer, and a thinker whose discourse will be greatly missed by his family, his friends, his readers, and his many students—from Oxford, Singapore, Canterbury, Berkeley, and Essex.

To write a work such as this is to incur a myriad of debts. First thanks go to my students, especially my graduate students at the Graduate Center–CUNY. I also thank Baruch College–CUNY, which awarded me a generous research grant during the writing of this book. In particular, I want to thank my colleagues at Baruch, including Gerry Dalgish, Ellen Block, Corey David Mead, and Jessica Lang, all of whom read the manuscript and offered opinions and ideas as well as encouragement. Dennis Slavin, Jeffrey Peck, and John Brenkman were helpful and supportive in this project: to them, I also extend my gratitude. I especially thank Peter Gruen, of the College of New Jersey, for his detailed reading and thoughtful suggestions—and for his listening to my near-endless prattling about grammar issues during our regular meetings at Eeentzy Eearth Café. And to Beata Williamson, who offered encouragement and suggestions, via email from the University of Gdańsk, I also extend warm thanks.

To the editors at Princeton University Press—Anne Savarese, Beth Clevenger, and Lauren Lepow, many thanks. Lauren's editing of this book was nothing short of amazing. And to Peter J. Dougherty, I owe a debt of gratitude. I especially appreciate Peter's help: he believed in this book and its 2005 companion volume, *The Imaginative Argument*, and helped shepherd them both to completion. The anonymous readers of this manuscript also deserve thanks, particularly for the care they took offering suggestions for improvements, almost all of which I took.

My greatest debt is to Kathleen M. Cioffi, my wife and companion of many decades and, I hope, of many more to come—someone whose sense of language is subtle and extraordinary, and who gave me support, insights, and patient critique. She would probably only respond to my thanks with a phrase that one of our Polish friends would often use: "Not for thank you." Well, thank you anyway.

Navigation Tips

? questionable usage

✳ nonstandard usage

bold type is used to identify terms that are included in the glossary, "Fifty Key Terms"

One Day in the Life of the English Language

Introduction

The Starting Idea: You and Your Audience

At one point in *Alice in Wonderland*, Alice finds herself at a tea party presided over by the Mad Hatter, and, after a particularly confusing remark of the Hatter's, she

> felt dreadfully puzzled. The Hatter's remark seemed to have no sort of meaning in it, and yet it was certainly English. "I don't understand you," she said, as politely as she could. (Carroll 100)

This same problem emerges with much written and spoken language today. Though definitely composed of recognizable English words, much language has "no sort of meaning in it." It doesn't work. This proves to be something of a problem. I will contend here that we want our language to communicate something—specifically, what we intend it to convey—yet often it fails when we don't pay enough attention to how we put words together.

Throughout this book, I will argue that you need to pay attention to putting words into sentences and sentences into paragraphs—as well as to creating larger, more complex messages, like papers, letters, blog posts, reports, emails, and the like. Part of that attentiveness involves employing, when necessary, Standard Written English, which this book outlines. (I often call this "formal English," though formal

English need not be written.) I am also striving to do something more ambitious here. In these pages, I am going to try to convince you that knowing the fundamentals of "correct" English has value in and of itself.

Now, you might wonder just how much such "correctness" ultimately counts: Is it important to master this stuff? I mean, does anyone really care anymore? In the Internet age? In most cases, isn't "correctness" only a superficial gloss, an add-on option, like magnesium wheels or a chrome-tipped exhaust on a car, something that's (maybe) nice but not necessary? Something, peradventure, even a bit overly flashy? If the basic content or idea being conveyed gets through, who cares about spelling, punctuation, or "grammar"?

Well, some people do. You care, or else you wouldn't be reading this book, taking a writing course, or looking for some answers. My students care. They often ask me, "Does grammar 'count'?" Yes, yes, it does. And I hope you don't merely "care," but go beyond that feeling into another realm, namely, that of having a deep concern for the words you craft, for the language that you float out into the world, for the verbal embodiments of your ideas.

Here is why grammar counts. While fairly often a version of your intended idea or message might seep or struggle through regardless of how imperfectly you write or say something, a lack of correctness has the potential to block or blight your message, to leave your reader or listener "dreadfully puzzled" (like Alice, at the Hatter's tea party).

What you're trying to communicate is not getting through. You yourself might have a good idea, but your words are not conveying it.

For example, sometimes verbal "errors" impede communication by distracting your audience from your message. Your audience might have to "translate" what you are saying or hold in mind two or three possible meanings while they listen (or while they read your writing), since your language lacks sufficient exactness. It resembles the situation in which you might say, "I was talking to Mike today, and"—and your listener has to hold three or four Mikes in mind while waiting for the detail that will pin down just which Mike you're talking about. So your listener takes in the message with one ear, in a manner of speaking, while simultaneously attuning the other ear to puzzling out a crucial player's identity. The message, in this situation, cannot command the attention it deserves.

Another kind of distraction crops up when a segment of your audience hears a particular usage—for instance, a double negative; a subject-verb error; a nonstandard verb or pronoun form, like "should have went" or "Me and him were …"; or a misused word—and swiftly dismisses you as someone whose ideas can't be any better than your usage. Their ears close up, their eyes glaze over, they not-too-surreptitiously consult their cell phones. They yawn.

When you speak or write, your words almost always produce responses, like yawning, or (let's hope) more engaged, complex, emotional responses in listeners or readers.

Ideally, these emotional responses are to your ideas, the content: the message itself. But the very way you phrase your thoughts and employ language itself generates affective responses. That is, your audience will respond emotionally to how you say things as much as to what you say—will judge you as a sayer, as a consciousness, as a person. And since your words create an image of yourself, an audience will naturally respond to that image at the same time that it responds to your words. It gets distracted by random associations prompted by your words or phraseology. (This is why you might have been told, for example, to avoid unintentional rhyme, so that an audience's attention won't be drawn to the sound of your words and the musicality of their rhyme rather than to the more important element, namely, your message. Unintentional rhyme is only one of many possible distractions, I should add.)

I'm urging you, therefore, to employ language that on its own will not spark negative emotional responses. It won't disperse or scatter an audience's attention. Nor will it provoke extraneous, irrelevant, or judgmental reactions and thus take that audience away from your point. Instead you want your language to clearly lead your audience directly toward that point and toward an understanding of it.

Unfortunately, you never really know for certain the makeup of your audience, or what it is listening for. Will this audience really care about your word order, vocabulary, and exactness of expression? Put yourself into your audience's position. Empathize. Think about who might be on the receiving end of your words. (Sometimes you need to do this very rapidly, even instantaneously.) If you decide that your listener or reader might notice and care about correctness—might really be paying attention to both what you say and how you say it—adjust your language to the occasion.

What kind of book is this, then? When I imagined this book, I wanted a volume that didn't just lay out the "rules"—we have lots of books that do that quite well—but one that did something in addition to that. I wanted to provide a human voice chatting about those rules, one that used real-world rather than manufactured language as its model, and one that tried to show how using language carefully can improve the quality of human interactions.

Certainly, errors in usage pale by comparison with errors in moral decisions, or, for that matter, errors made while conducting bypass surgery, piloting an airplane, drilling for offshore oil, or when deciding whether or not to invade another country. The things our culture seems to value highly for the most part have to do with safety, security, personal/environmental health—and events that involve dollar gain or loss. So what are we doing here?

Striving for greater usage accuracy and precision may help us toward something else, something that connects to crucial personal, cultural, and economic problems. Greater usage accuracy works toward a shared understanding.

At the same time, your attentiveness to language will change you. If you're motivated enough to improve your language use, the way you say and write things, the way you punctuate, the way you choose words, and the way you structure each sentence you utter or write, you'll find yourself fundamentally reprogramming your interaction with others. They will listen more attentively. They will see you anew. They might suggest ways to build on your ideas (instead of, say, ignoring yours and offering alternatives of their own). You'll discover, in short, that you are more effective at doing what you want to do.

A paradox of writing is that while you're essentially creating something for others, you're also trying to discover something for yourself, even something about yourself, about how you feel or think regarding an issue or idea. It's true, of course, that you consult with others, but writing also has a lonely and methodical, even a banausic, quality, more so once you have a draft and are revising, correcting, rephrasing, making sure that your language is exact.

It's sort of like working on a craft project that requires you to smooth out some uneven, raw, and unpromising surface. You might struggle with it for hours, clearing away encrusted dirt and cobwebs, taking out a smudge or imperfection here, a blemish or stain there. Sometimes, though, if you're lucky and after you've been laboring over the thing for hours or days, it reveals its true nature: it's in fact a pane of glass or of crystalline rock, and now that you've got it Windex-squeaky smooth, you realize that the real discovery isn't the surface-perfect thing itself, but what has suddenly emerged as visible, beneath or behind the thing you've been laboring over—namely, what you can see through it, and what others can also see. Maybe the best writing has this self-immolative quality. It metamorphoses into nothingness, as the things and ideas the writing refers to take on a shape and vitality independent of the words that summoned them up.

Really mastering the basics isn't just some abstract exercise, like memorizing the quadratic equation, the periodic table of chemical elements, or the sequence of U.S. presidents. It's more than that: language use creates as it reflects a world—as it creates and also reflects the people in that world. That's the message I try to convey to my college writing classes, and I couldn't find a textbook that really drove that home. So I wrote one.

Preview of the Following Pages

You will encounter three "voices" in the following pages. The first will be this voice, one offering general advice about language use. This voice isn't so much providing the "what" of English grammar and usage, nor even the "how" of it. Instead, it's addressing the "why" of the issue. Why is it important to be attentive to this or that language issue? Why will this or that change have an impact? To be more specific, this voice claims that learning these nuances and details of English has more than merely instrumental value, isn't just a means of getting to an end. Thus the voice will be chatty, anecdotal, even autobiographical at times, as it attempts to offer a context for learning formal English.

The second voice belongs to others and speaks in the example sentences I have gathered. It's the voice of "them," of the people "out there." These are real-world people. Almost all of the example sentences come from U.S.-based publications of a single day, December 29, 2008. What's so special about that day? Is it like September 1, 1939; December 7, 1941; August 6, 1945; November 22, 1963; or September 11, 2001? Nope. It's not, in fact, special in any particular way. Wikipedia has no entry for it as a special day (no December 29 was ever a special or newsworthy day, according to Wikipedia: an unlikely claim). We've all lived through it, and though it might have personal significance for some of us, I chose it as the source day for example sentences because of its very ordinariness.

So this second voice will be the collective one of real people—writers, politicians, scientists, reporters, professors, average men and women: people whose sentences have already performed a function in the world. Their sentences are "used" ones; "pre-owned," eBay might label them. They are not fresh, perfect, unopened-in-original-packaging ones created for the sole purpose of illustrating gram-matical principles. Instead, these example sentences have been riddled with the eye-tracks of many, maybe millions, of readers.

The third voice will be one directly commenting on these sentences from the newspapers, magazines, and web-sites. It's the voice of professor as language coach. It's an awkward position, to be commenting on and "correcting" people's (often writing professionals') usage, since it im-plies something flawed or "wrong" with it, so much so that it needs righting, adjusting, or editing. Yet I'm trying to make this voice, and the instruction it offers, as nonjudg-mental and as supportive as possible, and if this voice can point out a problem in published language, a problem you hadn't been sensitive to, or which you'd perhaps never before even noticed, it will have done you a great service. So don't take it personally if I point out a questionable usage that, habitually, you also employ. (But also, hey, think about it.)

To capture an image of one day in the life of the English language, I draw from eleven newspapers and websites, including the *International Herald Tribune*, latimes.com, nydailynews.com, the New York Times, seattlepi.com, sun times.com, sfgate.com, the *Trentonian*, *USA Today*, the *Wall Street Journal*, and the *Washington Post*. I also use six weekly magazines that carry the December 29, 2008, date: *National Review*, *New York*, the *New Yorker*, *Sports Illustrated*, *Time*,

and *Us Weekly*. (Some of these, by the way, are "double" issues, dated December 22/29 or December 29/January 5.)

December 29, 2008, as History

Am I creating a narrative of this day? Yes and no. My microcosmic selection offers random sentences, ones I've isolated because I want to use them to illustrate grammatical
principles. I think many narratives might be inferred from
the quotations I have culled, but I'm not consciously trying to create any particular or even discernible narrative of
the day, the month, the year, or the decade.

The day's language tells the tale of some events and issues that have not proven to be of ongoing significance,
and of some that have continued as part of our national
narrative. We often can't really tell what's historical and
what's just daily news that will swiftly disappear from the
collective consciousness, never to resurface. Will this event
or issue be the start of some important trend, the tip of
some huge, scary iceberg, or just a space-filler in a magazine or newspaper or news program? An additional com-
plicating factor is that what actually happened on December 29, 2008, is one thing, and what the newspapers and
magazines deemed significant enough to report, quite another. Thus the portrait of history that any single day's
publications paints will inevitably be much more incomplete, distorted, and patchwork than that found in history
books, which, usually written from a distance of years, can

better assess the significance of what happened during a given year, month, or day.

But still, reportage about current events amounts to a kind of history. This book will be looking at the English language that characterized and attempted to capture what was happening on our planet that December 29, thin-slicing, à la Malcolm Gladwell, the verbal universe in English that was on that day available to the average American via newspapers and magazines. It's only a sample of one day in the life of the language, but I'm hoping it's a representative one.

Three days from the end of the calendar year, that day saw much of the print media trying to frame and make sense of the striking and calamitous events that had taken place the preceding 363 days (it was a leap year). The *Trentonian* ran a feature entitled "2008: The Year in Review," though the events described covered only the first half of the year (the second half of the year was covered in a subsequent issue). It was a retrospective moment, December 29, and in many ways a "slow news day," yet on it the events of the previous days, weeks, and months reverberated and ramified.

As for those preceding months of 2008, three phrases might sum them up: natural disasters, ongoing violence, and financial meltdown—and a fourth, a proper noun that needs a category of its own: Barack Obama. All four remained epicenters of the news that third-to-last day of the year.

On December 29, the *New York Times* reported that China was still cleaning up after its devastating May 12 earthquake ("Romance, and Slow Recovery, in a Quake-Devastated Chinese County," by Edward Wong). *USA Today* ran an article entitled "Wet, Wind-Whipped Midwest Still on Alert." And the *USA Today* "reader photo," submitted by Kresta Meng Leimser, was captioned "A cumulonimbus cloud develops above a supercell thunderstorm near Lusk, Wyo., on a fall evening" (12A). In fact, the cumulonimbus in the photo looks very much like a mushroom cloud from an atomic bomb blast. Leimser's photo, which shows the cloud hovering above and behind some iconically American-looking silos and farm buildings, makes for a menacing—but an eerily apt—image.

Indeed, Mother Nature was sinister and deadly in 2008. Munich Re, the German reinsurer that keeps track of such things, calculated that some 220,000 people died from natural disasters in 2008 ("Timelines"). These included an earthquake (7.8–8.2 on the Richter scale; accounts vary) in China that killed close to 70,000 (an additional 18,000 were missing), and a cyclone in Burma/Myanmar that left 50,000 dead. The United Kingdom suffered a 5.2-magnitude earthquake, and on December 29 itself Yellowstone Park suffered a series of tremors; the significance of both was probably artificially inflated by the year's multiple natural disasters.

In the previous months, the United States had been experiencing terrible weather, with 111 deaths from tornadoes alone by the end of May. A bitterly cold winter, flooding, and hurricanes—at least one every month from July through December—rounded out the meteorological picture. At the same time, global warming continued, with a 160-square-mile portion of the Arctic shelf breaking up. Even the moon, by December, reportedly shone both larger and brighter, by a lot, than it had previously that year (NASA Science News).

The violence of living on this, the third planet from the sun, remained unabated, unrelenting, and deeply disturbing. On December 29 all the publications I looked at had numerous stories about deaths, atrocities, murders, and wars. "If it bleeds, it leads" certainly held true. The war in Iraq continued (it had started in March 2003); its cost at that point was estimated at three trillion dollars. During President George W. Bush's December visit to Iraq, an angry Iraqi journalist hurled two shoes at him. They missed. The journalist, Muntadhar al-Zaidi, was arrested, brutally beaten, tried, and imprisoned for nine months. (He was released early because of good behavior.)

In August of 2008, Russia and its neighboring state of Georgia had become embroiled in a conflict over breakaway regions South Ossetia and Abkhazia. Russia invaded Georgia, using tanks and aircraft, maintaining that "it was protecting pro-Russian South Ossetians" ("EU Launches Probe"), a claim that, regionally modified, would ominously reecho in the 2014 Ukrainian crisis. The *International Herald Tribune* of December 29 ran the prescient article "Tajiks Bleed in a Xenophobic Russia" (Tavernise), and the *Wall Street Journal* printed a front-page article, below the fold, entitled "As If Things Weren't Bad Enough, Russian Professor Predicts End of U.S." (Osborn), which reviews the slightly madcap ideas of Igor Panarin: "Americans hope President Obama 'can work miracles,' he wrote. 'But when spring comes, it will be clear that there are no miracles'." As if to at least partially confirm the Russian professor's prediction, early 2009 witnessed the emergence of the Tea Party in the United States, and the start of what would be a presidency marked by congressional stalemates, inactivity, government shutdowns, and angry, line-in-the-sand disputes between Republicans and Democrats.

The Mideast was roiled by the Hamas-Israel conflict. Hamas began by launching missiles into Israel, reaching the cities of Beersheba and Ashdod. Israel defended itself by launching missiles, killing close to 300 in the Gaza Strip. All major papers on December 29 ran stories about this as front-page news: "Israel Keeps Up Assault on Gaza; Arab Anger Rises" and "With Strikes, Israel Reminds Foes It Has Teeth" (*New York Times*); "Israel Pursues Strikes on Gaza; Toll Mounts and Outcry Swells" (*International Herald Tribune*); "Amid Gaza Violence, a New Task for Obama" (*USA Today*); "Israel Poised for Long Fight," "Food and Medical Supplies Grow Scarce on the Besieged Gaza Strip," and "Palestinian Deaths Near 300: Hamas Calls for Suicide Strikes" (*Washington Post*); and "Israel Pounds Gaza Again, Signals More on the Way" (*Wall Street Journal*).

Late November witnessed a massacre in India, where the militant group Lashkar-e-Taiba launched a cell-phone-coordinated attack on hotels and other commercial centers in Mumbai, killing more than 160. The December 29 *International Herald Tribune* revisited this event in "Mumbai's Torment Captured Click by Click" by Thomas Fuller, which presented a photographic record of the atrocity.

Earlier in the year, a suicide bomber had killed forty people during a "gathering of tribal elders and local officials in north-west Pakistan" ("Taking You Back"). In Afghanistan, on December 28, fourteen schoolchildren were killed in a bombing attack on a school bus, as reported in many December 29 papers. The Indian Coast Guard rescued two people off of the east coast of India, but "more than 300 people from Bangladesh and Myanmar . . . had jumped from a rickety boat that had been drifting for 13 days in the Indian Ocean and tried to swim to shore" ("Timelines"). This sad story made its way into the December 29 papers as well. The *New York Times* story, by Mark McDonald, carried the headline "Hundreds Are Feared Dead in Bay of Bengal." That fear was realized.

Meanwhile the financial world lay in tatters amid a global recession. It was declared as such on December 1 by the National Bureau of Economic Research. On September 15, Lehman Brothers, an investment firm so huge that it seemed immune to market fluctuation, filed for Chapter 11 bankruptcy. It had held $600 billion of assets. People were reeling. The U.S. government had to bail out Chrysler and General Motors, giving them approximately $17.4 billion in aid. The Emergency Economic Stabilization Act was enacted October 3, and $700 billion was earmarked to pay for bad loans and to bail out flagging banks. Bernie Madoff was convicted of creating an enormous Ponzi scheme that further weakened the U.S. economy and that of the world. He was charged on December 11 with securities fraud. His Ponzi scheme was valued at more than $50 billion, the largest financial fraud in history. Yet for their participation in wide-scale business practices that brought on the recession, Wall Street investors and bankers would suffer very little. It wouldn't be until 2013 that Credit Suisse banker Kareem Serageldin—the only Wall Street executive who would serve time for his criminal activities related to banking fraud—started a two-and-a-half-year prison term. (To offer a contrast, 839 people were "convicted in the savings and loan scandals of the 1980s," according to Jesse Eisinger of the independent nonprofit investigative organization ProPublica [38]. And those earlier scandals were minuscule in comparison with 2008's financial misdeeds.)

Not surprisingly, many news articles about the year's calamitous financial events appeared in publications on December 29. The *New York Times* ran two front-page stories devoted to the recession: "Veterans of '90s Bank Bailout See Opportunity in Current One" (Lipton and Kirkpatrick) and the more whimsical "Skaters Jump in as

Foreclosures Drain the Pool" (McKinley and Wollan). The *Wall Street Journal* ran a very long article that started on the front page, "The Weekend That Wall Street Died" (Craig et al.), while the *Washington Post* carried the first of a three-part, detailed article by Robert O'Harrow Jr. and Brady Dennis, entitled "The Beautiful Machine," which was under the kicker "The Crash: What Went Wrong." (A "kicker" is the journalistic term that refers to a smaller headline above the main headline; it often describes a series of articles or gives more information about a group of articles on the same subject.) Sequels in "The Crash" series would follow on the next two days. *USA Today* addressed a possibly different segment of the audience with its front-page "Bogus Money Goes Mainstream," which detailed the rise of counterfeiting "amid a souring economy" (Leinwand).

Yet perhaps the biggest news of the year was that in November, Barack Obama, an African American, had been elected the nation's first black president. He had campaigned on a platform that promised change. In seeking the Democratic nomination, he had vied with Hillary Clinton, the first woman who was a serious contender for the U.S. presidency. She would later be made secretary of state. Obama's vacated senate seat in Illinois was (illicitly) put up for sale by Illinois governor Rod Blagojevich, who was arrested on December 9 and eventually convicted. Running against Obama and vice presidential candidate Joe Biden were John McCain and his running mate, a new face in national politics, Alaska governor Sarah Palin, who dazzled listeners with her brashness, her non sequiturs, and her faux pas.

On December 29, Barack Obama was only president-elect, and George W. Bush was still officially president. In that limbo between an election and an inauguration, the world was looking to Obama for leadership, and anticipating a very different brand of U.S. politics from what had characterized the Bush presidency. Overseas reaction was pronounced. The *New York Times* ran "Gaza Crisis Is Another Challenge for Obama, Who Defers to Bush for Now" (Myers and Cooper), while the *International Herald Tribune* carried a Reuters article entitled "Brown Sees Obama as Inspiration for Britain," reporting British prime minister Gordon Brown's words, "I look forward to working with President-elect Obama in creating a trans-Atlantic, and then a global coalition for change" (3). On the home front, the *National Review* wrote of outgoing president Bush, "It is a pity he did not do better; we are about to do worse." The same editorial lamented the entrance of Obama's "economic team," labeling Lawrence Summers "a thoroughgoing redistributionist." Prudently, though, the *National Review* warned conservatives to back off from the harebrained theory that Obama was not born in the United States: "Conservatives do themselves no favors by inhaling vapors from the fever swamps" ("The Week" 8). The *Washington Post* provided a look at things to come with "Obama's Tax Cuts Likely Soon: Senior Advisor Says

Middle Class Needs 'Some Relief Now'" (Rucker). That relief would be a long time in coming.

Barack Obama was named *Time* magazine's Person of the Year. Other notable persons of 2008 included Fidel Castro, who stepped down as Cuba's president and transferred to his brother Raúl leadership of the country; Bill Gates, who resigned from his position at Microsoft; Radovan Karadžić, who was finally located after a twelve-year search and arrested for war crimes; Tarō Asō, who became prime minister of Japan; and Michael Phelps, who won eight gold medals in the Beijing Olympics. On the cover of the December 29 *Sports Illustrated*, the top line of print reads, "2008: BEST SPORTS YEAR EVER," and the inside article talks not only about Phelps but also about Tiger Woods and Usain Bolt and the Super Bowl–winning New York Giants.

Just the same, though, while December 29, 2008, might not have the historical resonance of, say, 9/11, it held great importance, was by no means a slow news day, for many—for those who, for example, lost their fortunes or their loved ones, who were fired or betrayed or stricken terribly ill, or who won the lottery that day. At first glance it might appear to have been a day that most people would "little note nor long remember," yet after having pored over many 12/29/08 documents, I now question the very concept of the "slow news day"—no day can be such for the billions of souls (6.7 billion in 2008) inhabiting this green-and-blue ball that hurtles, spinning, through space: every day sees its share of grief and joy, of tragedy and drudgery, of despair and elation.

Our culture does seem to value some days more than others, since what happened on them is of moment for more people. But at the same time, each day, no matter how momentous or ordinary, is enmeshed in, shaped by, and formative of history: it carves out a permanent place for itself along the time line. Just as the isolation of a single minute in a person's life might reveal an ordinary and apparently insignificant moment—or one of great pleasure, enlightenment, or horror—it is nevertheless still a moment that helps create who we are. Similarly, each day in the life of the world functions as part of an entirety, and can no more be dissevered from its place in history than can a single moment from a human life.

Thus picking a single day in history is a chancy business: December 29, 2008, had no forty-eight-point headlines, but what took place that day was part of an ongoing historical process. Entangled in history yet separate from it, that day still breathes strongly through the words that emerged on it, a small sample of which this book will share with you.

Two Disclaimers

I draw examples from publications across the range of political positions. Some of the quotations are from left-of-center writers (and publications), some from those to the right of middle. This random sampling does raise an interesting question: suppose I come across an example of a particularly well-expressed or elegantly phrased sentence, but that sentence expresses a political sentiment that I personally find repulsive. Should I include that sentence as an example of excellent English? Does praising the sentence's structure imply endorsement of its politics?

In a word, no. I'll just offer a general disclaimer here: I don't agree with the sentiments or politics of all the well-written sentences, nor do I think that the flaws of the questionable sentences inevitably imply questionable content. Perhaps in an ideal world, the beautifully phrased ideas will be also the most beautiful ones, and the ugliness of a notion will emerge through its rebarbative expression. But that's not, unfortunately, the case.

Second, most of my examples come from journalism, not from academic writing. In an attempt to excavate the language that was prevalent on a single given day in history, it seemed to me reasonable to look to print magazines and newspapers. My rationale for this is twofold: first, academic writing usually cannot be tied to a particular date. (Academic journals typically appear quarterly.) Second, on the sentence level, academic writing does not significantly differ from much journalism, especially not from the journalism in the *New Yorker*, the *New York Times*, the *Washington Post*, the *Wall Street Journal*, and the *National Review*. On the other hand, though, academic writing does differ from journalism in several important ways:

academic writing more clearly targets a specialist audience, hence usually employs specialized language; it is usually more heavily documented, almost always drawing on a wide range of references; it typically uses slightly more complex sentence constructions; and the journal articles that form the staple of academic writing run much longer than most pieces appearing in newspapers or magazines. But journalistic writing can be just as precise and lucid as academic writing—often more so—and regularly conveys complex ideas that are well expressed, eloquent, even inventive and striking.

Admittedly, much of the language I encountered proves far from what I would consider ideal. But I still see it as important. The way these many journalists and writers use language permeates our minds and our being. Their language has an iconic value. Today, for example, a front-page story in the *New York Times* includes the word *macabré* (Span A11). This caught me up short. *Macabre* has no accent. I wondered how many readers might see the misspelled word and then use it with an accented "e" in their own writing—or just imagine and accept it as correct that way. In striving to convey what "really happened," journalists' language takes on the truth value of its content.

Writers for publication need to take especial care because it is they who are the unacknowledged, unelected legislators of language use. And as their constituency, we need to be vigilant, constantly wary, of how their prose subtly indoctrinates as it informs us. As writers, we need to be aware of our own potential power.

I know that what I have captured here is only a limited sample, and that with three hundred or so sample sentences, I can provide only a small window into, a microcosmic snapshot of, a single day's language. But I'm not vying for exhaustiveness; I simply want an image of language as it's actually used—used well, used badly, typically used. I'm sure any other day's language culled from similar sources would reveal the same patterns (though a day from 1908—or 2108—would probably offer language markedly different from that which was prevalent in 2008).

On Using Sentences from the Real World

How does this differ from most books on this subject? Well, most authors of grammar guides fabricate sentences to illustrate various principles and ideas. Determined in large part by their made-up example sentences, such usage guides summon up zombie-like entities that inhabit a bland world of nonevent, a world only slightly evolved over Dick and Jane's from mid-twentieth-century grade-school readers. It's a world from which a dimension of reality—a sociopolitical consciousness, or just the news of the day, for example—has mysteriously drained away, so much so that the simulacrum left behind has only a cartoonish 2-D quality. Or if it's 3-D, you're not getting the disposable glasses.

Such context-free language does not represent English as it is or has been ordinarily used. Language as it's really used reflects a real, a complex, an often disturbing world. Actual experience is the armature that engines language, the inner spin that makes it spark and fire. And while some of my examples might initially distract the reader from grammatical issues, in a way that's just the challenge, just the point: language has to work properly and precisely under pressure of circumstance, often in the midst of turmoil, against imminent chaos.

Here are a couple of brief examples that hint at some of the difficulties in dealing with real-world language. I'll also take this opportunity to open a brief discussion of a very important "fundamental": **subject-verb agreement**. I'll talk about this more in chapter 1, but the general idea is that the subject of your sentence—that which is doing the acting, or being—determines what form of verb ought to be used with it. Ann Raimes and Maria Jerskey explain this concept in their popular textbook *Keys for Writers*:

> The principle of agreement means that when you use the present tense of any verb or the past tense of the verb *be* in academic writing, you must make the subject and verb agree in person (first, second, or third) and number (singular or plural). *A baby cries. Babies cry.* (425)

Well, this is a fair start, my only quibbles being that the entire "when-clause" is unnecessary; you need to worry about subject-verb agreement in nonacademic writing as well, and most importantly, perhaps, most readers don't have a lot of difficulty with sentences like "Babies cry" or "A baby cries." But before I dismiss the authors' strategy of using such sentences, I concede that their examples do have the value of illustrating the principle.

I'm more interested, though, in what might be called "non–baby sentences," sentences that provide a level of challenge for the reader, sentences that we might actually generate or perhaps puzzledly encounter. These sentences need not be long or complex. Here is one that appeared in the *New Yorker*, a magazine noted for its meticulous, even fastidious editing. The sentence describes the photographs at a Richard Avedon exhibition. I offer this three-word sentence as a starting point for discussing the challenges of real-world sentences:

? None are boring.

I place the question mark before a sentence whose effectiveness I question, and I should warn you that you'll see a lot of sentences so designated in the following pages. These sentences are questionable, iffy, at least by my lights, though perhaps not necessarily "wrong." Some readers might label them as "wrong"; others would pass over them and have no qualms. Again, it's important to note that professional writers and editors have already reviewed all of these sentences and deemed them acceptable. These sentences have been *published*. I'm not claiming that all these people don't know what they're doing. But maybe they (and you) should look again.

OK, then, back to "None are boring." *None* is the subject of this sentence. Is it plural or singular? This seems like a simple question, though not quite so simple as it was with *baby* and *babies*. Looking at the sentence carefully might get you thinking a bit more about the grammatical principle, about what's at stake here. What does that *none* signify? If it's plural, as the *are* verb implies, what does that say—about the photograph exhibition—that differs from a sentence in which *none* is seen as singular? A plural verb invokes the whole group, the entirety of photos in the exhibition. For me, the entirety that the plural summons seems to work against the claim that the photos making it up are not boring. The profusion puts me off. Thus I prefer the singular, "none is," because using a singular verb emphasizes how not a single, solitary one of these Avedon photographs is boring. And using *is* after *none* would have more impact too: it's a correct form that's rarely seen and might catch the reader up short, with the effect of driving home the point even more fully, of emphasizing the photographs' nonboringness, their real originality and excitement.

To be fair, Raimes and Jerskey don't limit their discussion of subject-verb agreement to "baby sentences." They acknowledge the complexity of the issue and look at many problematic cases. The trouble is, though, that their edicts about made-up sentences don't always quite work with "real-world" sentences. Most grammatical edicts prove to have exceptions. Here's what they say about "Subjects with *and*":

> When a subject consists of two or more parts joined by *and*, treat the subject as plural and use a plural verb.

> His instructor and his advisor *want* him to change his major. (431)

Fair enough. They go on, further, to point out that on occasion an *and* in a subject links together two aspects of the same, singular element:

> The restaurant's chef and owner makes good fajitas. (431)

This requires a singular verb: the chef and owner is one and the same person. Sounds good. Take me there right now.

But what about a sentence such as the following, which does indeed include *and* in the subject and has more than one element as part of the subject? It's also from a fastidiously edited publication, the *National Review*, and it's quite complex, so be forewarned that it's not for (or about) babies:

> **?** The memory of Reagan, and especially the élan of ascendant conservatism in the 1970s and 1980s that Buckley's memoir rekindles, burns hotter now that conservatives find themselves in the political wilderness again. (Hayward 42)

At first glance, it's a bit of a puzzle. This sentence seems to violate the *and* rule that Raimes and Jerskey accurately lay out. *Memory* is one part of the subject, and *élan* is the other. Therefore, it's a plural subject, and the verb should be *burn*, not *burns* (as in "they burn"). Or is it one of those two-part subjects that's *really* singular, like the one in the sentence about the fajita chef/restaurant owner?

Maybe. As I see it, you need to go beyond memorizing "rules"; you need to internalize how sentences work, and deal with each one individually. So let's look a bit more closely at this confusing sentence. What's it really about? What's burning? A memory can burn, sure. But can an élan burn? What is an élan, anyway? (Is it flammable?) Finally, I place Hayward's sentence into the "questionable" category, not so much because of its verb but because of what seems to me a minor punctuation/proofreading issue. One "memory" is of Reagan, but there's another memory—one of an "élan" (which means "vivacity," "ardor," or "enthusiasm"). It's not a compound *subject*, but a compound *memory*, a memory of two elements or entities. Here's a slight rewrite of the sentence that might better capture the idea:

> The memory of Reagan and, especially, of the élan of ascendant conservatism in the 1970s and 1980s that Buckley's memoir rekindles, burns hotter now that conservatives find themselves in the political wilderness again.

Memory (a singular noun as subject) requires *burns* (a singular verb as predicate). The intervening "*of*-phrases" don't make the singular subject plural.

Now, I know this might not seem to be an ideal example for a usage handbook, since the sentence is quite complicated and doesn't simply and clearly elucidate a grammatical principle. My only defense is that we're dealing with real-world language, and it's often muzzy, even caliginous. That's what this book is about.

I've not been stockpiling howler-type sentences laboriously gathered over years of reading. Instead, I'm looking at relatively ordinary written language from just one day. That it was written and edited by professionals might suggest that many of its inaccuracies or flaws are minor and unimportant. But I don't draw that conclusion. Rather, I note how often even professionals have trouble using English: their prose frequently obscures or even misleads readers about what's being discussed, described, or asserted.

What I'm arguing for, finally, is using rhetorical proficiency to get heard. It's crucially important to get heard, partly because language constitutes a form of power. (Not that having power is so terribly important, but if one word might characterize the contemporary human condition, it's power*less*ness, and we need to resist this state as much as possible.) The writer and scholar Ira Shor calls language power "soft power," "hard power" being, by contrast, ordnance like guns or bombs or tanks. But the two kinds of power are connected. "After the night of the long knives, comes the morning of the chalkboard," Shor points out ("Who Won"). But the process can be reversed too: soft power can precede and prompt the use of hard power. Amiri Baraka writes in "Black Art":

> . . . we want "poems that kill."
> Assassin poems, Poems that shoot
> guns. Poems that wrestle cops into alleys
> and take their weapons leaving them dead
> with tongues pulled out and sent to Ireland.
> ("Respected Poet")

I don't think Baraka is being entirely ironic here: this is an angry poem that literalizes the danger that the speaker wants his words to have. The poem is made scarier, too, because "wanting" to have "poems that shoot guns" is only a tiny increment away from creating such verbal weaponry.

While I don't fully share Baraka's anger or militancy, I do agree with him that words can have a potentially terrible power. However, if words have such power—and I think history proves that they do—they also can provide an anodyne to those in pain, a solace to those who grieve, and a source of great joy and insight. They can improve our collective lot. Thus we need to handle words with caution, and craft our language using the utmost care, for language has not just a power but even an explosive volatility—one about which most people remain blissfully, though possibly dangerously, unaware.

Formal Usage—Its Rules and Value

Abiding by usage conventions or writing "correct" prose may seem a small, perhaps tiresome, detail of modern life. Yet it's a detail that carries great significance for anyone who must write, and it's an area where innovation isn't routinely encouraged or accommodated. It is "rule governed." As I have said, people will often judge a piece of writing or speech by the accuracy of its usage, or by the precision with which it follows what they perceive to be the "rules." Innovation, generally valued in our culture, is in matters of grammar and usage usually seen as "wrong," possibly even uneducated, or, maybe, In Your Face. There are upsides and downsides that you might consider prior to "innovating" with your language use.

Paradoxically, the "rules of usage" don't exist per se. I know that there are lots of books that lay them out, but actual usage varies widely, adjusts to specific situations, and is in a constant state of flux. Most readers will note, too, that published writing often deviates from the "rules" I invoke. True enough. Many writers frequently and consciously violate "correct" usage, and some press so much on the margins of correctness that using their works as models would be misleading: they're attempting to creatively expand the remit of Standard Written English.

To complicate matters still further, most of the writing we encounter in our daily lives does not abide by the principles I will lay out here: text messaging, emails, blogs, tweets, advertising, journalism, street signs, the increasingly rare nonpictorial operating instructions, websites, poetry, fiction, "creative nonfiction" (to name a few genres) all have their own grammar and syntax, their own range of conventional and acceptable. Though such writing often has considerable value, it is not an ideal model of formal writing. Nor does speech serve as a model for formal writing: things we say are usually more colloquial, redundant, and imprecise than things we write.

Many of you already speak and write fundamentally sound and communicative English. For example, neither you nor the printed sources I perused use sentences such as this:

> ✱ Only of ran terrific inherent about plunge his understand powerful the creates to.

So we need not start at an extremely basic level, or at the level of a reader who has little knowledge of English. Just the same, it might be helpful for me to articulate, in relatively plain English, a few very basic linguistic concepts.

Often we can recognize a sentence as a sentence but not understand it (Lewis Carroll's " 'Twas brillig and the slithy toves / Did gyre and gimble in the wabe"; Noam Chomsky's "Colorless green ideas sleep furiously.") Or we can recognize a nonsentence but understand it perfectly. Then, too, we will occasionally encounter nonsentences that make no sense ("Furiously sleep ideas green colorless"). These are now even more common with the advent of voice recognition software. In fact, generating nonsentences is easy now: just read or speak a foreign language into a program that is set up for English. The results will come back with the caveat "Confidence is low." But your goal is to generate word strings that are both recognizable as sentences and understandable by an audience. We want our audience's confidence (in us, in our words) to be high.

It's important to note that sentences rarely appear in isolation. We as listeners or readers usually think we can understand—at least get the general drift of—what people are trying to say, even if their language is ungrammatical, very colloquial, disjointed, or flat-out slovenly. We look at the context, as well as for repetitions and expansions that confirm what we perceive as the message. There are limits, to be sure, and sometimes we have to ask for clarification.

English, like most languages, has its own sublanguages, dialects, and variations. Here, I will be presenting "formal" or "standard" English—not always the kind of English you might speak (or even write), but the kind that you will certainly have to use in many situations. To an extent, formal English provides a default language for situations in which you don't really know what kind of language would be most appropriate. Using this kind of English will rarely stigmatize or negatively mark you: it's usually the safest, most neutral, for you to employ. It's generally reliable as the form of English best suited to conveying your meaning to a wide audience. But it's not always or necessarily the "best" as in "most-appropriate-to-the-situation-and-audience" English, and certainly not the only English that you will ever use. In fact, in some situations you should probably avoid formal English, as it sounds too haughty, stuffy, stilted, or simply too "formal." You don't want to wear a tuxedo when you go out for pizza.

Language Use as a Reflection of Self and Social Class

Again, in almost all situations your language, spoken or written, reflects who you are. When you write an essay, an email, or even a text message, you at once communicate a content—that is, your thoughts—and also a version of yourself. Rhetorical theory calls this is an "ethos." How you project yourself as a "sayer" merges inseparably with what you say. You want to strive to project a positive, credible, authoritative ethos, something that might keep an audience listening and actively trying to figure out what you have to say. On the other hand, your subtle, penetrating insights will sometimes be lost if you routinely employ informal, ill-punctuated, or nonstandard English, since in these situations your language projects a not-so-credible ethos.

Let me illustrate this idea with an excerpt from a December 29, 2008, news story, "Caroline Kennedy No Whiz with Words." Kennedy had come under some scrutiny since she was being considered as a replacement for Hillary Clinton, who had vacated her seat as U.S. senator from New York in order to become secretary of state.

In a 30-minute session with The News on Saturday, Kennedy punctuated her answers with "you know" more than 200 times. "Um" was fairly constant, too.

Transcripts of her interviews with other media outlets showed the same problem. She said "you know" at least 130 times to the New York Times and more than 80 times on New York 1.

When The News asked if President Bush's tax cuts on the wealthy should be repealed immediately, Kennedy replied:

"Well, you know, that's something, obviously, that, you know, in principle and in the campaign, you know, I think that, um, the tax cuts, you know, were expiring and needed to be repealed." (Saul)

Poor Caroline. What level of credibility does she have? Admittedly, she's being judged on spoken language, which doesn't usually require the same level of exactness as the written variant—except for (and here is an important exception) people who run for public office or whose profession requires it. Newspapers and reporters mercilessly attacked Kennedy for the way she spoke. I wonder to what extent her withdrawal from consideration for the senate seat emerged from the perceived gap between her language and her ideas—from her own suspicion that she could not verbally convey a confident and certain intellect, and from her dismay at being ridiculed for it. (For the record, she cited personal and family reasons for withdrawing from consideration in early 2009.)

Some writers contend that language use provides a sure and exact marker of educational level. Such a marker may or may not be important to you. For example, the following comment, which appears in the "Backtalk" section of the *Trentonian*, seems to be from someone who lacks a formal education:

> ❓ It's 3 o'clock in the afternoon and I can't get no-where because of all these people going across the Calhoun Street Bridge. (Going Nowhere)

"Educated" people generally avoid double negatives ("I can't get nowhere"). Of course it's possible that "Going Nowhere" has had plenty of formal education but is assuming another persona since she or he does not want to be seen as a "pointy-headed intellectual," a term used disparagingly elsewhere in the "Discussion" section of the *Trentonian*.

In fact, language usage, pronunciation, and punctuation almost always convey more than just the "meaning" intended by an author. The following letter writers' language undermines their ideas, I'd say:

> ❓ say vnny, you don't have to pay the high ticket prices to subsidize the players high saleries, just stay home and watch on the television, that's wat i do! (Steveack2004)

> ❓ I had one person with a "questionable" SS card although I brought it up it was like talking to the wind. The job was min. wage so who cares right? (BklynAli)

Both of these are relatively easy to understand, yet the manner of their expression limits their impact. Steveack's twenty-nine-word sentence contains ten basic errors (three capitalization errors, two comma splices, an apostrophe error, a comma error, and three spelling errors). And the fact that BklynAli uses "SS" to refer to "Social Security," not to the *Schutzstaffel*, the security echelon of the Nazis (the usual reference), is also significant: he's culturally indifferent, ahistoric. (Am I being too tough on him? Maybe. I've asked various people about this, and I've received varying responses: some say "SS" just means Nazis; others contend that an "SS card" is just a Social Security card. Again, gauging the audience is key.)

Steveack's and BklynAli's are "voices of the people," admittedly, real people's voices; were they a bit more refined, they might seem more worth our while to read. Now they're just funny examples of language use by clueless yutzes. The *Trentonian* editors know this too, and I'd wager they're having a bit of fun at these letter writers' expense.

But many usage errors emerge, quite simply, from lack of vigilance on the part of the writer. Look carefully at your writing. Adjust it, revise it, polish it. You might want to recalibrate the standard of what's acceptable to you. Look for rough edges that need smoothing off; look for ways to perfect your expression of ideas. If you yourself notice roughness, it's almost certain some of your audience will too.

Interestingly, language like Steveack's and BklynAli's often forms the basis for humor. The following sentence, from "Paulson, Bernanke and Trichet Walk into a Bar . . ." parodies an email scam, mocking Treasury Department secretary Henry Paulson as it does so:

> "I am ministry of the Treasury of the Republic of America. . . . My country has had crisis that has caused the need for large transfers of funds of 800 billion dollars US. . . ." (Alderman)

Alderman's parodic jibe links poor English with speakers who have questionable—maybe even criminal—motives and modi operandi. Poor English accompanies a pathetic attempt at deception. These speakers are self-deceived, I think, about their own "cleverness" and that of their schemes. And their language use only underlines that self-deception. That's why they're funny. This is also funny because the scam Alderman invents is coming out of the U.S. government, which had just been through a financial crisis.

Does language reflect social class? I know that many Americans do not believe we have any social classes. Some people have more money than others, but fortunes can be made, and incomes can increase rapidly. Language use seems to be independent of wealth or income. I believe, though, that the way we use language connects closely to educational experience, and at least today, Americans with wealth have access to a higher quality of education than do Americans at or below the poverty line. And it's likely that people judge and categorize you (your social class, your education, your intelligence) by the way you speak and write.

Still, I can't claim that the English I'm presenting here is that which is spoken and written by all successful members of society, or by those in positions of power or authority. We can hardly "misunderestimate" the many Bushisms generated by President George W. Bush—though in some sense he is the exception that proves the rule. And Caroline Kennedy's use of English might have been tolerated or ignored were she not from a wealthy, powerful family, or if she had been born male rather than female. Our society is so complex and the kinds of success and power so multifarious that it would be a mistake to label one dialect of the language—formal English—as that used by those who've succeeded or who are members of the upper class.

It has often been remarked that it's not language but power and money that actually drive the changes in our society. If so, then why fool people into thinking that success would be theirs were they only able to speak and write with accuracy, exactness, and force? Well, to begin with, I'm not in the business of making appointments to the Supreme Court or giving out seven-figure checks. But a better response would be that of scholar and critic Gerald

Graff, who writes about power and money, "For those who don't have either, rhetorical proficiency is crucial" (260). I'm hoping to offer a way toward that invaluable "rhetorical proficiency"—a way toward using English that might help you achieve the rewards you want, even though at the moment you might feel powerless or be in debt up to your eyeballs.

"If you don't have grammar, you don't have sense"

While accurate grammar is not strictly necessary for communication, it can make that communication more effective. This book aims to help you hone your ability to write English into an edged tool that, to borrow and modify a phrase from Washington Irving, will only grow sharper with frequent use. (Reflecting the sexism of his era, Irving applied it, in "Rip Van Winkle," to "a woman's tongue.") If you write emails, blogs, letters to the editor, holiday letters to send with late-December cards, or just a daily journal that no one but you ever reads, then this book might help you when you're wrestling with grammatical difficulties. Perhaps this small book might even better your career prospects, might improve your ability to communicate what you want, might secure you greater credibility in a larger arena of discourse—whether college, government, law, business, medicine, letters—where writing is the coin, the password, the app, of the realm; where writing defines, even substitutes for, the writer him/herself.

In the following pages I will be arguing that grammar is more than just a superficial "form" to our thoughts. In fact, I maintain that the form and content of our language merge in the communicative message we send out; the grammar of our expression helps determine to what extent its content gets understood. Pulitzer Prize–winning playwright Margaret Edson gets at this idea when she writes, "If we weren't teaching grammar as a way to bring the voices of our students forward, for a redemptive purpose, then why teach, why live? . . . If you don't have grammar, you don't have sense. . . . You don't have one another. You can't say 'I love you' without grammar" (Haberman). And we usually have more complicated things than "I love you," to say (though I certainly don't want to downplay the complexities of that apparently simple sentence).

Now you might object, and contend that you thought this book wasn't so much about *what* you say, as about *how* you say it. But I want to emphasize here that what you say and how you say it are ultimately inseparable, like conjoined twins sharing a heart. People see the gestalt rather than the component parts. To change the metaphor, just as you're usually seen as a human being, not a pile of cells or a collocation of atoms, your writing's content and proficiency will be taken in together, as an entirety.

Part of the difficulty of "correctness," and of the "rules" of Standard Written English, is that these precepts make up a malleable, constantly reshaping template. That template is created of dead plant dye on paper—ink—or in something even more evanescent, electronically generated pixels; it's not carved into stone tablets delivered from the Mount. It's a huge challenge to have to deal with the paradoxical situation that grammar is important, even crucial and necessary for living in society, yet it's also constantly shape-shifting, like a "metamorph" from science fiction stories or films. As the linguist Anne Curzan asks in a recent article about the "correct" forms of usage, when books or teachers or "authorities" claim thus and such is the correct form, we have to ask ourselves, "Says who?" I'll go a step further and ask, "And why should we listen to them?" These are questions that you yourself must figure out how to answer. To do so, you have to be on top of what's going on with language use within the area or discipline in which you are using it, but more importantly you need to carefully and maybe even laboriously make sure that your ideas convey just what you mean and don't summon up other, conflicting ideas.

Standard Written English hasn't come about because an aristocracy employed it, nor by dint of legislation. Rather, it has evolved in order to drive and power the social mechanism. It has what anthropologists call an adaptive value. Thus as society changes, the concept of what's "correct" changes, too, along with the very arbiters of that change. Communicative needs, fashions, and technologies change. Employing a Standard Written English will help you communicate effectively across all those changes. And people know this. That's partly why there are close to a thousand grammar handbooks on the market, why writing courses are required at virtually every college in the country, or why a book such as Lynne Truss's *Eats, Shoots & Leaves* can become a best seller. And even though language is constantly changing, there is some bedrock value to a core grammar and usage, a deep structure, an underlying form beneath or behind all the possible shapes our language can assume. Finding that form, especially on a wide-scale basis, will transform our society, will quite simply make it work more efficiently, with less misunderstanding.

My angle is that you have to work hard to make sure that your language conveys its ideas but doesn't distract, doesn't lead your readers into an absurd "other" universe, doesn't occlude your sense. In a recent *Times Literary Supplement* article about language use, "J.C." remarks, "It might be old fashioned to invoke 'breeding,' but we have yet to hear an argument that favors incomprehensibility over clarity." This might sound a little bit snooty, but the point stands. We need to use language that is above all comprehensible and lucid. We have a personal, even a moral, obligation to do so—to say what we mean, to say it lucidly if not plainly, and to hold others to the same high standard.

That's the goal. I know it's lofty: a personal, pedagogical Mount Everest. Let's hope that up on top the air won't be thin, but instead thick with meaning, dense with oxygenated discourse.

I want to start by providing you with a working vocabulary, namely, the parts of speech, to describe sentences in English. Most of these terms should be relatively familiar. I'll move on to discuss sentence structure, punctuation, and diction. I hope that even if the points I make are not "new news" to you, perhaps some of the example sentences will live and breathe, for they are sentences that have already done some work, have already been read by thousands (in some cases, maybe millions). They are, if nothing else, actual. Imperfect, rough, sometimes plain, sometimes poetic, they connect English usage to a spacetime that generated this very moment we're now experiencing. In a way, they've helped create who we are.

Chapter 1

Actants, Actions, Ongoing States:
Nouns, Verbs, and the Sentences They Form

Why Learn the Parts of Speech?

Nouns, verbs, adjectives, prepositions—isn't all this just mumbo jumbo? Words just stand for things, right? So why bother with all this jargon?

In *Gulliver's Travels*, Jonathan Swift deals with this very issue. The "scientists" in part 3 of his 1726 novel have worked out a curious system of communication: people can carry around objects that they can show one another and thus mutely communicate. Speaking words wears out the lungs, the scientists have concluded. No need for multiple parts of speech here—people just show each other objects (nouns) and get their ideas across through those things. Only "women . . . the vulgar and illiterate . . . the common people" rebel against this innovation. Swift's joke is that nouns can't convey meaning by themselves, so using the system burdens one with donkey-loads of items. Here is how he describes it:

> The other project was a scheme for entirely abolishing all words whatsoever. . . . since words are only names for things, it would be more convenient for all men to

carry about them such things as were necessary to express a particular business they are to discourse on. And this invention would certainly have taken place, to the great ease as well as health of the subject, if the women, in conjunction with the vulgar and illiterate, had not threatened to raise a rebellion, unless they might be allowed the liberty to speak with their tongues, after the manner of their forefathers; such constant irreconcilable enemies to science are the common people. However, many of the most learned and wise adhere to the new scheme of expressing themselves by things, which has only this inconvenience attending it, that if a man's business be very great, and of various kinds, he must be obliged in proportion to carry a greater bundle of things upon his back, unless he can afford one or two strong servants to attend him. I have often beheld two of those sages almost sinking under the weight of their packs, like pedlars among us; who, when they met in the street, would lay down their loads, open their sacks, and hold conversation for an hour together; then put up their implements, help each other to resume their burdens, and take their leave. (Swift)

The joke is that in a materialistic culture, the things that people own speak louder than what they say. As we acquire more stuff, we become more communicatively burdened or blocked—less articulate, maybe less human.

It's also fairly clear that whatever "communicating" is taking place has to be fairly primitive. From a linguistic perspective, the whole project of communicating through only nouns would be limiting, if not impossible. Swift's scientists have engineered a ridiculous method: that's also what makes the passage funny. In English, fortunately, words are not just denotations of things. We use words for action, for joining, for emphasis, for description, and even for abstract ideas. Perhaps wealthy "sages" don't have to do too much communicating and have all the time in the world, but the rest of us regular folks, Swift's "common people," don't. So we need multiple parts of speech.

Naturally this leads to the complications inherent in language use, which Swift's "sages" seem to be rebelling against. One of the problems with parts of speech, for example, is that we can't definitively divide up the dictionary into nouns, verbs, adjectives, and the like. Words find their ways into multiple categories. Any noun can probably be a verb, at least in some context: almost every day on my New Jersey Transit train, I hear the announcement, "The last car will not *platform* at New Brunswick," using a new verb, *to platform*, which means to stop at a place where, when the doors open, a platform will be right there, level with the floor of the railroad car. An example I recently heard on the radio also comes to mind. A man who bought his mother's old car complained about how much he had to pay her: he said, "My mom *bluebooked* me on the car" ("My

Big Break"). (And, curiously, many verb-derived words, called "verbals," function as nouns, or as adjectives, for that matter.)

Some linguists don't see the parts of speech as being as separate and distinct as I do (or as distinct as perhaps you were taught). Rather, they envision nouns, verbs, prepositions, and the like as existing on a "quasi-continuum." This view, put forth in the 1970s by John Robert Ross, is sometimes called "squish grammar" or "fuzzy grammar," and in it Ross posits a kind of hierarchy of parts of speech: verb—participles—adjectives—prepositions—nouns:

> Proceeding along the hierarchy is like descending into lower and lower temperatures, where the cold freezes up the productivity of syntactic rules, until at last nouns, the ultimate zero of this space, are reached. (317)

Verbs have many tenses and forms (conjugations), while nouns can be only singular or plural. Ross concludes that "the distinction between V[erbs], A[djectives], and N[ouns] is one of degree, rather than of kind" (326), an idea that you might find persuasive and possibly helpful in terms of envisioning how the language works.

To give you some idea of how slippery all these categories are, let's look again at "Garden Path Sentences," which I introduced above. These are confusing, leading the reader down the wrong path, often because the reader misapprehends key words' parts of speech. In the sentence "The old man the boat," for example, most readers take in the first three words as article, adjective, noun, and expect the next part of the sentence to be about what the old man does. But the sentence should be taken in as article, noun, verb, with the meaning "The old people make up the crew of the boat."

Here's the key: you need to figure out how words fulfill varying duties within a sentence. You need to intuitively grasp the inner workings of the English sentence.

While I can't cover every case, every nuance of the language (I refer you to Jespersen, Quirk et al., or Huddleston and Pullum for authoritative and complete guides), I can urge you to scrutinize more self-consciously both your own sentences and those of others. Seeing sentences as composed of various elements that work and interconnect in clearly established and logical patterns will, I hope, transform the way you envision and use language. But the goal isn't to make you into a pedantic nitpicker; instead, it's to help you see and internalize the patterns of the English sentence. I want to sharpen your understanding of the language you produce and the language you encounter, to make you a better listener, and to enhance your writing's communicativeness, exactness, and power.

Fundamentals

Nouns

Definition: Typically defined as "a word for a person, place, or thing," a **noun** is usually the easiest kind of word to add to your vocabulary in a language. Remember that a "thing" might be an abstract concept, that is, something intangible, imaginary, or even nonexistent: liberty, hatred, righteousness, hell, nirvana.

Verbs

Definition: A **verb** is usually described as a word denoting action. Verbs can also show a state of existence (with a *to be* verb, such as *am, are, is, was, were, been, being*) or possession (variations of *to have*). The *International Herald Tribune* article "Pardon of Jailed Official Angers Sarkozy's Foes" includes the following sentence, whose verbs denote slow-motion, offstage-sounding action, but action just the same:

> Jean-Charles Marchiani, 65, helped free French hostages in Lebanon in the 1980s and Bosnia in the 1990s, and served in the European parliament and as a governor in the south of France. (Derschau)

Helped free and *served* constitute the "action" of this sentence. Verbs can be words of "action" that's internal, action that is metaphoric, action that doesn't involve movement, or action that takes place over a long period of time.

Verbs embody and depict events taking place, incidents occurring, states of mind, and states of being. They show, as if filmically, what happens, is happening, happened, will happen, could happen, would happen. They also can "link" one noun to another or to an adjective, setting up a rough equivalence.

Nouns and Verbs Together

Typically a noun and verb work together to create a sentence. But the noun has to function as a **subject**, and the verb must function as a **predicate**. The noun has to be the entity doing the action or existing, while the verb enacts what that noun is doing.

We know we have a full sentence via something called "sentence sense," a term that some teachers and writers use, suggesting that recognizing a sentence is like smelling, feeling, tasting, hearing, seeing, or balance: it can't be taught; it's almost instinctive, innate. It's sort of a seventh sense.

Here is one way to envision a sentence: If you enter a crowded room, and you have only a brief window of time to speak (i.e., a short interval during which everyone will momentarily hush and listen to you), what kind of utterance should you make? Only a full sentence will effectively convey a relatively clear and complete idea. This could be simply an **interjection**—"Yes!!"—or it could be an **imperative** (command), such as "Get out!" or "Party!" all of which are complete without additional sentence elements. Were you to shout something that could not be construed as a sentence, it would probably provoke puzzlement or laughter: "Mxyzptlk!" And a declaration such as "Among!" or "Perhaps!" might have some limited communicative value, though I'm not sure either would convey a "relatively clear or complete idea" to a roomful of people. Perhaps this marks a limit to the crowded room scenario.

Think of a sentence as a Stand-Alone Linguistic Unit of Thought or Expression: a **SALUTE**. In what I am calling a "typical sentence," a "SALUTE," you need a subject (note that in the command form this is implied: "[You] get out!"); you need a verb working with that subject; and that verb needs to have a tense: past, present, or future (or a perfective variant, i.e., with *had*, *has*, or *have*). But remember, the sentence has to be a SALUTE. It's something that might depend on antecedent or subsequent language, but it does not have to do so. While it is almost always offered within the context of a paragraph, a book, a speech, a conversation, it's also independent, self-contained, and nearly autonomous.

Short Sentences Often Acceptable

Sentences can be very short yet still "full" and correct. Here, actress Keri Russell describes the house her husband renovated (and also describes her husband himself):

> "It's so beautiful. He's such a stud. It's done. . . . And he did it." (Freydkin)

These three sentences are all complete ones, even though they are only between two and four words long.

Standard Pattern of English Sentences

In English, sentences most often take a subject-verb-object pattern. Thus the listener or reader usually knows—right

away—who or what is doing the action, as in this headline:

Online Piracy Menaces Pro Sports (Arango)

Online piracy functions as the subject in the sentence. What
is it doing? The headline makes it clear. Online piracy menaces. And what does it menace? Pro sports.

Interestingly, even though nonnative speakers might
jumble word order, they usually still retain the subject and
verb. In "Tajiks Bleed in a Xenophobic Russia," a Tajik is
quoted:

"No, never I go," he said in English, walking through the
mud in the village to a relative's house to repay a debt
his dead brother owed. (Tavernise)

This Tajik man's meaning is evident, perhaps because he
keeps subject and verb close together, even retaining the
subject-verb order.

I think it's true that many people dismiss your ideas if
you don't couch them in accurate language. But as a listener, you should not yourself engage in such behavior.
Even if someone speaks very heavily accented or imperfect
English, he or she often has something of great value and/
or insight to impart. My advice is paradoxical, perhaps:
while others might not be listening, you should be. You
must listen beyond and through the errors—always keeping in mind that others might not be listening beyond or
through your errors.

To make *Star Trek*'s Klingons sound more alien, the linguist who invented their language used an object-verb-subject pattern (Zimmer). And *Star Wars*'s gnomic Yoda always started with the verb or object. Chad Hagy offers a good analysis of Yoda's sentence structure:

> In most of his phrases, he begins with the verb that we would normally put in the middle of the sentence. He then ends the sentence with the words that we would typically begin the sentence with. So, for example, the phrase "You will be a great Jedi" becomes "Be a great Jedi, you will."

This deviation from standard English sentence structure is supposed to evince the workings of Yoda's strange but wise and otherworldly mind.

Subject-Verb Agreement

In the introduction, I briefly alluded to the complexity and slipperiness of subject-verb agreement. Some verb forms are used for plural subjects, others for singular subjects. Some are for what we call "first person" (to go with *I* or [plural] *we*), "second person" (to go with *you*, singular or plural), or "third person" (to go with *he*, *she*, *it*, or [plural] *they*). On the surface, this seems very straightforward.

Consider, for example, the forms of the verb *to be* in the present tense (see below). You need to use the form of the verb that matches (or "agrees with") the subject of your sentence. For example, you would never say, "They am here." Of course, few writers or speakers make mistakes like that. (Or do they? Just recently I noted a graffito on Twenty-Third Street in New York City: "My love you!" What kind of thought does that represent? Is something missing? Your *what* love me? Or is it saying, "I love you!" Seems a significant distinction. I mean, if I'm an object of love, I really want to know from whom.)

Subject-verb agreement has great importance because it reinforces as it clarifies your meaning. And when the verb is somewhat distant from the subject, that verb's form should recall to the reader whether the subject is singular or plural.

Nonagreement of subject and verb, though, is not only confusing but also stigmatizing: it marks you as being insufficiently attentive to your language, maybe even someone who's forgotten the subject of the sentence by the time you come to the verb: a good thing, this is not.

To Be (present tense)

	Singular	Plural
1st Person	I am	we are
2nd Person	you are	you (>1) are
3rd Person	he, she, it is	they are

Fine Tuning

Subject-Verb Agreement with Indefinite Pronouns

The **indefinite pronouns** *neither* and *no one* take singular verbs, though they may seem conceptually plural.

But *none* proves trickier. Most editors, including those at *USA Today* (from which the following is taken), accept a plural verb after *none*, and I think they are right to do so here. Using the plural rarely interferes with clarity and often makes more sense, since the *none* often refers to a multiplicity of people, entities, or things.

> Five films opened nationwide over the weekend, and four beat expectations. None, though, *were* bigger than *Marley*, which had been expected to come in third place. (Bowles)

Many English teachers and editors will say that this should read, "None, though, *was* bigger," because *none* is equivalent to *no one*, which takes a singular verb. This is a convenient explanation, but it's simply not always true: sometimes *none* means "not any," the case in the example sentence, and *not any* conveys plurality.

Sometimes, though, *none* means "not a single, solitary one," and the writer wants to emphasize this fact. In that case, *none* should take a singular verb, as in "None is boring," my revision (in the introduction) of a critic's assessment of an Avedon photograph exhibition.

The indefinite pronouns *some* or *any* may take either a singular or a plural verb, depending on whether they refer to just one thing or to more than one.

Subject-Verb Agreement When Prepositions Intervene

Often a **prepositional phrase** (a phrase beginning with a **preposition**, a word like *for, with, from, about*, or the like—see glossary for a more complete list) intervenes between subject and verb. When determining whether the verb should be singular or plural, though, you need to go back to the subject itself, ignoring the material in the prepositional phrase. Prepositional phrases like *in addition to, as well as, in combination with*, or *along with* provide only weak jointures, ones that lack the solidity of *and*. Thus they can't pluralize a singular subject.

David J. Lynch, in "Formerly Soaring Trade Stomps on the Brakes," breaks this rule:

> **?** A trio of bilateral trade deals with Colombia, Panama and South Korea *continue* to idle in Congress.

Since *trio* denotes a singular (though admittedly three-part) entity, the sentence should end, "*continues* to idle in Congress." (We would probably not ever say, "A trio are here.") Another option would be to make the subject plural, as in "Bilateral trade deals with Colombia, Panama, and South Korea continue to idle in Congress."

But how about this following situation: is *handful* singular or plural?

> ❓ A handful of graphite drawings—"Study for a Christ in Limbo," "Sacrifice of Isaac," and "Studies for the Head of Leda" all on loan from the Casa Buonarroti, in Florence—make this show worth a visit. (Rev. of Michelangelo Exhibition)

"A handful . . . make" seems to me awkward, though I can see why the editors let it stand. The handful being alluded to consists of three drawings, which might seem to constitute a plural entity. Further, if *makes* had been used ("a handful . . . makes"), it might have seemed to diminish the size of that handful. But handfuls are quite small, aren't they? That's the whole thing about a handful: it's not very much. So we have here a disjunction between the smallness of a handful and the plural verb, which might be implying a magnitude or multiplicity. I think I would have changed "A handful of" to "Three striking," or something similar:

> Three striking graphic drawings—"Study for a Christ in Limbo," "Sacrifice of Isaac," and "Studies for the Head of Leda" all on loan from the Casa Buonarroti, in Florence—make this show worth a visit.

The following are two correct usages, each of which shows careful attention to sentence structure. The first sentence is taken from "Palestinians Need Israel to Win."

Hypocrisy, the subject, agrees with the verb, *is*, which I've italicized. The *together with* phrase does not affect the verb:

> The U.N.'s hypocrisy, together with growing media criticism of Israel, *is* reinforcing Israeli concerns that territorial concessions, whether unilateral or negotiated, will only compromise the country's security and curtail its ability to respond to attack. (Oren and Helevi)

(Note: Michael Oren, coauthor of the source article of this quotation, soon thereafter served as Israel's ambassador to the United States from 2009 to 2013).

In "Will '09 Be OK? Watch January," Adam Shell also demonstrates verb-form vigilance, a kind of vigilance for which people are, sadly, rarely complimented.

> Historically, stock performance in the first five days of a new year, and January overall, *has been a good predictor* of how the full year will go.

Why is this so important? If Shell had written *have been good predictors* instead, would his meaning have been lost or misunderstood? Even slightly?

Maybe. I think if he had used the plural, then his phrase *and January overall* would gain a sudden importance. And because that phrase is separated by nine words from *stock performance*, it seems to me that readers would not necessarily think of January's stock performance as being part of the subject, but would instead think of other aspects of "January overall"—maybe the weather, the political events, the upcoming inauguration—as being good predictors of the whole year's economy.

Some people won't notice any missteps or mistakes you make. It's/Its/Its' all the same to them. How nice. On the other hand, these same people will also almost surely fail to appreciate your elegant language constructions or your expressive powers. The difficulty is that you don't know the exact makeup of your audience. I suggest that you assume (or pretend) that everyone notices, everyone listens.

Subject-Verb Agreement with *There is/There are*

As I mentioned above, English sentences usually start with the subject. But this is not always the case. When you start with *there is* or *there are*, the subject follows, and you have to make sure that the form of the verb you pick agrees with it. If you have a singular subject, use *there is*; if your subject is plural, use *there are*.

It's easy to flub this. For example, a complex, long (forty-nine-word) construction from the *Wall Street Journal*'s "Murders of Black Teens Are Up 39% since 2000–01," flounders because a plural element follows *there is*:

> ❓ Mr. Fox said the cuts in law-enforcement programs and activities geared toward youth disproportionately affect African-Americans because they are more likely than their white counterparts to come from communi-

> ties where *there is* inadequate adult supervision, high
> rates of single-parent homes, inferior schools and wide-
> spread gang activity. (Fields)

I think this should be *there are*. Fields probably opted for
there is because *inadequate adult supervision* is singular, and
having that immediately follow *there are* sounded odd
("there are adequate adult supervision"). He should probably have reordered the list, starting with a plural element
after *there are*: "…where there *are* high rates of single-parent
homes, inadequate adult supervision, inferior schools, and
widespread gang activity." Alternatively, he could have just
used *with* instead of *where there is* or *where there are*. Sometimes just shortening and simplifying sentences clears up
their problems.

Here are another couple of examples of how pesky this
construction can be. The first is from John Fritze's "Groups
Send Wish Lists for Economic Bill," and I think we want
there are a lot of people rather than the singular (note that
this is recorded speech, though, so the "rules" for usage are
a bit looser):

> **?** "When Congress has got a pocketful of walking
> around money, *there's* a lot of people who are trying to
> take them for a ride," said Steve Ellis with Taxpayers for
> Common Sense.

Speaking in a colloquial manner, high school senior
Gabby Brice also opts for a singular verb with *a lot more*

responsibilities. Here he is quoted in "Having to Put a Senior Season on Hold":

> ❓ "*There's* a lot more responsibilities than doing your homework every night." (Sandys)

This would also sound better with *there are* (*there're*) instead of *there is*. Some might argue that *There is . . . a lot* is perfectly acceptable, since *a lot* is singular. It seems to me that it can be singular or plural. You just have to decide, depending on what follows the *a lot*, if you want to invoke pluralness or singleness. *A lot of people* (singular) means maybe a voting bloc, or a collective, but that significantly differs from what *a lot of people* (plural) usually means.

Subject-Verb Agreement in Unusual Cases

As I mentioned above, having an *and* in a sentence does not always make for a plural subject. Peter S. Goodman, in "Print Cash Today and Fret Later," cites poor fiscal policy but abides by good grammatical principles:

> Borrowing and spending beyond ordinary limits largely *explains* how the United States got into such economic trouble.

Goodman presents *borrowing and spending* as a single linked, conjoined action, so it takes a singular verb.

A similar situation emerges in a sentence quoting California representative Darrell Issa, but the three-part entity he invokes has a plural resonance:

> **?** "I'm taking President-elect Obama at his word that waste, fraud and abuse *is* something he wants to tackle," Issa said. (Dilanian)

Waste, fraud and abuse is something he wants to tackle just doesn't work for me; I see these three things as being separate ideas that establish a plural subject. The sentence should probably end, "waste, fraud, and abuse are things he wants to tackle." (Note that I'd include a comma, too, after *fraud*.)

But at the same time, I can understand how someone might say, "No, 'waste, fraud and abuse' all occur together. They form a set of linked problems and are hence singular." Well, I can see this: maybe. But I'd prefer that that three-part set be a more recognizable singular entity, like the name of a law firm, before I comfortably imagine it as taking a singular verb.

Here is another situation, from "The War on Terror Has Not Gone Away," in which I think an editorial intervention would have helped:

> **?** Indefinite detentions may offend our principles, but speedy trials for suspected terrorists *presents* no less a moral dilemma. (Rosenbaum)

"Trials . . . presents"? Keep in mind that the subject of the second main clause (*trials*), not the object (*moral dilemma*), should determine the verb. But, again, the author might argue that his locution *speedy trials for suspected terrorists* is a concept, and therefore singular. You can see how these things might be open for debate. In this case, I think that those taking the side of the writer would have the weaker position.

All too often writers push their nonpluralizing beyond acceptable limits. Something bothers me about the way the following sentence sounds, but it's probably borderline acceptable. Instead of *was*, I would likely use *represent* (agrees with plural *interceptions* but does not sound weird—as *were* might—before *the single stat*).

> ❓ But his six interceptions *was* the single stat that allowed the Redskins to avoid a losing record and perhaps even a coach-endangering mark. (Boswell)

Sometimes, determining whether the subject is plural or singular takes a little work. (Sports writing conventions differ from the norm. *Six interceptions* is acceptably singular if it's a statistic. *Runs Batted In*, usually called "RBIs," should technically be "RBI." Actually, it should be "R'sBI." Just try that out on a baseball fan.)

What I am arguing here, though, is that subject-verb agreement can be especially subtle, and as a writer, you need to take some time with it. In the following sentence, about female genital mutilation, taken from "For Kurdish

Girls, a Painful Ancient Ritual," the author sees the subject as plural, a questionable choice.

> **?** The practice, and the Kurdish parliament's refusal to outlaw it, *highlight* the plight of women in a region with a reputation for having a more progressive society than the rest of Iraq. (Paley)

The problem is that the comma after *practice* essentially isolates that noun, *practice*, as the subject, and the following phrase (*and the Kurdish parliament's refusal to outlaw it*) functions parenthetically, even though there are no actual parentheses. Again, though, I'm not labeling the sentence as "wrong": I'll let you decide. I'd argue that the commas surrounding *and the Kurdish parliament's refusal to outlaw it* cause the reader to pause and hesitate a bit too long. I would have enclosed the element in dashes and used a singular verb—or just removed the commas and kept the plural one. A third possibility would be to use *as well as* instead of *and* after *practice*, again with a singular verb form. Each of these revisions makes the subject more clearly just *the practice* or more clearly *the practice and the refusal*. As it stands now, the sentence's subject flutters between plural and singular. I don't think that fluttering really helps out the author in terms of conveying a meaning.

Another interesting situation emerges when the subject is split into two parts, as in "correlative constructions." These are not used very often in popular writing, though they do frequently appear in academic prose. Correlative constructions include *Either . . . or . . .* , *Neither . . . nor . . .* , and *Not only . . . but also. . . .* The usual practice is to make the verb agree with the part of the subject closest to it. In "Vision, Honor, Action: The Right Man Was in the White House on September 11," Mark Steyn (correctly) writes,

> The "war on terror" concept will die with his administra-
> tion: Neither Barack Obama nor the European leaders
> he finds congenial *think* it a useful model. ("Vision,
> Honor, Action" 30)

If the two elements had been reversed, the verb would change:

> The "war on terror" concept will die with his administra-
> tion: Neither the European leaders he finds congenial
> nor Barack Obama *think*s it a useful model.

Splitting the subject this way adds complexity—sometimes a virtue—and allows for more emphatic expression. In some ways, a correlative construction is a rhetorical device intended to heighten the drama of what one is writing or saying. There is nothing wrong with that, though I recommend not using more than one correlative construction every couple of pages.

Passive vs. Active Voice

Many of your teachers and professors will discuss the matter of verb "voice," or will expect that you know which voice to use in most writing situations. The active voice, most typically employed in everyday speech, basically states and makes clear who's doing the action. The passive omits that agent. It reverses the usual word order in English, a maneuver that buries the subject of the sentence, in effect almost hiding that entity. Here is a randomly selected sentence, the opening sentence of "'Stimulus' Doesn't Have to Mean Pork," from the *Wall Street Journal*:

> President-elect Barack Obama says he will create or protect some three million jobs by spending a massive amount of federal dollars to build roads and other "shovel ready" government projects across the country. (Winston)

This is a straightforward (**indicative**) sentence structure, but let's put it in the passive ("passivize" it) to see how it changes. Winston's version has vigor and directness, both of which are good things. Will it lose those in the passive voice? In the passive voice, the object comes first and a *to be* verb is inserted along with a past participle:

> Some three million jobs across the country will be created by President-elect Barack Obama, he says, by spending a massive amount of federal dollars to build roads and other "shovel ready" government projects.

It seems to me this sentence suffers in the transformation; Obama is seen less as a vital implementer of change and more as a kind of remote manipulator of events. He seems somehow diminished by the use of the passive to describe his plan. However, that remoteness (or impersonality) may be something that you, as a writer, want to convey. "Spending," in the passivized sentence, loses its agent (who's spending?), which makes it a little wiggly as to who's doing that spending—a problem not evident in the original.

Here is another example, again from the *Wall Street Journal*:

> On Friday, the dollar slipped against the euro, with one euro buying $1.406 late in New York. (Slater)

Again, a good sentence, clearly showing a subject (*the dollar*) and a predicate (*slipped*), and effectively communicating its meaning. To convert this into the passive, one must take the object and put it first. The thing doing the action, then, is either omitted or buried toward the end of the sentence:

> Against the euro, the dollar was weakened on Friday, with one euro buying $1.406 late in New York.

I'm not sure this sentence loses much by being passivized. When human agents are absent, the active/passive distinction carries less weight.

On the other hand, in a sensational *Trentonian* story entitled "'Little Michael's' Mom Found in Suitcase," the passive voice appears throughout. I'll provide some sample sentences from the article. The grisly story is about the murder and dismemberment of a young woman, Amy

Giordano, and the writer's use of the passive raises a lot of unanswered questions, which I will pose following each excerpt I quote:

> Amy's boyfriend, Rosario DiGirolamo, 33, married and living in a mansion in Millstone, was arrested and charged with murder and tampering with evidence.

OK, but who arrested and charged him? Where did this take place? Whose mansion was he living in? To whom was he married?

> On the Wednesday before Thanksgiving, however, DiGi-rolamo's bail was posted by a bond company, and he walked free to the anger of many who had been follow-ing the case.

A "bond company" posted his bail. Fine. Who are they? Did he pay them? Who was behind this bailout?

> Stipulation was made by authorities that he remain con-fined to his parents' home in Brooklyn and be moni-tored by an electric tracking device.

What authorities made this stipulation? Was there a trial or an arraignment?

> Russo said DiGirolamo was involved in her death and dumping, and DiGirolamo was charged with murder.

Well, he was "involved"—does that mean he killed her? He "was charged," but, again, by whom?

What's interesting about all these sentence constructions (and many others in the same awful story) is how they only apparently reveal details about the case but in fact end up concealing them. There is very little known, evidently, but readers of the *Trentonian* are provided with an illusion of knowledge about the murder and the alleged perpetrator. However, just looking at these four sentences, one wonders exactly what went on.

The trouble with the passive, and the reason so many writing teachers recommend against it, is that it tends to be, in a word, deceptive. It deletes (or hides) the actual agents of action and just presents what happened, as if almost scientifically and emotionlessly. Often, when used in nonscientific writing, it tends to obscure rather than clarify what it describes.

But guess what? Here, that's acceptable. I would argue that in this DiGirolamo case, the *Trentonian* does the right thing by using the passive voice. The story also does not carry a byline, I want to note: it's written by "*Trentonian* Staff." Newspapers must be wary of lawsuits and often tend to use legal-sounding, passive-voice language, so that they cannot be accused of judging an alleged perpetrator before his trial. They need to be indirect.

So the question for you, if you find yourself frequently using the passive, is as follows: what are you trying to hide? As grammar maven Bryan A. Garner points out, the passive "fails to say squarely who has done what" (613), which failure is sometimes a virtue, but usually not.

(Update: Rosario DiGirolamo pleaded guilty to the murder and was sentenced to twenty-five years in prison. His appeal was denied in 2012.)

Deep Focus

Appositives and Gerunds

An **appositive** is a word or group of words that repeats a noun or noun phrase but uses a different expression: it invokes the same thing in a different way, but at the same time adds some information. In "A Relentless Push to Approve Loans: At Washington Mutual, the Policy Seemed to Be: Don't Ask, Just Sell," the writers employ an appositive:

> In a financial landscape littered with wreckage, WaMu, a bank based in Seattle that opened branches at a clip worthy of a fast-food chain, stands out as a singularly brazen case of lax lending. (Goodman and Morgenson)

A bank based in Seattle that opened branches at a clip worthy of a fast-food chain stands in apposition to *WaMu*. The noun phrase establishes what might be called a presumptive equivalence, or, as linguist Gerard Dalgish labels it, a "nonassertive equivalence" ("Syntax"). It restates the noun, as it adds to and complicates it.

Typically appositives don't provide absolutely essential information, but serve to embellish and/or reinforce a sentence's ideas, as the above example demonstrates. Goodman and Morgenson's appositive complements and reiterates how WaMu was "brazen" and "lax." Supplying background or contextual information, appositives also help orient the reader.

You might object that their writing is redundant. Maybe. Keep in mind, though, that sometimes redundancy can be useful. By building in some redundancy, you make sure that your points get across, if not the first time, then the second or third. Just try to avoid *obvious* redundancy, which readers might see as "padding" or overinsistence.

One cautionary note I should provide here is that if a noun phrase is singular, its appositive (should you set one up) also needs to be singular.

Another interesting feature of English is that sometimes verb forms can function as nouns. For example, the following sentence contains words ending *-ing*, which look like present progressive forms of a verb. But here, in "Securing the Sea-Lanes: China's Gunboat Diplomacy," *stopping* (= "prevention of"), *declaring* (= "a statement of"), and *keeping . . . at bay* (= "containment of") function as nouns:

> The primary mission of the People's Liberation Army Navy remains *stopping* Taiwan from *declaring* independence, as well as *keeping* U.S. forces at bay in any ensuing war. (Medcalf)

Such verb forms, pressed into service as nouns, are called **gerunds.** A gerund is just one type of "verbal," which is a verb form functioning as a nonverb part of speech. In the last phrase of the above sentence, *ensuing*, also a verbal, functions as an adjective, and is called a **participle**—more specifically, a present participle. (I should note that some linguists would contend that the *-ing* words I've labeled gerunds actually function as verbs in the example sentence. And it used to be that grammarians separated out participles as a distinct part of speech, neither an adjective nor a verb: "some have injudiciously ranked them with the adjectives," Goold Brown writes in his 1863 handbook [99]. As I said, there are disputes about these issues.)

Possessive Forms before Gerunds

In general, it's best to use a possessive form before a gerund. I'll spend a bit of time on this, so be prepared. I fear that this usage is disappearing from the language. Can we resurrect it, or prevent its demise? This may sound like a pet peeve, I realize, so feel free to skip or skim this section (though I would prefer you did not).

Here are some correct uses. The first is from "Soviets Stole Bomb Idea from U.S., Book Says," and it's a usage most people would employ:

> Priscilla McMillan, an atom historian at Harvard and author of "The Ruin of J. Robert Oppenheimer," said *her weighing* of old and new evidence had come down on Dr. Sakharov's side as the main inventor. (Broad)

The next example is less obvious, but still clear and correct. In the article "India, an Exporter of Priests, May Keep Them," Laurie Goodstein writes,

> His prosperous family was not particularly supportive of *his* joining the priesthood, he said.

Some writers might be tempted to write, ". . . of *him* joining the priesthood." But keep in mind that gerunds function as nouns (as *joining* does in the above sentence by Goodstein). We would never use anything but the possessive were we to substitute for *joining the priesthood* a more obvious noun form, such as, say, *clerical membership*:

> ✳ His prosperous family was not particularly supportive of him clerical membership.

His would clearly be the correct pronoun to use before *membership*.

Former British prime minister Tony Blair, writing an article on Nicolas Sarkozy for *Time*, correctly uses a possessive form (*Nicolas's* would also be correct; see chapter 5) before the gerund:

> *Nicolas' reaching out* to the U.S., under President Bush, was not expected except by those who knew him. (90)

And in the same issue of the magazine, this usage appears again. It's not just "British English," but clearly something that *Time*'s editors are scrupulous about. Craig Robinson,

writing about playing basketball with Barack Obama, remarks,

> There's been a lot of talk about *Barack's building* a bas-
> ketball court somewhere in his new home.

Using the possessive before a gerund makes your meaning clearer—and less often invokes what I call an "absurd
universe." Let me further clarify what I mean by *absurd
universe*, a concept I will be revisiting. As an example, I'll
use the following sentence, which is from "George, Abe,
Rick & Barack," by William Kristol, and it abides by the
possessive-before-gerund rule:

> What's more, in a radio address this past week, Obama
> cited George *Washington's crossing* of the Delaware River
> on Christmas night, 1776, as a lesson for us today.

Here is what happens, though, if I purposely damage this
sentence by undoing the possessive—and you will need to
read this carefully, in order to notice how it's been severely,
if not fatally, damaged:

> ❓ What's more, in a radio address this past week,
> Obama cited George Washington crossing the Delaware
> River on Christmas night, 1776, as a lesson for us
> today.

Note that in my rewrite, the grammatical function of *George
Washington* is not clear. Or to put it another way, *crossing*

could be read as a present progressive form, relating back to Obama, as if he gave the radio address while he was crossing the Delaware in 1776, or as if he were giving a citation or maybe a traffic ticket to George Washington.

Of course, that's absurd; no sane person would entertain such notions for long—that's why even the mangled-by-me sentence still basically succeeds in conveying its intended meaning. It just doesn't work as well as it should: it could be misunderstood, if only for a split second, giving a quick and zany glimpse of an absurd universe, where President Obama is handing out tickets to George Washington. You most likely don't want to write sentences that give readers any opportunity to imagine an absurd universe. Unless you actually want to evoke such a universe, that flash of absurdity can distract your reader, subtly undermining your attempt to communicate a meaning.

An example of this possessive-before-gerund problem emerges in *USA Today*. In "They're over 'The Hills' and on Their Own," Brody Jenner describes his attitude toward male friends. This is speech, by the way:

> ❓ "It's just you being a friend to me and I'm being a friend to you." (Carter)

Here's how this would sound if Jenner respected the possessive-before-gerund rule:

> It's just your being a friend to me and my being a friend to you.

I think that this rewritten version causes fewer pauses on the part of the reader. It's a clearer expression of a thought. Even what *it* refers to (not stated but implied in both sentences) seems less problematic in the revised version, which succeeds better in describing an ongoing, existent state— something that I think is hinted at in the original, but which Jenner's pronoun use prevents from surfacing. Jenner's sentence sounds to me almost tentative, temporary, a friendship acted out rather than real. Or maybe Jenner is subconsciously conveying the idea that all Hollywood friendships have that provisionality. The rewrite I offer implies, I think, greater permanence.

A more difficult situation emerges in the following, perhaps hypercorrect, sentence, from "A Failure of Nerve, and a New Beginning," in which Diana Michèle Yap discusses her serious medical condition:

But I remember our being in bloom.

Yap is talking about remembering being healthy and mobile; *in bloom* attempts to convey how short-lived and transitory is that period of life. But to me, the whole sentence sounds a little stilted, stuffy. Wouldn't it be better to say, "I remember being in bloom"? or "I remember having been in bloom?" Part of the problem is with the concept of "in bloom": what does that mean? The image makes the sentence a bit confusing—perhaps intrusively poetic.

One of the (many) difficulties with English is that while

you want to be "correct," you don't want to seem to be straining to be correct.

Splitting Infinitives—Acceptable? Yes

An **infinitive** is the base form of a verb. In English an infinitive consists of two words, such as *to run, to go, to find*. In some cases the particle *to* is dropped, such as when auxiliary or helper verbs such as *can* are used: "she can run, win, lead." In many other languages, including the languages from which English was derived, the infinitive consists of just one word. This fact is often cited as the reason not to split infinitives. If the Latin or Greek word that the English one is derived from is just one word, we should try to make our infinitive as close to one word as possible, specifically, into two adjacent words. I'm not sure that this logic has an, ahem, algorithmic coerciveness.

One of the most famous **split infinitives** in English comes from the TV series *Star Trek*. "To boldly go where no man has gone before" places *boldly* between *To* and *go*, and it might not be accepted by some editors or teachers. (Obviously they would not be Trekkies.) Bryan A. Garner calls this a "justified split" (768). Some writers contend that the *to boldly go* construction deemphasizes the boldness of the quest, draining the *boldly* of impact. I'm not sure it does. Are the nonsplit variants, *to go boldly* or *boldly to go*, stronger, more forceful, more clear? It's hard to say, since *to boldly go* has imprinted itself on my memory and just sounds right.

Don't worry about splitting infinitives. Some people will no doubt "correct" you for your split infinitives. Editors have corrected me. But they are overcorrecting. Harvard linguist Stephen Pinker expresses the idea succinctly and powerfully: "In English," he writes, "infinitives like 'to go' and future tense forms like 'will go' are two words, not one, and there is not the slightest reason to interdict adverbs from the position between them" (A33). Even though he is at Harvard, I think his opinion is now in the majority.

Just the same, I offer you an example of a split infinitive that one might unsplit. I don't give it a question mark, though; it's neither wrong nor confusing. It could be improved, I think. A letter to the *New York Times* concludes,

> Our economy will come back, but if we are to truly reclaim the greatness that was awe-inspiring to the rest of the world, we must climb out of the morally corrupt hole we have dug ourselves. (Lowenstein)

Omitting *truly*, eliminating the split infinitive, might strengthen this writer's message, as it would moderate his tone somewhat ("awe-inspiring"? "morally corrupt hole"?). This omission would be a stylistic choice, though, not a matter of "correctness." It might inspire the writer to rethink his inflated language throughout. Sometimes split infinitives work as flimsy mechanical devices—like a megaphone, maybe—to bolster a weak concept or sentence: useful things to have when you need them, but required only if you fear your natural voice is too tiny for the task.

Some audiences have incorrect or out-of-date notions of "accurate" formal grammar, and they will look down on people who, say, split infinitives. So do I recommend that you *not* split infinitives if you suspect or know that your audience will disapprove? Nope. Just go ahead and keep splitting them. Do so with brazen impunity. The nonsplitter camp is diminishing in number, and if enough articulate, forceful, effectual people self-consciously split their infinitives, then maybe this ridiculous prohibition will die a natural death. Caving to the nonsplitters only perpetuates a pointless prohibition.

Verb Tense Conventions Vary with Genre

When discussing literary texts—films, novels, short stories, poems, plays, stories based on true accounts—use present tense. Pretend that the events you describe are happening right before your eyes, as if on a lighted stage—you know, with props, actors, sound effects: "Hamlet laments, 'To be, or not to be. . . .'" "Gatsby thinks that he can repeat the past." As a writer, it's as if you are actively witnessing what's being enacted.

If you discuss past historical details of an author's life, though, use the past tense. If you discuss elements of the work's backstory, also use past tense.

Verb Tense Issues: Perfect Forms

Many writers have difficulty with verbs in the **perfective** form. In fact, newspapers tend to shun perfect tenses. Present perfect, past perfect, and future perfect all indicate a tense (past, present, or future) and at the same time signal something else, namely, when the event being described has been or will be completed.

The present perfect suggests something has started in the past and continues on up to the present moment (and possibly longer): "I have been a stamp collector for ten years." Past perfect indicates the start and completion of an action in the past: "I had been an anthropology major for two years, but then I discovered English." Of course you might use simple past, as in "I was an anthropology major...," but that would carry less of a sense that there was a definite end to that period. As might be expected, this tense is used less often than the present perfect. And the future perfect is used to show how an action started either in the future or earlier will be completed in the future: "If I live long enough, I will have been married for seventy years in January 2044." This tense is used still less often than either of the others.

Timelines for these tenses:

Action described marked with ×'s;
Now (indicated by **N**) is the present moment at which the sentence is uttered or written. The | indicates the point at which the action ends.

Present perfect

Started in past, continues beyond:

————×××××××××××××××××**N**×××××→

Or stops in present:

————×××××××××××××××××**N**|

[Randy] Johnson *has won* five Cy Young [pitching awards]
and is five victories from win No 300. ("Sportsline")

Note that at the time of writing (2008), it was possible that
Johnson still could have won more Cy Young awards; the
present perfect does not prevent that possibility. (Age did.)

Past perfect

Started in past, completed in the past:

————×××××××××××××××××|————**N**

But a few survivors came away from the experience
with the knowledge that they *had stared* apocalypse
in the face and found the strength to come through it.
(Marciano)

Future perfect

Started in past, starts in present, or will start in future;
completed at future point:

————×××××**N**×××××××|

or

————N×××××××××××|

or

————N————×××××××|

> If a somewhat stable and democratic Iraq endures,
> Bush *will have forged* a historic accomplishment. He *will*
> *have replaced* an enemy with an ally, a dictatorship with
> something better. (Lowry 21)

Aside from *will*, other helper words such as *may*, *must*,
might, *could*, *would*, or *should* can be used with the same
verb form as in future perfect (*could have* [*could've*], *would*
have [*would've*], *should have* [*should've*], etc.), each offering a
slightly different (often wistful) reimagining of past events
("He could have been a star"). I mention these only because they are frequently misspelled as **should of*, **could of*,
*would of—or even **shoulda*, **coulda*, **woulda*. Editors watch
for such errors and usually catch them.

The "What if?" Verb Mood: Subjunctive

The **subjunctive** causes many writers considerable heartache, though in English its use is diminishing. It survives in
expressions such as *as it were*, *long live the Queen*, and *if it*
please the court. In a book review, Wyatt Mason praises the
subjunctive as indicative of carefully constructed prose:

> The precision of the subjunctive—which literate people
> bother with less and less, the simple past tense in-
> creasingly and diminishingly employed in its place—is
> never arbitrary, and its presence suggests that if atten-
> tion is being paid to a matter of higher-order usage,
> similar intention lurks behind. (14)

The subjunctive is one of three verb "moods" (or "modes")
in English, the other two being the indicative (normal
speech), and the imperative (command form). A few other
verb forms, I should point out, are sometimes seen as
moods. These include the infinitive verb form (called the
"generalizing" mood); as well as verbs linked with words
called "modals"—*may*, *might*, *can*, and *could* (the "potential" mood); *should* and *would* ("conditional" mood); *must*
and *ought* ("obligative" mood). It's interesting and useful
that people have labeled these moods, but I won't be using
the terms in the rest of this book.

The subjunctive is trickiest. It is used when the speaker
or writer asserts a matter contrary to fact ("If I were a rich
man . . ." Note that simple past would be "If I was a rich
man"). This mood also occurs in situations where a sentence starts, "I wish . . ." and in sentences where there is a
recommendation, demand, order, suggestion, or require-
ment being voiced about another agent's actions. We form
the present subjunctive by dropping the final "s" on the
verb, as in "I propose that John follow up [not "follows
up"] on the issue." With *to be* verbs, present subjunctive is
be and past subjunctive *were*.

The following sentence from *New York* magazine needs to have a subjunctive form, I believe:

> **?** The transformation of the Knicks into a team that, while still not all that good, is a joy to watch reminded us that anything really is possible here [in New York City]—if it *wasn't* why would there still be 22-year-olds so desperate to stay they were offering to pay $100 a month for the privilege of sleeping in a corner? ("Reasons to Love" 5)

Weren't instead of *wasn't* would strengthen the contrary-to-fact nature of the supposition.

A pair of examples from the *Trentonian* also illuminates the issue:

> If a special prosecutor *were* to be appointed to investigate possible criminality involved in detainee interrogations, "extraordinary renditions" or terrorist surveillance, it's not only Bush-era top officials who'd have to hire lawyers to defend themselves, but lower-down intelligence operatives as well. (Kondracke)

> **?** Defense lawyers attempted the spin that the defendants were merely indulging in a little R&R, having some fun—as if going down to a shooting range while yelling "Allahu Akbar!" *is* [should be *were*] a common way of blowing off steam. ("Ft. Dix Jihad")

Here is an example of the subjunctive used after the verb *orders*. (Note that the indicative would be *are*, which would likely sound strange even to people who have never heard of the subjunctive):

> So at irregular intervals, the International Earth Rotation and Reference Systems Service, based in Frankfurt, orders that the world's atomic clocks *be* stopped for a second. (Vinciguerra)

Sometimes the subjunctive is the same form as the past, which of course makes it even more difficult (and unnecessary) to distinguish the two:

> If you *were* to count the percentage of Americans who actually watched in a theater, "Twilight" was probably closer to the performance of "Congo," a jungle thriller from 1995. (Cieply, "When Megahit")

In most sentences that use the subjunctive, there is considerable complexity. The following sentence is correct, but a bit unwieldy. I would recommend splitting it into two separate ideas, probably after "funds."

> ❓ Davis-Bacon mandates, which effectively require that the actually "prevailing" union wages (often much higher than the actually prevailing market wage) *be* paid to workers on any construction project receiving federal funds, also drive up the costs of roads and other federal transport projects. (Winston)

Sometimes writers overcorrect. The subjunctive is not required with every use of *if*. I think Tony Blair might be better off with the indicative here. Writing about French president Nicolas Sarkozy, Blair states the following:

> ❓ Fourth, he showed, as President of the European Union, that he knows how to take center stage and get action. The differences within Europe over exactly the right action to stimulate the European economy will remain. But under his [Sarkozy's] leadership, Europe looked as if it *were* acting in concert.

I think *was* would be better in the last line, since Blair is commenting on a state of affairs that existed and was not contrary to fact; he is saying, "Europe was actually acting in concert, at least temporarily," not that it looked to be but was not.

Chapter 2

Words That Modify and Orient: Adjectives, Adverbs, Conjunctions, Prepositions, Articles, Interjections

---

The Power of Small Words Well Deployed

While nouns and verbs form the pith and pulsing essence of all sentences, the small modifying and orienting words (the subject of this chapter) are often crucial to the meaning of each sentence you write, and thus must also be handled with great care. They often determine meaning. For example, when the Tajik man says, "No, never I go," his word order is nonstandard, but it gains power because of the use of *never*. *Never* gives his sentence its meaning. He will *never* leave. *Never ever*.

Writing is about more than merely conveying your basic meaning. You want to convey the texture and nuance of your ideas. Remember, we're not like Swift's sages, who just carry around sacks of goods that we show to others. We actually need to use language. And to help you do this, you should master the use of words that give flavor, color, richness, warp and woof to your language—namely, the parts of speech that form the basis for this chapter.

Adjectives

Fundamentals

Adjectives Defined

"What is an **adjective**?" the poet Anne Carson writes. She elegantly answers her own question:

> Nouns name the world. Verbs activate the names. Adjectives come from somewhere else. The word *adjective* (*epitheton* in Greek) is itself an adjective meaning "placed on top," "added," "appended," "imported," "foreign." Adjectives seem fairly innocent additions but look again. These small imported mechanisms are in charge of attaching everything in the world to its place in particularity. They are the latches of being. (4)

So much rests on these small words. What's the difference between an "incisive" analysis and an "insipid" one? Between a "fortunate" accident and a "fatal" accident? Between a "terrible" marriage and a "terrific" marriage? It's just one word but all the difference in the universe.

Adjectives give specificity, add information, and lend vividness to your sentences. They modify (shape, narrow, sharpen, color, animate, limit) the meaning of a noun or pronoun—or of another adjective. As mentioned above, certain verb forms, known as participles, sometimes function as adjectives. Some typical forms of adjectives include "comparatives" (usually ending in *-er* or preceded by *more*) and "superlatives" (usually ending in -*est* or preceded by *most*). Note that some comparatives and superlatives require *more* or *most* because the addition of -*er* or -*est* produces something too hard to pronounce. For example, *beautifuler* and *beautifulest* don't work, at least not yet, as substitutes for *more beautiful* or *most beautiful*, since multisyllabic adjectives become tongue twisters, and it's problematic which syllable would receive stress. In the case of these two words, the second "u" would probably be elided, as in "She's the beautiflest person I know, beautifler than me." Generally, longer adjectives require "more" or "most."

Adjective Placement and the Misplaced Adjectival Modifier

Try to place adjectives as close as possible to the word or words they are modifying. If you don't do so, you risk confusing your reader—as this sentence might:

> ❓ Prabhu's photos show two police officers in pressed khaki uniforms wearing formal, wing-tip style shoes. (Fuller)

Notice that sometimes a group of words can work as an adjective or "function adjectivally." *Wearing formal, wing-tip style shoes* functions as an adjective. But placed where it is, it's confusing: it seems to be modifying *uniforms*. Are the uniforms wearing the shoes? Admittedly, most readers would realize that's not the case. But it's an example of the "absurd universe." This kind of error is called a **misplaced**

modifier. You need to construct a sentence less prone to misreading. One possible revision might be the following:

> Prabhu's photos show two police officers wearing pressed khaki uniforms and formal, wing-tip style shoes.

Although it's most common to see adjectives placed before the nouns they modify, sometimes words, phrases, or clauses that function adjectivally appear after the nouns they modify, as in the previous example and also here:

> We've made men bolder, women stronger, and shrinks poorer. (Harley Davidson advertisement)

You have to make sure, though, that this placement does not cause confusion. Usually the problem gets worse if you have piled up your modifiers. Here's a sentence that requires multiple readings to make sense of:

> ❓ Among the dead were seven teenage students at a UN-run school killed in an air strike while waiting for a bus, said Christopher Gunness, a spokesman for the United Nations Relief and Works Agency. (Silverman, Kalman, and Kennedy)

Let's see. Clearly, the UN-run school was not killed; the students were. Nor was the air strike waiting for a bus; the unfortunate students were the ones waiting. How to rephrase this?

> Christopher Gunness, a spokesman for the United Nations Relief and Works Agency, reported that an air strike killed seven students while they were waiting for a bus to [or from?] a UN-run school.

Interestingly, while rewriting this sentence, I noticed that a possibly crucial piece of information was missing: were the students going to school or coming home? Often when you work to clarify your modifiers, new issues emerge.

In the following sentence, the phrase *to be with him* functions as an adjective, and the author is intending it to modify *she*. But it seems to me that *to be with him* ends up modifying the thing right next to it, namely, *plans*:

> ❓ "He's been going through a hard time, and she's supporting him. She has even *canceled plans to be with him*." ("Hot Stuff: Kate & Owen")

Did Kate Hudson cancel other plans in order to spend her time, instead, with Owen Wilson (the meaning implied by the first sentence)—or did she cancel out quality together time? These are basically opposite meanings, so the sentence should probably be rephrased:

> To be with him, she has even canceled other plans.

Sometimes using adjectives in a cavalier manner will have an unintentionally comic effect:

> ❓ [Jim] McKay is likely to be remembered most for his work at the 1972 Munich Games, when he began a

15-hour stretch *behind the desk in a damp bathing
suit*—he had been in a sauna when the news broke—
watching the horrible fate of 11 Israeli hostages unfold.
(Bechtel 62)

From *Sports Illustrated*, this sentence makes it sound as
though the desk is clad in a damp bathing suit: unlikely and
absurd, I know, but I get this mental image of a big, drip-
ping wet Speedo draping the front of a mahogany desk . . .

Forms of Verbs—Verbals—That Function as Adjectives

Don't look only at morphology, or "form" of a word; look
most closely at syntax—how the word functions in its sentence. Understanding how words work within a sentence,
how they fit together, improves your writing. Remember
that "verbals," such as gerunds (verb forms used as nouns)
or participial phrases (verb forms used as adjectives), cannot function as predicates.

The following sentence is stuffed full of *-ing* words—
verbs and verbals of various kinds. It's from "The Weekend
That Wall Street Died." *Trading* and *remaining* are adjectives, *filing* is a gerund, while *soothing*, *slamming*, and *sowing* are verbs:

Rather than *soothing* markets, Lehman's bankruptcy *filing* roiled them—*slamming trading* partners that had direct exposure to the firm and *sowing* fears that Wall
Street's *remaining* giants weren't safe from failure.
(Craig et al.)

The next example passage, from "Mumbai's Torment Captured Click by Click," describes a horrific situation. Notice how important the verbals are, how they make the scene especially vivid and shocking. The first word (*captured*) and *sprawled* function as verbs; the other participles function adjectivally. A photographer going into the Taj Mahal hotel in Mumbai after the terrorist attack on it

> *captured* images of restaurant tables *abandoned*—there are *half-eaten* meals on plates and *shattered* glass is everywhere. By the swimming pool, a Western couple *clad* in white are *sprawled* lifelessly near an ice bucket and some wine glasses. (Fuller)

Make sure that, when your writing includes participles that end in *-ed* or *-en*, you retain those endings. Many people who learned English only by hearing it spoken tend to truncate these participial forms in writing. Note, too, that not all participles end in *-ed* or *-en*, but they differ from the standard verb form: *felt, put, swum, begun, bent* are a few examples.

Fine Tuning

Order of Adjectives

If you string together more than two adjectives, especially when they are all modifying the same noun, you need to determine the most logical sequence for them. R. Jeffrey Smith writes, in "Under Bush, OSHA Mired in Inaction,"

> In the summer, the agency decided against moving further toward the regulation of crystalline silica, the tiny fibrous material in cement and stone dust that causes lung disease or cancer.

Tiny and *fibrous* are both adjectives modifying *material*. What is the most logical order? What do you see as essential and important? I think we can guess the crystalline silica is tiny, but more significantly, it's fibrous. So Smith put *fibrous* closest to the noun being described, wanting, I think, to emphasize the icky, insidious quality of this stuff that people breathe into their lungs.

Typically, according to a standard grammar text that bases its findings on how native speakers actually speak, long adjective series follow this order:

> opinion | size | shape | condition | age | color | origin
> (Celce-Murcia and Larsen-Freeman 394)

Smith accurately places size (*tiny*) before shape (*fibrous*).

You probably don't want to use too many long adjective strings in your formal writing. Here is an example I'm making up, used to describe an automobile, a Nash, my family once owned:

> It was a horrible, big, bulbous, battered, old, gray American car.

The sentence seems to work fairly well, following the adjective order Celce-Murcia and Larsen-Freeman specify.

But in general, avoid more than three consecutive adjectives, unless you are striving for some special or strange effect. (In an earlier version of this book, I recommended that you avoid Nashes as well, but one of my colleagues noted that no one knows what Nashes are anymore, reminding me that language must connect both to a changing world and to an ever-evolving audience. Besides, a Nash in tip-top shape is likely worth a fortune.)

I should point out, too, that any adjective string should use words that don't just repeat the same idea. Each adjective needs to describe a different aspect of the thing being modified. Here, describing a character named Jara, Roberto Bolaño skillfully demonstrates this precept in a *New Yorker* story published on our "one day in the life":

> So I explained to him who I was and, while I was at it, who he was, too, thereby creating a Jara to suit me and him, that is, to suit that moment—an improbable, intelligent, courageous, rich, generous, daring Jara, in love with a beautiful woman and loved by her in return. (81)

The six-adjective string in the middle of the quoted passage, which itself is in the middle of a very long sentence, manages to offer six mutually exclusive attributes. I've suggested above that usually such long strings should be avoided, but Bolaño's sentence demonstrates that rules often find fulfillment in their brilliant violation—you have to be brilliant in order to violate them. This is from fiction, but it can provide those of us who have less artistic genius a lesson in prose style. (And fiction and nonfiction are growing closer and closer, what with the emergence of "creative nonfiction," not to mention "gonzo journalism" or the nonfiction novel, or "faction.")

Relative (Adjective) Clauses

Like verbals that function as adjectives (participial phrases), relative (adjective) **clauses** (groups of words introduced by *who, that, which,* and *where*) also modify nouns. "Spaniards in Huge Rally Emphasize the Family" contains the following sentence:

> The service started with a message from Pope Benedict XVI, who urged Spanish Catholics to keep their families strong.

This includes the relative clause *who urged Spanish Catholics to keep their families strong,* which functions as an adjective modifying *Pope Benedict XVI.* By putting the comma before the relative clause, the author created a **nonrestrictive** (or nonessential) clause, that is, one not necessary for conveying the basic meaning of the sentence (namely, that the service started with a papal message). The relative clause gives extra—though not "essential"—information: the sentence still makes full sense without it. That nonessential material does give additional, more detailed and specific information, but it's sort of tagged on at the end. The principal meaning, what the subject "verbs" or "is verbing," let's say, exists apart from the information in the nonessential clause. Note that nonrestrictive or nonessential clauses are usually set off with commas.

You need to be careful, though, with the placement of these kinds of clauses. The following confuses me, and probably would confuse some other readers as well:

> ❓ Muniz's own art isn't shown, but it tends toward re-conceptions, like a *Mona Lisa* made of peanut butter and jelly, *that depend on such echoes.* (Sudarsky)

Using a comma before *that* makes the modifying phrase seem to modify what comes directly before, namely, the PB & J. Putting *that depend on such echoes* directly after *re-conceptions* would help put the emphasis onto the PB & J *art*, rather than on the PB & J itself:

> Muniz's own art isn't shown, but it tends toward recon-ceptions that depend on echoes, like a *Mona Lisa* made of peanut butter and jelly.

Deep Focus

One of the . . . *and* The only one of . . .

An interesting situation emerges when we use the phrases *one of . . .* and *the only one of . . .* , since both of these often precede relative clauses. Note the correct verb forms in the two following examples:

> One of the religious leaders who *have* been less vocal in demanding female circumcisions is Hama Ameen Abdul

Kader Hussein, preacher at the Grand Mosque of Kalar and head of the clergymen's union in Germian. (Paley)

I hope the Giants are focusing this week on Philly since they are the only one of our three potential opponents that *is* scary. (Jersey Joe 1)

You need to ascertain what is being modified; this will allow you to decide on the correct verb. In Paley's sentence about female circumcision, the relative (adjective) clause—which starts out with *who*—modifies *religious leaders* (plural); hence the verb within the relative clause has to be plural as well (*have*).

But in the sentence from Jersey Joe, the relative (adjective) clause—*that is scary*—modifies *the only one* (*Philly*); therefore, the verb has to be singular (*is*). This is made a bit confusing, I suppose, because Jersey Joe treats *Philly* as both a plural, a team ("they are"), and then as a singular opponent ("the only one that is"). By the way, I would have included a comma after *Philly*, though I don't think most people would consider the sentence wrong without one.

Adverbs

Fundamentals

Adverbs Defined

An **adverb** modifies verbs, other adverbs, or adjectives. Adverbs answer the questions "When?" "In what way?" "Where?" "How?" as well as other essential questions. I can imagine a whole book about adverbs. They are "morphologically and syntactically the most diverse grammatical structures in English," according to Celce-Murcia and Larsen-Freeman (491), which means you can't identify them by how they look, and they appear all over the place in sentences. Adverbs can modify single words, phrases, or whole sentences. Often they can be identified by the *-ly* ending, though not all words ending in *-ly* are adverbs, and there are many adverbs that do not end in *-ly*. *Folly*, for example, is a noun, and *well* is often an adverb.

Like adjectives, adverbs have base, comparative, and superlative forms, such as *hard, harder, hardest*; or *lazily, more lazily, most lazily*; or *badly, worse, worst*. Sometimes one is tempted to come up with strange variants of comparative or superlative forms. On December 29, 2008, the *New Yorker* printed a previously unpublished Mark Twain short story, and it uses the word *oftenest*:

> Sometimes we suppress an opinion for reasons that are a credit to us, not a discredit, but *oftenest* we suppress an unpopular opinion because we cannot afford the bitter cost of putting it forth. None of us likes to be hated, none of us likes to be shunned. (50)

This would, I think, fall under the category of "poetic license," though *oftenest* and *oftener* do appear in dictionaries. Wiktionary notes that these words have been in "declining use since 1910." I'd recommend *most often* and *more often* as substitutes, though the choice is ultimately up to you.

Well vs. Good

In its coverage of the arts, the *New York Times* ran an article describing late 2008 film releases. In an effort to garner more Academy Award nominations, studios often wait until year's end to release their best, most star-studded movies. Michael Cieply's headline captures this notion in a succinct phrase, and he also uses the adverb correctly:

Star-Filled Year-End Releases Draw Well

In general, adverbial forms seem to be falling out of favor, especially in spoken English, but try to preserve them as much as possible in your writing. Cieply's headline was not "Star-Filled Year-End Releases Draw Good," you should note. (But, on the other hand, a colleague advertising a car wrote in her classified ad in a small-town paper, "The car runs well," and she got no calls the first week of the ad. She revised it to "Car runs good," and ten calls came the next day. Audience is crucial.)

If you think that the *well/good* distinction doesn't matter, well—you are probably in the majority. To many people, it doesn't matter one whit. This group of people do not make such distinctions. They are called "levelers." But to a segment of your audience, the *well/good* distinction matters *a lot*. This group is called "sharpeners"; they sharpen distinctions, as opposed to leveling them. (Sometimes the terminology is different: "levelers" are called "lumpers," and "sharpeners" are called "splitters.")

Adverb Placement and Misplaced Adverbial Modifiers

Like seasoned partygoers, adverbs move around and mingle. Often they open a sentence; equally often, they close one. But in general, it's good practice to keep them fairly near the word or phrase they modify, especially considering that adverbs can modify so many different types of words. Here is an example of how an adverbial phrase is (in my opinion) confusingly placed.

> ❓ Culiacán is home to Mexico's most notorious drug kingpins, and thugs fight daily with Kalashnikovs, rocket-propelled grenades and homemade bombs. (Grillo)

Here it sounds as though the thugs are struggling against Kalashnikovs, grenades, and bombs. I'd rewrite the second clause slightly more emphatically (and I hope more lucidly) as follows: "and armed with Kalashnikovs, rocket-propelled grenades, and homemade bombs, thugs go into combat every day." Note the comma after *grenades*, about which more later.

If an adverb is placed next to a sentence element it could conceivably modify, some readers will take it to be modifying that adjacent element. In the following, *for months* might seem to be modifying *those close to the couple*, but I don't think that's O'Leary's meaning:

> ❓ Though they renewed their wedding vows this past October, signs of strife have been apparent to those close to the couple *for months*, especially at the family's sad Thanksgiving dinner in L.A. (O'Leary 44)

Were the signs of strife apparent for months or were those apparent only to people who were close to the couple for months? I would place *for months* directly after *October*.

> Though they renewed their wedding vows this past October, the couple has been showing signs of strife—apparent for months to those close to them, and especially visible at the family's sad Thanksgiving dinner in L.A.

Readers will *pounce* on a meaning—often, the very meaning they want to hear—and move on. You need to do everything you can to make sure that that meaning matches your intended meaning. Think about what you're using the adverb to describe, specify, or modify, and try to make this absolutely apparent.

End-of-clause modifiers often prove troublesome. Here, a sentence about Susan Sontag ends with a prepositional phrase functioning as an adverb, but it might be misread as an adjective:

> ❓ As a lonesome genius, she felt the usual agonies of precocious teenhood *with superhuman intensity*.
> (Anderson 102)

Was Susan Sontag's a teenhood with superhuman intensity, or did she feel the agonies with this intensity? "She felt with superhuman intensity the usual agonies of precocious teenhood" would be a better word order, I think.

Some grammarians rail against the "split verb," a term that includes both the split infinitive and the situation in

which a modifier—for instance, an adverb—comes between an auxiliary and the main verb, as in *should willingly
have agreed*, or *should have willingly agreed*. But this splitting, as I've suggested above, is far less problematic than
leaving the reader confused about what's being modified,
as in the following, from "Agriculture Experts Urge More
Aid for Women Who Farm," which refers to an African
woman farmer, Mazoe Gondwe:

> ❓ Gondwe, who was flown by the development agency
> ActionAid to Poland for UN talks on climate change
> *this month*, said she wanted access to technology that
> would cut the time it took to water her crops and till
> her garden. (Rowling)

I've given this a question mark because the sentence can
confuse, if only briefly: are these talks on this month's climate change, or was Gondwe flown to those talks this
month? I expect *this month* modifies *flown* (answers *when*
she was flown); however, thirteen words separate *flown*
and *this month*. That's probably too long to make your
reader wait. Furthermore (just to sharpen the editorial
pencil to a still finer point), is the agency called "Action-
Aid to Poland" or just "ActionAid"? The *to Poland* prepositional phrase functions as an adverb, but what it modifies
is unclear. Readers want a meaning as quickly as possible.
And maybe the talks were really on this month's climate
change. We can't be 100 percent certain. Let me suggest a
revision:

With her trip funded by the development agency Action-Aid, Gondwe was flown this month to Poland, where she attended UN talks on climate change and requested access to technology that would reduce the time it took for her to water her crops and till her garden.

Here is another adverb placement problem. *According to . . .* phrases usually function as adverbs, answering the questions "In what way?" or "How?" But if the *according to* phrase isn't closely tied to the element it's supposed to be modifying, then—well, take a look:

❓ The Border Patrol caught 705,000 people along the U.S.-Mexico border in fiscal year 2008, which ended Sept. 30, according to agency figures. (Frank, "Fewer Caught")

It sounds as though we have to check agency figures to determine that the fiscal year ended on September 30. I suspect the agency figures actually recorded the number of people caught. A revision might involve starting the sentence, "According to agency figures. . . ."

President Obama, interviewed by *Time*, attaches an adverb to the very end of a prepositional phrase:

❓ Sorting through our policy with respect to Iran *effectively*—that will be a priority. ("The Interview: Person of the Year Barack Obama" 68)

It probably would be best to have opened with the adverb, *effectively*, which would then be placed next to the verb it's modifying. Ending with it makes it seem too closely linked to *Iran*, as if "Iran effectively" were some variation of the country, like Iran and its sphere of influence.

I'll provide here a few more examples of misplaced adverbial modifiers. I have italicized portions that seem to me problematic.

> ❓ Sotheby's closes with a busy week that begins with a sale of *mostly Israeli art* (Dec. 16), spanning and even predating the creation of Israel. ("Auctions and Antiques")

Is the art 95 percent Israeli? Paintings from Israel, frames made somewhere else, maybe in Greece or Borneo? Or is there a mixture of art from Israel and art from other countries?

I have italicized the fragment in the following example. It's at once titillating and confusing:

> ❓ It is so easy to get laid as a New Yorker out of town. *Easier than Brooklyn, even.* ("Brawndo")

Intriguing, especially for someone (like me), born in Brooklyn and working in New York—maybe a typical reader of *New York* magazine. But exactly what (or who) is "easier than Brooklyn"? I think the message is that it's easy for a New Yorker to get laid when s/he goes out of town— it's even easier than it is for a Brooklynite who goes out of town. But, alternatively, it could mean that it's easy for a New Yorker to get laid when s/he goes out of town: in fact out-of-town action is even easier to find than what's available in Brooklyn. The adverbial phrase is maddeningly vague.

As with misplaced adjectives, misplaced adverbs will sometimes evoke comic, absurd-universe results. Here is an example from a non–December 29 source, a sentence from a *New York Times* article from late 2012, perhaps proving that copyeditors still had some of the same blind spots they had four years previously. In an article about a man who makes exotic motorcycles, Alix Browne describes a workshop/studio in L.A.

> ❓ Within the confines of a 14-foot corrugated metal fence, they created an oasis, but their front door was strewn *with human feces and used needles almost daily.* (114)

The prepositional phrase that starts, "with human feces" modifies *strewn*. But when I first read it, it sounded as though the door itself had been using needles. A few readers have told me that no sane person really thinks this, but if only a small portion of the audience could misread your sentences, and a revision is fairly effortless, it seems a good plan to revise.

On the other hand, while I have been contending all along that you don't want your language to cause your readers to pause, stop, go back, and reread, some excellent writing has this as one of its goals. Here are a couple of curious sentences that didn't confuse me, exactly. But they gave me pause; their condensed complexity was intriguing. I had to reread them, and the rereading was rewarding:

> Conservatives don't need telling. (O'Sullivan 18)

> The experience of sheerly responding pleases. (Schjeldahl 113)

Interestingly, these come close to being "Garden Path Sentences" but are not so confusing that they defy understanding. They inhabit an interesting borderland between "Garden Path Sentences" and overly elliptical, or too-poetic, usage—and end up being successful. Sometimes, pushing your sentences to the edge of comprehensibility gives them energy and makes them succeed. You just have to make sure they don't go over that edge.

Fine Tuning

Conjunctive Adverbs and the Comma Splice

Here are some common **conjunctive adverbs**: *accordingly, additionally, anyway, besides, certainly, consequently, doubtlessly, finally, furthermore, hence, incidentally, indeed, instead, likewise, meanwhile, moreover, namely, nevertheless, now, otherwise, similarly, still, then, thereafter, therefore, thus, undoubtedly*. These words modify a phrase as they join that phrase to the one following.

Here is an especially important point. If you use one of these words after a full sentence, and follow it with another main clause, you will have to use a semicolon as well (either before or after the conjunctive adverb). If you use just a comma, that's called a **comma splice**, and is considered a misusage:

> ❓ If you had money on Atlanta and Arizona both going to the playoffs this year—let me know which Island you can now afford. I'll be there for your New Year's soirée.
> The answer to the question posted is probably the dangerous Cardinals passing game, however, the Arizona defense has been so suspect of late that it's the Falcons rushing game that I believe will make the ultimate difference. (Leibowitz)

The second sentence contains two grammatically complete sentences, which, if you want to include in their entirety in just one sentence, need to be separated more sharply than with just a comma.

The break comes either before or after *however*. Used this way, *however* always implies a contrast. Where do you want that contrast to be? Putting in the semicolon before *however* anchors that word to the second clause; placing it after *however* anchors it to the first clause and to the sentence that precedes it. These are two somewhat different meanings, each emphasizing a different contrast that the writer is noting:

> The answer to the question posted is probably the dangerous Cardinals passing game, however; the Arizona defense

has been so suspect of late that it's the Falcons rushing game that I believe will make the ultimate difference.

The answer to the question posted is probably the dangerous Cardinals passing game; however, the Arizona defense has been so suspect of late that it's the Falcons rushing game that I believe will make the ultimate difference.

I know that many would think that these two sentences differ so slightly in meaning as to be functionally equivalent. But not me. I think the semicolon belongs before the *however*. (If Leibowitz had omitted the commas altogether, this would be called a **fused sentence**—probably a slightly worse error, but also one that would reveal an inability to recognize sentence boundaries.)

The comma splice is quite a serious error, yet it appears with surprising frequency, both in papers that students turn in for their college courses and in the popular media. Here are just a few that I came across in December 29 publications:

❓ "She's mellow and down-to-earth, he's very moody." [An "inside source" tells *US*, in reference to Kate Walsh and Alex Young; "Hot Hollywood"]

❓ "Weakness is a contagion, strong people rightly shun the weak." (100) [Susan Sontag's early journals, quoted in a review by Sam Anderson]

❓ "I can tell you're having a girl, they steal the mother's beauty." [Emily Nussbaum, on pregnant women in New York City]

❓ "I don't have any room in midtown, it's a pain in the neck!" [Jesse Oxfeld quoting "financier turned frankfurtier" Nicholas Gray]

❓ "I did not recognize myself," she [Janet Jackson] said of her 60-pound gain. "My thighs got hefty, I got this big stomach." ("Body News")

❓ Out with the old, in with the new. Oxford University Press publishes a "junior dictionary," widely used in British schools and popular with parents. ("The Week" 10)

Closest to acceptable, I think, is the final example, since the main clauses are short, and since the expression's proverbial quality might come through better with a comma. Some people would accept the others too, but I find them awkward. I had to reread them to make sure what they were saying, since I didn't automatically pause at the comma, as I ordinarily do if processing an end punctuation mark or semicolon. Their authors aren't clearly signaling where one main clause ends and another begins. Worse, since most are transcriptions of speech, by failing to use a semicolon or divide the main clauses into separate sentences, the writers undermine their subjects' credibility.

People often ask me, "Why is the comma splice such a big deal? Why do people think that it matters so much? Can't they figure out what the sentence means?" Actually, I can usually figure out these sentences. They usually convey a generally understandable "content." But that content takes a bit of time to get to—and more importantly, it usually lacks exactness. Having a comma in a sentence where (say) a semicolon is needed causes that sentence to momentarily flutter out of focus before it resolves into its more or less intended meaning plus something else.

The "something else" that such a sentence also conveys is that the writer does not know—or care—about sentence boundaries, proofreading, or the standard use of punctuation. The comma splice usually conveys a linguistic carelessness, a preference for stream-of-consciousness writing that reflects an unedited process of thought, a slapdash method of composition. If that's what you want to reflect, then the comma splice is your friend. Stream-of-consciousness writing isn't really appropriate in most communicative or rhetorical situations. We have many ways of joining main clauses, ways that more clearly indicate and establish—with considerable precision—the linkages and relationships between and among them. Since comma splices communicate linguistic laxness, this fact will work against the content that's being conveyed, and will often stigmatize the writer.

Deep Focus

The Adverb However *and Its Problems*

However can also function as an **interruptive**, a word that temporarily stops the flow of a sentence. R. Jeffrey Smith in "Under Bush, OSHA Mired in Inaction" uses the word as a kind of throat-clearing element to signal a contrast:

> Wainless persisted, *however*, and over the next two years sent four drafts to Henshaw's office to meet what another OSHA official described in an internal e-mail as "requests for minor changes" by the agency's deputy director.

Alternatively, *however* can mean "in whatever manner," as in "The Beautiful Machine," an article about how Howard Sosin and Randy Rackson contrived their grandiose scheme to change the way Wall Street operates:

> [Tom] Savage respected Sosin, but saw no reason to follow Sosin and Rackson out the door. "I think what was clear was that, *however* things should work out, there was a business at AIG Financial Products and Sosin didn't need to be there for it to be successful," Savage said. (O'Harrow and Dennis)

As you probably know, this business did not in fact work out so well, but the sentence is good.

Some people have been taught never to start a sentence with *however*. This seems to me another one of those prohibitions that have no grammatical basis. Bryan A. Garner points out that it's a stylistic, not a grammatical, objection. But then he goes on to say, "*However*—three syllables followed by a comma—is a ponderous way of introducing a contrast, and it leads to unemphatic sentences" (428). I disagree. I think it's fine to start a sentence with *however*, provided that a comma follows it, and a full sentence follows that. Or you can use a structure similar to the one in the quotation above ("However things should work out, there was a business at AIG Financial Products.") Keep in mind that some will disagree. However unassuming it might appear, *however* is a word around which problems seem to have accumulated.

Conjunctions

Fundamentals

Coordinating Conjunctions

Coordinating **conjunctions** include *and*, *but*, *so*, *or*, *for*, *nor*, *yet*. Once, a student of mine pointed out that *else* can also function this way. True enough, but such a use is slightly archaic: today's writers will typically use *or* in combination with (or instead of) *else*.

Some people use the mnemonic FANBOYS to recall these words, but I prefer **ABS OF NY** as a way to recall the coordinating conjunctions. Like abs (i.e., the rectus abdominis muscle), these words, a seven-pack of conjointure, knit together and help establish your sentences' core strength. NY—the venue from which so many words emerge—is, at present, the publishing capital of the country. And here, words matter, at least to some fairly sizable segment of the population. (I know this derivation is slightly whacky, but if it helps you recall the mnemonic and the words, it's done its job. Of course, if FANBOYS has a resonance for you and you can best remember the coordinating conjunctions using that mnemonic, great. If you like neither, there are 5,038 additional options—maybe you'd prefer the slightly more edgy FABNOSY or SONAFYB.)

Conjunctions can be used—again, with a preceding comma—to join two **main clauses** to create a compound sentence. Examples abound. I've highlighted the coordinating conjunctions in the following. About New Year's resolutions, Stephen Prothero writes,

> We are getting flabby, *so* we resolve to work out.

And on the weakening of the dollar, Joanna Slater points out,

> That is good news for U.S. exporters, *but* it is raising concerns in places like Japan and Germany, which are both gripped by recession.

Note that a main clause is essentially a sentence that can stand on its own. We can break down Prothero's sentence into its two component sentences in this way:

1. We are getting flabby.
2. We resolve to work out.

Slater's might be broken down as follows:

1. That is good news for U.S. exporters.
2. It is raising concerns in places like Japan and Germany, which are both gripped by recession.
   *[Here we have a main clause plus a **relative pronoun** that introduces a relative clause.]*

Note that each pair of sentences might be logically joined with any one of several different coordinating conjunctions. "We are getting flabby, and we resolve to work out," "We are getting flabby, but we resolve to work out," or "We are getting flabby, yet we resolve to work out" are all acceptable. (*For*, *nor*, and *or* don't seem to convey a cogent idea.) Each variant has a slightly different meaning.

Fine Tuning

Conjunction Placement

Contrary to popular belief, it is just fine—totally acceptable—to start sentences with coordinating conjunctions. The prohibition against doing so is just another "rule" that seems honored in the breach, i.e., rarely. It is really fine to start a sentence with a conjunction, but it's probably not a good idea to start many—or the majority—with conjunctions. (You have probably noticed that I start many sentences with *and*, a few with *but*, and even fewer with *so*.)

The "rules of English" that we were taught, still remember, and even live by provided guidelines for grade-school students, namely, children who were gradually acquiring an understanding of formal English, and who had to be weaned from their childish language. For example, we were taught not to start sentences with conjunctions such as *and* or *so* or *but*. We were taught not to end sentences with prepositions and not to split infinitives. As far more sophisticated users of language, we understand why these rules were created, and though we don't invariably break them, we also understand that it's not necessary to blindly or mechanically obey them. In fact, we realize how important it is to routinely question these rules, and to discover their margins and limits.

Subordinating Conjunctions and Fragments

Subordinating conjunctions include such words as the following: *after, although, as, as if, as long as, as though, because, before, even, even if, even though, if, if only, in order that, now that, once, provided, rather than, since, so that, than, that, though, till, unless, until, when, whenever, where, whereas, whether, while, why.*

Placed before a sentence, these words have a transformative power. They make that sentence into a dependent or subordinate clause, that is, into a group of words that must be then attached to a full sentence. On their own, they are not a sentence, but a fragment. For example, if you take a sentence such as

> Finally we saw a lighthouse.

and precede it with *when*, you no longer have a sentence.

> ✱ When finally we saw a lighthouse.

To produce a correct and comprehensible sentence, you must now append a full sentence, such as "many jumped into the water," as does Mark McDonald, in an article entitled "Hundreds Are Feared Dead in Bay of Bengal":

> When finally we saw a lighthouse, many jumped into the water.

In most contexts, **sentence fragments** are viewed as errors, evidence that you have not internally grasped the concept of a sentence. Using them reveals your "sentence sense" is a bit off. When employed for rhetorical effect, they can occasionally be acceptable, but you should be cautious about using fragments in your writing.

If you stretch or break the rules, make sure your language is so successful that no one notices—or cares—that you've done so. For example, while in general it's safest to use full sentences, many skilled writers flout this rule. Clearly in the following, Pat Caputo is using fragments for a special verbal effect—and I think he almost succeeds. I especially like the last, one-word sentence:

> ❓ Their fans will never forget it. Or the headache it will bring in memory. The Lions of '08 will live forever as all-time bottom feeders. Plankton.

The problem is that Caputo employs the fragment four other times in the same article, all in a space of two paragraphs, which also include a comma splice. Not recommended.

Each of your sentences should contain a subject and a verb whose tense locates the expression in time. This strategy helps to create a complete parcel of thought, something that can stand on its own, what I am calling a SALUTE (Stand-Alone Linguistic Unit of Thought or Expression). Remember that a gerund or a participle, even though it looks like and is derived from a verb, cannot function as a predicate.

To rephrase, when you use a subordinating conjunction (like *while, if, when*, as listed above), make certain that you have a full sentence *in addition to* the clause that includes the subordinating conjunction. And to repeat, putting a subordinating conjunction before a main clause renders that clause a non-SALUTE (a "SALUTE-not"?), in fact a dependent unit of thought insofar as it depends upon—relies upon, requires a connection to—a main clause, that is, to something which could by itself be a SALUTE.

Deep Focus

Fragments in Disguise

Sometimes a sentence will be more or less acceptable on its own, but because of the context provided by preceding material, it functions as a fragment. That is, if we look at it in isolation, it's a SALUTE, but in its place within a paragraph, the sentence is not a Stand-Alone Unit of Linguistic Thought or Expression. It is a function of the preceding material. In *USA Today*'s "Savvy Shoppers Eschewed Gift Cards," the following appeared:

> ❓ Consumers figured out that for the $100 they would ordinarily spend, they could get far more merchandise than before. Or get something far more expensive that had been deeply discounted.

If you were to isolate the second sentence and look at it carefully, you'd probably see it as a correct imperative: *get something* is command form, the subject *you* implied. But a command form here makes no sense. The preceding sentence sets up something else. That second sentence should just proceed from the first, continuing its mood (indicative), its syntax, and its tense. The second sentence's placement thrusts it, in short, into what I call the "context-generated fragment" category. The first sentence's structure establishes a syntax and tense (conditional) with its "could get far more merchandise than before." Thus the second sentence—which should not be set off with a full stop and capital letter, but just joined to the first with a comma—continues that syntax and tense with, "or get something far more expensive...."

This represents something of a colloquial style, I should point out, and appears oftener in newspapers like *USA Today* or magazines like *Us* than in the *New York Times* or the *New Yorker*, but it's proliferating more and more in our culture.

More typically, writers will generate long sentences and then decide to break them simply because of their length. The resultant pair of sentences works together as a unit, but one of them, typically the second, fails to attain SALUTE status. It's only a portion, an appendage, of the first. Here is an example from Carlos Alberto Montaner, writing for the *New York Daily News*:

> This must be the objective now: Cuba's peaceful transformation into a stable democracy with freedoms and respect for human rights.

So far, so good. But the passage goes on with a new sentence:

> ❓ A nation similar to Costa Rica, with good relations with its neighbors and the United States; a nation that, far from expelling its people for lack of opportunities, is able to absorb the thousands of exiles who would return to Cuba if living conditions were acceptable there.

This second sentence is trying to lay out what the "stable democracy" of Cuba might look like; it's an elaboration of the noun phrase ending the previous sentence. In short, the whole sentence is an appositive, but maybe because it was so lengthy, Montaner (or his editor) decided it could stand on its own. It can't. It does seem to be, paradoxically, a "complete thought," but just the same, it doesn't work as a SALUTE.

Why not? It has no predicate. The whole sentence is really just a noun phrase. To modify it, I would simply add a predicate to this second sentence:

> Cuba must evolve into a nation similar to Costa Rica, with good relations with its neighbors and the United States—a nation that, far from expelling its people for lack of opportunities, is able to absorb the thousands of exiles who would return to Cuba if living conditions were acceptable there.

(Note that I dropped the semicolon, which struck me as unnecessary, and substituted an em dash.)

Another good alternative would be to append the second sentence to the first, thus clearly establishing the second sentence as an appositive. The only problem with this is that you'd end up with an appositive within an appositive, which seems a bit awkward, though not impossible ("a stable democracy" = "a nation similar to Costa Rica" = "a nation that...is able to absorb the thousands of exiles"). To mark those two appositives, one-em dashes would probably be preferable to commas:

> This must be the objective now: Cuba's peaceful transformation into a stable democracy with freedoms and respect for human rights—a nation similar to Costa Rica, with good relations with its neighbors and the United States—a nation that, far from expelling its people for lack of opportunities, is able to absorb the

thousands of exiles who would return to Cuba if living conditions were acceptable there.

Maybe the most interesting thing about these fragments is that they reveal the fallacy of the oft-taught notion "a sentence is a complete thought." In fact, it's often *not* a complete thought; sometimes a complete thought requires many sentences. And sometimes a complete thought is present, but the linguistic expression of it is flawed, so much so that it cannot actually stand on its own as a sentence. I refer interested readers to David E. E. Sloane's work "A Sentence Is Not a Complete Thought: X-Word Grammar."

Prepositions

Fundamentals

Prepositions Defined

Prepositions are small, somewhat hidden fixture-type words. When I taught in Poland, one of my students there told me that she remembered prepositions as the words that describe possible relationships between a plane and a cloud. A plane can fly *in* a cloud, *into* a cloud, *through* a cloud, *around* a cloud, *behind* a cloud, *between* a cloud and something else, *above* a cloud. It can be flying *before* a cloud, *below* a cloud, *outside* a cloud. Not every preposition works in this formulation, but it's a striking memory device, or at least gets one off the ground as far as prepositions go.

These words usually denote placement or relationship of things—objects, ideas, or actions—to other things. They include words such as *about, above, across, after, against, along, among, around, as, before, behind, below, beneath, between, beyond, by, concerning, despite, down, during, except, for, from, in, into, like, near, of, off, on, onto, out, outside, over, through, to, toward, under, until, up, with, according to, along with, apart from, as for, because of, by means of, except for, in back of, in case of, on top of, outside of.*

Prepositional Phrases

Usually, prepositional phrases—which include a preposition, a noun or pronoun, and perhaps an adjective—function as adjectives or adverbs. In this sentence, from "'Firm and Patient,'" a *New York Times* editorial, the prepositional phrase (*about the off-again-on-again North Korea nuclear deal*) functions as an adjective modifying the noun *advice*:

> President Bush has offered good advice about the off-again-on-again North Korea nuclear deal.

In the following sentence, from "Suicide Bombing Kills at Least 36 in Northwest Pakistan," the prepositional phrase functions as an adverb specifying when the Pakistani president insisted:

> Pakistani President Asif Ali Zardari insisted *over the weekend* that his government is committed to battling the Taliban and al Qaeda, and said he doesn't want a war with India. (Hussain and Rosenberg)

Here is a front-page-story sentence that should probably move its terminal prepositional phrase modifier (*for decades*) closer to what it's modifying. (The adverb here is answering the question "How long?") But note that the pyramiding of prepositional phrases tends to clog up the sentence. It really is hard to keep them straight. In my rewrite, I eliminate one of these phrases:

> ❓ Enter Obama, who in 22 days will walk into the Oval Office and assume the mantle of Middle East peacemaker played with little success by U.S. presidents for decades. (Wolf and Stone)

> Enter Obama, who in 22 days will walk into the Oval Office and assume a role that for decades has been unsuccessfully played by U.S. presidents: Middle East peacemaker.

(The original sentence contains a mixed metaphor, which I will come back to later.)

If a sentence makes your reader pause, stop, go back, and reread, be aware that, unless you are writing poetry or "literary" prose, many readers simply won't bother. Your ideas will thus be lost on some segment of your audience.

Fine Tuning

Preposition Placement

Again, make sure that you structure your sentence so that it's clear what a prepositional phrase modifies. (Also, bear in mind that if a pronoun serves as the object of the preposition, then that pronoun must be in the objective case, as in *for me*, *to him*, *with her*, and the like. See **pronoun case** in the glossary.)

Most difficult to manage are multiple prepositional phrases. In "Weaker Dollar Worries Japan, Germany," the following appears:

> **?** Of course, there are upsides to a having a stronger currency in some corners of the globe. (Slater)

This sentence is reproduced exactly as it appeared; perhaps the extra *a* (in *to a having*) survives as a trace of incomplete editing. (Or didn't you notice that?)

The problem is that *in some corners of the globe* is adverbial (answers "Where?") and makes more sense, I think, following *of course*, rather than following *currency*. I would recommend this rewrite:

> Of course, in some corners of the globe, there are upsides to having a stronger currency.

Now you might say this means exactly the same as the original. But look again. The original version's *in some corners of the globe* modifies *currency*, which I think most U.S. readers of the *Wall Street Journal* would see as what? The dollar.

My revised sentence places the prepositional (adverb) phrase (*in some corners of the globe*) at the opening, after *of course*. Placing the adverbial phrase there establishes scope: in some corners of the globe—that is, all over the place, or in some as yet unspecified places—it's good to have a strong *local* currency.

In the original article, Slater's next sentence provides more context, proving that the currency being discussed is not the dollar, but the currency of "emerging markets": "The dollar's turn downward has brought a modicum of relief in emerging markets, where currencies have been battered in recent months."

Readers process a sentence over time, in the word order it appears in. So the early portion of a sentence sets up what might be called a "meaning-field," establishing the scope of the sentence and the limits of its meaning. And since your "lead" or opening clause often sets up your meaning, don't allow any ambiguities to creep into that lead. At the same time, make sure it's effectively worded and proofread.

Deep Focus

On Ending Sentences with Prepositions

As I've mentioned, many people were taught not to end a sentence with a preposition. This rule is certainly not one that need always be adhered to—or, rather, not a rule to which one need always adhere. Don't worry if one of your sentences ends on a preposition, and keep in mind that sometimes rephrasing it makes things worse.

Surprisingly, on December 29, 2008, this very grammatical issue was the subject of an op-ed piece in the *International Herald Tribune*. Jan Freeman writes,

> John Dryden, in a 1672 essay, suggested that a prepo-
> sition at the end of a sentence—a natural occurrence in
> English—was a less than elegant phrasing; his opinion
> launched a fetish that persists today.

Dryden's grammatical "fetish" might persist today, but it's worse than a mere fetish. In fact it seems to me that many people believe knowing such a rule makes them somehow automatically authoritative. Once, when he ended a sentence with a preposition, Winston Churchill was "corrected." Never at a loss for words, Churchill responded, "That is the type of arrant pedantry up with which I shall not put!" (qtd. by Garner 654).

It is true that English usage is "rule-governed." But knowing the rules is only the first step. And some rules are actually misguided or out of date. You need to figure out which fall into that category and which are legitimate guides. The next step is seeing where those rules (almost any rules) fail to work effectively; that is, you need to determine their margins. The final step, taken with caution, I might add, is creatively violating the rules—for rhetorical effect or individual expressiveness.

Articles

Fundamentals

Articles Defined

Articles are a subset of a larger group of words that are labeled **determiners**. Other determiners include quantifiers, such as *some*, *many*, *a lot*; demonstrative adjectives such as *this*, *these*, or *those*; and possessives, such as *my*, *your*, *her*, *our*, or *their*. They are placed before nouns, with the intent and effect of narrowing and specifying some detail about that noun. Articles have a fundamentally adjectival function: they modify the noun following them. They indicate, among other things, what knowledge the writer and audience share about that noun. Many languages do not have articles, but we have three: *a*, *an*, *the*.

Native speakers of English generally have little difficulty with these, but the rules for article use are surprisingly complex. If you have to explain these, say, for a nonnative speaker, you need to consult either an ESL text or an unabridged dictionary. . . or run and hide—or possibly all of the above. Basically, native speakers internalize a very complex system of rules, and to get speakers of other languages (especially languages that do not use articles) to follow these and to see them as "natural" is exceptionally difficult.

Articles precede the noun they modify. *A* refers to one of many, but the speaker/writer cannot assume the listener/reader can figure out *which* one of the many the noun refers to. *The* usually precedes a noun that the audience knows has a certain singularity and specialness. Consider the following, from the *New York Times* "Footnotes" section in "Arts, Briefly":

> On Sunday *the* cast of *the* current London production of Harold Pinter's "No Man's Land" honored Mr. Pinter, below, who died on Wednesday. Michael Gambon, *a* star

of *the* play, led *a* tribute at *the* Duke of York Theater.
(Bloom)

All of these articles are necessary and correct. Note how
they are used. They give a bit of extra information: "*the*
cast"—there is only one, or the writer can assume that the
reader can figure out which cast is referred to. (If *a* had
been used, it would have suggested that there were several
casts); "*the* current London production"—again, only one
is going on at the moment; "*a* star"—there are several
stars in the show; "*the* play"—again, only one; "*a* tribute"—this might be a *the*, but using *a* indicates that more
tributes are possible, and this might be one of many; "*the*
Duke of York Theater"—there's only one Duke of York
Theater.

Deciding when to use which article (*a*, *an*, *the*) or no
article (linguists call this the null article [Ø]) proves troublesome. Whether you use *a*, *the*, or Ø before a noun depends on many factors. First, what do you want to say?
What meaning are you trying to get across? *A* (and when I
refer to *a*, I will by implication also be including *an*) and
the are sometimes interchangeable—either is OK—but
they carry different connotations. As I mention above, *a*
has a generalized quality to it, an "any old thing" aspect: it
suggests individual singleton-ness, but it's nonspecific. *The*
is more exact and specifying. (Memorable quotation from
the TV show *Dr. Who*: "You're *the* Doctor Who?" a character asks the doctor, who apparently had been plagued by a

fabricated double of himself. The doctor responds, smiling, "The definite article.")

Fine Tuning

A *or* An?

In general, you should use *a* before words that start with a consonant or a consonant sound, and *an* before words that start with a vowel or a vowel sound. Curiously, it's the sound, not the spelling, that determines which you should use. For example, before "U.S." you should use *a*, since the sound is of a "y": YOU ESS. The following sentence, which includes *an U.S.* does not seem to work:

> ✱ A spokesman for the U.S. army, Captain Charles Calio, said the soldier was killed by a roadside bomb that targeted *an* U.S. convoy. ("Iraq Bomber")

Should you use *a* or *an* before a word like *historic*? This reminds me of an incident at an English Department faculty party I once attended. When Sandra Day O'Connor was named to the Supreme Court in 1981, *Time* magazine featured her on the cover along with the headline "An Historic Occasion." At the party, my dean at the time made a point to show the faculty that cover of *Time*. "Isn't that the worst possible pomposity imaginable?" he asked us. When we balked and looked at the carpet, he strengthened his statement: "I will never, never, never be so pompous as to use the word *an* before any noun that starts with an 'h'!"

The whole room fell silent for maybe ten seconds, until one of my colleagues cleared his throat and remarked, "Well, we will see in *a* hour if you are *a* honest man!" That particular colleague has now taken a job elsewhere. So has the dean.

Takeaway message? Be careful about making categorical statements regarding grammar, since its rules are riddled with exceptions, conditions, and qualifications. (And probably it's best not to "correct" or ridicule your boss's use of language.)

To repeat, use *an* before words that sound as if they are starting with vowels, even if these words actually start with consonants. (This is the case with "h-words" when you hear that "h" as a vowel, as in *hour* and *honest*, or, maybe, in *historic*.) Use *a* before words that sound as though they start with a consonant, even if they actually start with a vowel ("a uniform," "a U.S. convoy").

Oh, and one more thing. In case you were wondering, *the* is pronounced "thee" (a long "e" sound) when it precedes a noun starting with a vowel (thē ostrich, thē aardvark, thē umbrella)—or when you want to emphasize the importance of the noun that follows it: "To Sherlock Holmes, she is always *the* woman" (6), his story "A Scandal in Bohemia" begins. In all other instances, *the* is pronounced so that it rhymes with "duh" (thə).

Interjections

Fundamentals

Interjections Defined

Words such as *oh*, *ahh*, *eek*, *arg*, *gak*, *ugh*, *yuk*, *Arggggggahhhh hhooooooooooooooooooooh!* Found in comics, children's books, and pornography, these are supposed to reproduce involuntary utterance and are best avoided in formal writing. Their graphic equivalents, called emoticons (Wikipedia has a very extensive list), are also more appropriate to emails, blogs, and notes than to writing that requires a modicum of formality.

Chapter 3

Who Is He/She? Pronouns

A Whole Chapter on Pronouns?

Apologies if a whole chapter on **pronouns** seems excessive. But I have discovered that pronouns cause considerable difficulty, and this difficulty seems to be increasing. At any rate, I promise to keep the chapter short.

These small words, which should be fairly simple to master, raise a number of problems because their use requires that you carefully review previously written material, that is, the words directly prior to the pronoun. To be a good user of pronouns, you must be a good editor. That's the hard part: great attentiveness is required. You need to be willing to reread your own writing—and you need to judge it with an objective, unjaundiced eye.

The problems of pronouns ramify because singular forms specify gender (male, female), yet we do not have a "gender neutral," singular pronoun that can apply to both or either gender—except for *it*. Yet *it* cannot or should not refer to people. For instance, we would never say,

> ✱ A student should bring *its* text to class.

> ✱ Every person should express *its* opinion.

And let's hope it never comes to that. At present, *it* refers to things, animals, or infants ("Is it a boy or a girl?" "It's so cute." "What's that thing in its eye?")

Fundamentals

Pronouns Defined

Pronouns are words that substitute for nouns. We use pronouns to avoid odd, possibly boring, awkward, or confusing repetitions of nouns.

A Small Emendation

I think it might be useful here to quote Rei Noguchi, a linguist who contends that the above definition or something similar is inadequate:

> Most grammar books state explicitly that a pronoun is a word that "substitutes for a noun." Yet this traditional definition of a pronoun is clearly incorrect, or at least incomplete, since a pronoun can substitute not just for a noun (e.g., *boys→they*) but also, among other things, a noun phrase (e.g., *the noisy boys in the back of the room→they*) or any construction that functions as a noun or noun phrase, including other pronouns (e.g., *he and she→they*). (43)

I like this. But the clarity challenge still remains: the pronoun stands for, replaces, recalls, or invokes *something*, usually (though not always) something preceding it, and you have to make clear to your reader exactly what word or word group the pronoun replaces. If you don't think your reader can figure out what word or phrase the pronoun is replacing—or, worse, if you yourself are unsure—you should take the time to restructure and revise the sentence. (Note too that *I* and *you* do not require an antecedent.)

Pronoun "Case"—Definition of Pronoun Extended

Yet another difficulty with pronouns is that they come in several different forms (pronoun cases and classes), and these forms have differing functions within sentences. I'll provide a brief list.

Subject pronouns . . .

are words that can function as the subject of a sentence: *I, you, he, she, it, we, they*.

Object pronouns . . .

receive action or are objects of a preposition: *me, you, her, him, it, us, them*.

Reflexive pronouns or intensive pronouns . . .

emphasize either a noun or a pronoun; they include *myself, yourself, himself, herself, itself, ourselves, yourselves, themselves*. The following sentence refers to the now-infamous administration of former OSHA director Edward G. Foulke Jr.

> For his part-time advice over a 22-month period begin-
> ning in May 2006, OSHA paid [consultant Randy] Kimlin
> $513,403, a salary higher than that received by Vice
> President Cheney, any member of Congress and Foulke
> *himself* during that period. (Smith)

Reflexive pronouns can also sometimes be used to show
that the receiver and doer of the action are one and the
same. Here is a now all-too-oft-repeated scenario, and a
regrettably familiar appearance of the reflexive pronoun.
It is from "U.S. Soldier Killed in Baghdad's Sadr City":

> A roadside bomb killed a U.S. soldier in Baghdad's Shi-
> ite slum of Sadr City on Sunday, and an Iraqi was killed
> when a suicide bomber riding a bicycle blew *himself* up
> amid a mass rally against Israel's airstrikes on Gaza.
> (Heintz)

Possessive pronouns . . .

include words such as *my*, *mine*, *your*, *yours*, *its*, *his*, *her*,
hers, *our*, *ours*, *their*, and *theirs*, and they indicate possession.
Contrary to what might seem to be logical, possessive pronouns do *not* take an apostrophe.

Relative pronouns . . .

include *who*, *whom*, *that*, *which*, and *where*. They usually
introduce relative clauses, which function as adjectives.
Locating the noun that they modify is sometimes a bit
challenging, but it's often necessary to do so in order to

determine the form of the verb that follows: "The houses that I like are too expensive for me." "The house that I like is too expensive for me."

Indefinite pronouns . . .

also form a class, and include words such as *one*, *someone*, *somebody*, *no one*, *none*, *nobody*, *everyone*, *everybody*. These are usually singular, but prove troublesome to writers because they are often used in a way that's conceptually plural. And to make matters even more difficult, sometimes a plural verb with them is preferable to a singular verb.

Pronoun Antecedent Clarity

The most widespread and significant difficulty with pronouns, the one that really causes confusion, is the following: what word or word group does the pronoun replace? Since pronouns perform a substitute-for-the-noun (or noun phrase) function, readers frequently have trouble determining what sentence element a pronoun is substituting for.

Lydia Davis writes, in her essay "Foucault and Pencil," about why the philosopher Michel Foucault's writing is difficult to understand. It has to do, at least in part, with his use of pronouns. She narrates her thought process:

> Understood more clearly at which points Foucault
> harder to understand and at which points easier: harder
> to understand when sentence was long and noun

identifying subject of sentence was left back at beginning, replaced by male or female pronoun, when forgot
what noun pronoun replaced and had only pronoun for
company traveling through sentence. Sometimes pronoun then giving way in mid-sentence to new noun, new
noun in turn replaced by new pronoun which then continued on to end of sentence. (336)

Pronouns carry considerable weight within their sentences,
since they are standing in for previously specified (or in
some cases subsequently specified) nouns. The reader has
to know which nouns your pronouns are standing in for.
Davis is suggesting here that Foucault is difficult not merely
because his ideas are abstract and original, but because he's
a tad sloppy with his writing.

Here's another philosopher whose pronoun use tends
to trip one up. In the following epigram about teaching,
Ludwig Wittgenstein writes,

> ❓ A present-day teacher of philosophy doesn't select
> food for *his* pupil with the aim of flattering *his* taste, but
> with the aim of changing it. (Wittgenstein 17e)

To whom does the second *his* refer—teacher or pupil? The
first *his* clearly refers to the teacher, since there is only one
possessive-possible noun that precedes it (*philosophy* and
food are not really possessive-possible). Seven words later,
there's another *his*, and in that seven-word bridge, another
possessive-possible noun emerges: *pupil.* Do both instances

of *his* refer to the same noun (teacher), or is it possible that the second refers to the pupil? Does Wittgenstein mean that philosophy teachers should try to change the tastes of their students? Or is he saying that in teaching philosophy, the teacher should endeavor to change his or her own tastes, should learn by teaching, should adapt to the audience and to the material as it's experienced anew?

Actually, there is a clear-cut answer to this conundrum. We just have to consult the original German (and a multilingual speaker who can help us out). In fact, the original German lacks the ambiguity of the translation, so we discover that the first meaning is the one Wittgenstein intends: the word that the second *his* replaces is *pupil*. Teachers should work to change their students' tastes. Well, OK, though I confess this revelation provided for me the less interesting insight. I suppose I also learned that English is sometimes more ambiguous than German.

Just to give you the technical term, the word for that substituted-for element is *referent* or **antecedent**. The antecedent might well be very clear and apparent to you as you write, but to readers, it's murky. You must put yourself in your reader's place—is there any possibility that the sentence could be confusing, or that the antecedent could be misunderstood? If so, rephrase the sentence. Again, *I* and *you* do not typically require antecedents. Most people will recognize to whom these pronouns refer. However, with other pronouns the antecedent needs to be manifestly clear. "But most people will know what I mean, or who the pronoun refers to." I often hear this defense. I fear, however, that we cannot count on its truth. An audience will usually gravitate toward what it wants or expects to be your meaning. Hence be especially careful of any ambiguous language, as it will typically be interpreted by your listeners or readers as a confirmation of their own predispositions, prejudices, or expectations.

The following sentence is unambiguous. From "Child Neglect Cases Multiply as Economic Woes Spread," the sentence contains the pronoun *her*, which clearly has the antecedent *Banita Jacks*:

> In the District, there was an 18 percent increase in child neglect and abuse investigations, but officials said the case of Banita Jacks, the Southeast mother accused early this year of killing *her* four daughters, had a large effect on hotline calls. (St. George and Dvorak)

You need to be especially careful when you discuss mayhem, murder, atrocities, deaths; when writing about people who are killed, maimed, shot, blown up, decapitated. Your reader must know who did what to whom. If you yourself notice the possibility of misreading or confusion, a significant percentage of your audience will also misread or be confused.

One common writing problem emerges when two or more names appear in a sentence: any pronoun following these has the potential for confusion. For example, the following sentence has two possible referents for *they*— namely, *bankers* and *Americans*:

> ❓ Mortgage bankers gave loans to Americans for homes *they* couldn't afford. (Craig et al.)

It may be that the mortgage bankers themselves could not afford the homes for which they were giving out loans, but I think it's the borrowers who can't do the affording here. Trouble is, both referents make sense; that's why it's especially important to make sure it's clear which one you want.

Here are two (I think) preferable versions: "Mortgage bankers allowed many Americans to take out unaffordable home loans," or (the alternative but at the same time complementary meaning) "Mortgage bankers could not afford to lend out as much money as they did in home loans to Americans." Note that I use *lend* as a verb and *loans* as a noun. And *afford*, in this version, takes on an equivocal meaning, especially in light of 2008's economic meltdown. (In some sense, none of us could afford the banking policy or behavior being described.)

Here's another interesting example of a pronoun with two possible antecedents. In "Navy, Environmentalists Reach Deal over Sonar," Steve Marshall writes, in reference to an agreement,

> ❓ It doesn't require sailors to adopt additional measures to protect animals when *they* use sonar.

Who is using the sonar—the sailors or the animals? Dolphins, bats, and the navy all use sonar. While the article's headline indicates it's about the navy's use of sonar, the sentence still remains ambiguous. I'd suggest something like this:

> The agreement doesn't require any additional protective measures for animals endangered by sailors using sonar.

In the following sentence, from *Time*, it's a bit hard to figure out who is clutching whose hand. The article is about Sarah Palin:

> ❓ And when *she* finished and the crowd screamed and danced, *she* twirled across the stage with the baby in *her* arms, signaling to women everywhere that nothing was going to stop *her*, and to conservatives everywhere that nothing would make *her* abort a Down-syndrome baby, and *her* daughter stood there with *her*, clutching *her* boyfriend's hand. (Gibbs 94)

I think the daughter is clutching the hand of her own boyfriend, but the sentence could be misread as describing the daughter's clutching Palin's boyfriend's hand. All seven preceding pronouns clearly refer to Palin herself. The last one, however, in reference to Palin's daughter, trips one up. I mean, we can eventually figure this out, but in the time span of that "eventually," we envision a scene more wild and anarchic than even that which evidently took place.

The following sentence, from "Focus on Medical Mistakes," provides an example of a sentence that lacks an antecedent for *it*:

> ❓ Doctors run more tests because *it* benefits patients, not because of liability concerns. (Weisbrod)

I'd recommend a rewrite of some sort, such as substituting *doing so* for *it*.

Why bother, you ask? Does "Doctors run more tests because doing so benefits patients, not because of liability concerns" convey anything different? Nope. Actually, the original strikes me as close to acceptable. Some writers and teachers would no doubt accept it. But I can't. Let me offer a more extensive rewrite than just substituting *doing so* for *it*. This rewrite conveys the same idea with more precision, I think, giving the writer more credibility with an audience and allowing for less possibility of momentary confusion:

> Doctors run extensive tests, not just from a fear of malpractice suits, but because they feel that such testing leads to more accurate diagnosis.

Interestingly, as I rewrote this, I realized that in fact contemporary MDs do fear lawsuits, a possibility that the original as much as brushes off, burying at the sentence's end the quite important, even crucial, noun phrase "liability concerns." The original's claim, while the same as that of the rewrite, is almost covert. That's why I inserted *just* in my rewrite—it seems to me that the sentence is a bit more honest that way.

As long as we are on the subject of health care, here's another pronoun issue. The pronoun *it* proves troublesome in the following editorial from *USA Today*, "Lawyers' Bills Pile High." The sentence concerns malpractice settlements:

> ❓ States need tougher error-reporting systems in which each hospital's track record is made public. Sealing settlements from public view, a common practice, makes *it* impossible to study and should be eliminated.

The "sealing" makes what, precisely, "impossible to study"? I think the author needs to repeat the antecedent for *it* and write something like this:

> Sealing the details of malpractice settlements from public view, a common practice, prevents the study of those records, and that practice should be abandoned.

Another somewhat confusing use of *it* (in the possessive form, *its*) appears in a *Time* article about Baghdad:

> ❓ In the U.S. a different story is drawing to a close: one that began with Bush standing defiantly atop a heap of rubble at ground zero and started *its* downward spiral when he stood before an ill-advised banner reading MISSION ACCOMPLISHED. (Ghosh)

I don't think I am willfully misreading this to say that it sounds as though that heap of rubble had started its downward spiral. After rereading the sentence a few times through, though, I think it's the "different story"—the one of the Iraq War's downward spiral—that is being alluded to. A simple insertion of *that* before *started* would help clarify the sentence.

(I note that *it* provides an ongoing challenge to writers. Here, in a May 18, 2014, front-page article in the New York *Times*, a statue on the Wellesley College campus is reported to have added to a controversy about what's known as "trigger warnings":

> ❓ The issue arose at Wellesley College this year after the school installed a lifelike statue of a man in his underwear, and hundreds of students signed a petition to have *it* removed. (Medina 15)

What exactly were students clamoring to have removed? Underwear or statue?)

Sometimes, a sentence's construction obscures its actual meaning to such an extent that the writer can advance illogical, inchoate, or deceptive claims. Such language use abounds: it creates an apparent explanation or idea, but when examined closely, it's empty or vacillating—or both. Learning to recognize such linguistic deformation helps you avoid it yourself. The following sentence implies someone was killed and then (magically? bionically?) later escaped. You don't want to create such an "absurd universe" situation:

> ❓ Another young villager was walking with Azizov when *he* was killed that evening, but *he* managed to escape. (Tavernise)

A possible revision is as follows:

> Azizov was killed, but another young villager, who had been walking with him when they were attacked, managed to escape.

And—one more gruesome example, this from "Mexican Officer Accused of Working with Cartels"—inadvertently gives a brief glimpse into a world even weirder than our actual world:

> ❓ After torturing and decapitating the unarmed soldiers, the killers left *their* heads on public display with a message warning the military to discontinue antidrug operations. (Dillon and Betancourt)

Whose heads? A simple insertion of *victims'* after *their* would have helped clarify this sentence, the impact of which is undermined by the image of vicious killers somehow recanting, and putting their own heads on display.

I know that no one is really confused (at least not for long) by this sentence. They don't think the killers put their own severed heads on display. So why do I single out the sentence as being unclear if no one is tripped up? I do so because momentarily, maybe just for a few thousand nanoseconds, people might misread or misconstrue the sentence. And in that brief interval, the image is ever-so-slightly undermined. We read along, imaging up an awful scene, but then an odd absurdity—one lasting no longer than the flash of a flashbulb—blurs everything. We blink, and it's all back to normal. Or is it?

Mia Farrow produces a slightly less shocking but still problematic sentence construction in the following quotation in a *Time* advertisement for UNICEF and Canon:

> ❓ I have heard heart-rending stories of mothers who died of hemorrhage or infection—deaths that could have been prevented if only *they* had had access to basic health services.

Deaths should have access to basic health services? After the em dash, Farrow should probably have written something like "deaths that could have been prevented if only the women had been given access to basic health services," a revision that would have made explicit the antecedent of *they*.

Long sentences often trip people up, since the referent for the pronoun can easily disappear in the pileup of words. Nancy Gibbs creates, in the "Commentary" section of *Time* magazine, a sentence that has a few too many *they*s, *them*s, and *their*s in it:

? Years ago, I started saving all those T shirts from soccer league and school plays and breast-cancer walks, even after *they* no longer fit. *They* are in a box in the attic, awaiting the day my girls head for college and we patch *them* into a soft, stretchy quilt made entirely of *their* adventures and allegiances. Maybe someday we'll do the same for *their* sons and daughters, make a map of moments on *their* way to forever.

The *them* refers to the T-shirts, not the girls, and the last *their* refers to her girls' sons and daughters—facts that gradually become clear, but only after one studies the sentence awhile.

But Gibbs's sentence is less confusing than this following one, from *National Review*, in which a plural pronoun is used with a singular antecedent:

? Radio was new then, and the young Carter toyed with *them*—homemade—on the roof of his building. (Nordlinger 47)

The sentence should probably have begun, "Radios were new devices then, and the young Carter toyed with them...."

Finally, *They say* or *It is said* constructions lack authority and force, and hence should probably be avoided, unless the pronoun's antecedent is very clear from the context. Here are Neil Gaiman's words:

❓ "With trying to make superhero movies over the years, it has always been that you simply couldn't do it. *They* would say, 'You will believe a man can fly,' but you really wouldn't. Now, you pretty much can." (Boucher)

Who says this? Who are the "they" saying, "You will believe"? Producers? Ad agency writers? Screenwriters? Can/should we believe "them"?

Fine Tuning

Pronoun-Case Problems

Since there are so many different categories or cases of pronouns, you need to be quite careful to use the pronoun case that joins with or fits into your sentence structure. A sentence such as "Us hated they" is obviously nonstandard and strange, and few native speakers would generate it, unless they were trying to be, well, nonstandard and strange. But pronoun-case problems extend beyond such obvious errors.

People are often somewhat confused by sentences such as "Tell John or me" (not *I*); or "It was finally decided by the two-person team, John and me" (again, not *I*). Since *John and me* is in apposition to *two-person team*, which itself is in the object position, the pronoun must be an **object pronoun**. When you are in this situation, eliminate the "other person" named in the sentence and try out the new, shortened version. Reduce "Tell John and I" to "Tell [~~John and~~] I." Would you ever say "Tell I"? But "Tell [~~John and~~] me," or "Tell me," is natural sounding and acceptable.

Do problems in speech "not count" since they disappear along with the utterance itself? I'm not sure. It strikes me that spoken words—often forgotten by the speaker—can linger with peculiar poignancy. I'm not recalling "grammatical errors," but other remarks or offhand comments made by friends, family, or acquaintances. The fact that I remember and am even slightly haunted by these words argues that spoken words matter. Curiously, when spoken aloud, error-clogged sentences often seem to make sense and can be readily understood, but in writing, these same word strings generate confusion. The following is from a writer of "cell-phone novels," so I guess we need to cut her some slack:

> ❓ "Where *me* and my friends live, in the country, there aren't any universities," Mone wrote. (Goodyear 62)

Even in speech you should probably avoid using something like *me and my friends* as a subject, or the word *ain't*, or double negatives, or obvious errors in verb form (like *I don't got no time*), though I know that within certain social situations you might want to adopt the role of a down-to-earth, average Joe/Josephine, cell-phone-novel-writing kind of person.

"Fronting"

Subject-verb-object is the typical sequence or "order of parts" in English sentences, but it's not the only possible order. "Him I must see" is a perfectly good sentence in English, with the slightly unusual word order emphasizing the object. So you should reserve that structure for those times when you really want to make a special point, when you want to call attention to the object of your sentence—or when, for some reason, you want to sound like Yoda.

I recommend striving for a sine-wave pattern of intensity in your sentences. By this I mean that you should strive to alternate between areas of high-wattage linguistic brightness (say), and places where it's just standard candlepower. Or to put it another way, there should be places where your language has a special—almost poetic—evocativeness, power, and crispness, and others where it allows your reader to rest. If your prose is all at the same level, it becomes dull, insipid, maybe slightly exhausting.

Correct but Awkward Pronouns

Sometimes the correct case sounds awkward. For example, one oft-repeated rule is this: after *to be* verbs, use the subject case:

> It is I.
>
> It is we.
>
> This is she.

These three sentences are all correct, though to me they are slightly awkward or foreign sounding when used in speech. Once when I was teaching and I explained this rule, one of my students said, "If someone knocked on my door, and I said, 'Who is it?' and they answered, 'It is we,' I wouldn't open the door!"

In speech, it often sounds better to use "incorrect" grammar. However, in writing, it's best to avoid the "nonstandard." Written and spoken English employ somewhat different principles, even—according to some linguists—a different grammar.

Though **subject pronouns** should follow *to be* verbs, the rule is often broken. James Surowiecki remarks in the *New Yorker*, for example,

> ❓ The real problem for newspapers, in other words, isn't the Internet; it's us.

Some editors or teachers would contend that this sentence should end, "it's we," since the nominative (or subject) case should follow a *to be* verb. True, that's the rule. But what would I write? Actually, I would end the sentence, "It's we. We are the problem." It seems to me that would be slightly stronger and would have the advantage of being grammatically standard, something I probably need to strive for more than Surowiecki does.

A similar structure emerges in "Veterans of '90s Bank Bailout See Opportunity in Current One":

> "It is a good time to be me," said John L. Douglas, a partner in Atlanta at the law firm Paul Hastings and a former lawyer for bank regulators who helped create the agency that administered the last federal bailout, the Resolution Trust Corporation. (Lipton and Kirkpatrick)

Douglas's sentence was in fact the "Quotation of the Day" for the *New York Times* on December 29, 2008. What would we think if Douglas had followed the nominative-case-after-*to be*-verb rule, saying, "It is a good time to be I"? I'm not sure that statement would have merited QOTD status. People might even be confused and think that he was talking about the Roman numeral I, as in "It's a good time to be Number One." (I don't mark this with a question mark, though, because it is spoken English.)

But I wonder if, even in written English, the nominative-case-after-*to be*-verb rule is out-of-date. Maybe. I think that, once again, you as a speaker and writer need to judge what your audience expects, as well as what level of exactness and formality is needed. You need to assess the occasion and purpose of your language, and then come up with the appropriate usage.

Pronoun Reference with Indefinite Pronouns

Usually, the indefinite pronouns *each, everyone, no one, none* are singular, despite their apparently plural conceptual force. The following, from the *Trentonian*, should probably take singular pronoun forms (*his or her*), largely because that usage reinforces the emphasis of *none*, namely, "not a single person":

> ? It is made clear at the outset of each kaizen exercise that no one will lose *their* job as a result of the efficiencies that result, although some state agencies have shrunk their staffs through attrition following kaizen improvements. ("The Kaizen Kraze")

The next sentence, from "Discounts Not Enough to Revive Online Retail Sales," also cries out for revision; I'd argue that the writer should maintain a singular pronoun, *itself*: (Note too that the sentence displays a problem with **parallel structure**.)

> ? ComScore's Mr. Lipsman says each of the sites is known for separating *themselves* from the field—Amazon by offering some of the widest variety of goods, while Apple provides innovative products and WalMart proffers some of the lowest prices. (Worthen and Vascellaro)

Here is a rewrite of this sentence, in which I alter the pronoun and address the lack of parallelism:

> ComScore's Mr. Lipsman says each of the sites is known for separating itself from the field—Amazon by offering a wide variety of goods, Apple by providing innovative products, and WalMart by maintaining some of the lowest prices.

Words tend to point in different directions—that is, each word has its own trajectory, moving through the "space" of meaning. In each sentence you write, though, you want to make sure all these trajectories converge. For example, if one word emphasizes the "singleness" of the subject, then you want to continue using words that maintain that emphasis.

Here's another interesting wrinkle of indefinite pronoun use. If you use a word like *everyone*, *no one*, or *each* as an antecedent at the start of a sentence, and the sentence goes on into a new clause, then—strange but true—it seems to be preferable to use a plural pronoun to refer to that singular indefinite pronoun antecedent. (I have to say, though, that when I presented this to a group of college professors, they disagreed, and one exclaimed, "Says who?") Still, I accept the following, which uses the usually singular pronoun *anyone* as an antecedent for *their*:

> "When I was an active priest and pastor, we welcomed anyone to our little church who had a sincere desire to love God and serve *their* fellow human beings." (K. Smith)

Just as we would say, "Everyone was shouting, so I told *them* [not *him*] to shut up," so we generally accept *their* in Smith's sentence, even though its antecedent, *anyone*, is singular. (Nonetheless, it might be better here to simply pluralize the antecedent and say, "our little church welcomed all people who had a sincere desire to love God and serve their fellow human beings.")

Who vs. *Whom*

Some relative pronouns, specifically *who* and *whom*, cause considerable confusion. If you are stumped, here is a relatively simple five-step process you might employ. One of the good things about writing is that you usually have time to go back and apply such a process. In speech, you have less time and have to decide very quickly.

1. Separate out the relative clause in which the word appears.
2. Find the noun that that relative clause is modifying. (Remember that relative clauses function as adjectives and are sort of attached to a noun or a noun phrase.)
3. Then, after you've found the thing being modified, look at the verb *within* the relative clause.
4. Figure out whether the noun being modified functions as a subject of that verb (doing the action) or as an object of it (receiving the action).
5. If it's a subject, then use *who*; if an object, use *whom*.

Maybe this sounds complicated, though it seems easy to me, since I automatically revert to it all the time. But I'll provide an example. The sentence about Craig Clark, the so-called King of the option ARM at the bank WaMu, contains two relative clauses, which I italicize:

> Clark, *who now works for JPMorgan*, referred calls to a company spokesman, *who provided no further details*. (Goodman and Morgenson)

The first *who*-clause is straightforward; probably no one would say, "Clark, whom now works for JPMorgan." But to follow my procedure outlined above, first find the noun that the relative clause is modifying: *Clark*. Now locate the verb within the relative clause: *works*. Does *Clark* function as the subject, if paired with this verb, or as the object of this verb? "Clark works" seems to be the general sense here. Since *Clark* is the subject, a *who*-clause containing the verb should include the subject pronoun *who*.

Let's look at the second *who*-clause. *Who provided no further details* functions as an adjective modifying *spokesman*. Now look at the verb in the clause: *provided*. Is the close-mouthed spokesman the object of the providing, or the person who is providing? In fact, he's the person providing, so *who* is correct. (Even though the spokesman provides nothing [thanks a lot], s/he is the providing party, the subject.)

When *who* or *whom* is obviously an object, or the object of a preposition, as in the following, use *whom*. This sentence alludes to Agnes Kalibata, Rwanda's minister of state for agriculture. She

> said government land reform and credit programs specifically focus on struggling female farmers, many of *whom* are bringing up children alone, their husbands having been killed in the 1994 genocide. (Rowling)

Whom has fallen out of favor in speech, and using it (orally) might sound a little old-fashioned or almost scolding, like a precisian teacher. (I don't think you'll too often hear "many of who," however.) Still, in formal writing, you probably should preserve the *who/whom* distinction. Sorry if that sounds evasive. Here, the writers opt not to preserve the distinction:

> ❓ "I must get an e-mail a day from people *who* I worked with back then about what to do about the current mess," Mr. [Eugene] Ludwig said. (Lipton and Kirkpatrick)

I worked with back then is the clause to focus on. What does it modify? *People*. OK, then. The verb in the relative clause is *worked*. What is the relation of *people* to *worked*? Is the sentence saying the people worked? I don't think so. Is it saying, "I worked with people"? This seems to be the case: *people* is the object. Hence the word should be *whom*. Another way of using this method is to ask yourself, would one say, "I worked with *they* back then" or "I worked with *them* back then"? Since it's the latter, *whom* is correct.

But it's only fair to point out that the sentence is offering a transcription of speech, so *who* might be acceptable after all—more conversational, more down-to-earth. Actually, the sentence does not need either a *who* or a *whom* at all: "I must get an email a day from people I worked with back then." (Often, trimming your sentences improves them.)

Why ever use *whom*, then, if it's out of favor and so few people know how to correctly use it, anyway? Good question. I think that sometimes, perhaps on important occasions, your audience will indeed know how to use these words correctly, and will notice if you do not.

Once, when I was making this point, one of my students raised her hand in class and said, "You know, you're not just teaching us English here. You're teaching us how to be English TEACHERS." I paused a beat before I realized she was right. "Yes, exactly right. In fact, most of you will be English teachers," I said. It was a general education class, with not an English major in sight. They all guffawed. Since then, one of these students, teaching English in Japan, wrote me to tell me I was correct (and to ask for career advice). More, of course, have married and have had children. What language do they teach those children? What level of correctness do they want their children's language to demonstrate? It might be true that using correct English is no guarantee of getting ahead or succeeding, but weak language skills tend to work against people. In some ways it's just a matter of pragmatics: clear, fundamentally accurate expression makes for a more smoothly working social mechanism, and maybe just as importantly, such language use helps people to become creators of that mechanism, rather than just creatures of it.

Deep Focus

Using *I* and *You* in Formal Writing

Often students have been instructed not to use *I* or *you* in their writing, and they ask me where I stand on this matter. My advice is that in formal letters, essays, reports, and the like, *I* is acceptable, but should be used sparingly. Why so?

Remember that if your focus is on an argument about texts or issues, your own position should be obvious and not require use of the first-person pronoun. If you find yourself using *I* in every paragraph, for example, you should step back and look at your argument. Are you writing an argument or a narrative? Presenting a logical, persuasive idea or telling a story? Seldom will you repeatedly need to use the first-person pronoun in a formal argument.

(I feel compelled to note here that one of my colleagues, Mary Louise Penaz, pointed out that in the blogosphere, it's crucial to use first person, to identify yourself, say who you are, and speak from that identifiable position. It's a way of giving yourself authenticity.)

You I suggest you avoid altogether. It is usually too chatty and informal. This book, you may have noticed, uses *you* (and *I*), but here I am striving to reproduce a chatty, open discussion or classroom, not the scholarly alembic of formal written prose.

Gender-Biased Language

Another pronoun-related problem comes from the relatively recent increase in attention to **gender-biased language**. Traditionally (that is, when I was a child, but this tradition continues, to an extent, today), English teachers taught students to use the male pronoun if the antecedent did not specify gender. Here is an example of this old-fashioned, outdated rule. Terry Wood advises website creators,

> ❓ "You need to be able to talk to the user in a way that makes *him* want to come back." (Jones)

Even if you don't agree that this is gender-biased or sexist, you have to admit that not all people visiting websites ("users") are male. So something is a bit off or misleading in the sentence.

Nor are all illegal aliens male, either, as the following, from "Tensions Up with Border Fence," might inadvertently imply:

> ❓ But in urban areas, where most of the border is under video surveillance, agents can spot someone trying to climb or cut the fence and have a few extra seconds to catch *him* before *he* enters the USA and disappears into a city, Cordero says. (Frank "Tensions")

And some managers are likely to be women, too, a fact not really respected by James Freeman, writing a review of a book by Sam Wyly:

> ❓ A division manager at a Wyly company does not have to seek headquarters approval for daily decisions on hiring or marketing; in fact, he enjoys a remarkable degree of autonomy.

(I'm not certain, though, that Wyly has any female managers, so in fact that sentence might be factually accurate.)

Texts and writing handbooks since the early 1980s have identified gender-biased language as an area of concern. When I bring it up in classes, I'll often hear the objection, "Oh, get over it—you are so-o-o-o P.C.!" Perhaps. But I point out that to a certain extent, the concern for gender neutrality is simply an attempt to make language reflect, as accurately as possible, the actuality of the situation. If you are talking about a population that has both genders in it, then your prose should respect that important fact. At the same time it's necessary to reinforce, through our use of the language, that the female half of the population is not just a subset of the male.

I suggest one of three options: (1) alternate use of pronouns (say, in one paragraph using male pronouns, and in the next paragraph using female pronouns); (2) use *his/her*, *she or he*, or something similarly slightly awkward but increasingly acceptable; or—my preference—(3) modify the sentence so that the pronoun can be plural and non-gender-specific (this involves making the antecedent plural).

Sometimes you'll find that you can modify the structure enough to eliminate the problematic pronoun altogether. For example, the Terry Wood sentence above (about website users) might be rewritten in the following way:

> You need to be able to talk to users in ways that will increase the likelihood of repeat visits to your site.

Keep in mind, too, that most professions are no longer confined to one gender. Cosmetologists, nurses, and teachers are often male; doctors, judges, and Olympic boxers, female. (There is no rule concerning transgendered or intersexual persons, who at present individually choose a preferred gender pronoun.)

Sometimes, trying to avoid gender-biased pronouns results in curious, almost nonsensical sentences. Here's an example of one such linguistic creation I discovered in an advertisement for American Airlines:

> ❓ Win Enough Travel and Money to Put Any Concierge through the Paces.

What exactly are "the paces"? The expression "put him through his paces" or "put her through her paces" is being recalled here, but American Airlines' revised version seems to be recalling something else, maybe involving horses? I'd suggest a revision along the lines of "Win Enough Travel and Money to Work the Heck out of Any Concierge," though as I write this, I realize that it's probably a good thing I don't write advertising copy for a living.

There is another option: new pronouns altogether. An erstwhile colleague, the linguist John Herum, suggested that a new pronoun, *herm*, be introduced, which could serve for *him or her*. I noted the similarity between this pronoun and Professor Herum's name.

Alternatively, one could use a word I see on a bookmark that seems to have found its way onto my desk: "The Epicene hu." Produced by the Archangul Foundation (specifically, Professor D. N. Deluna), the bookmark extols the virtues of this new pronoun:

Pronounced with a short *u* sound.
The stylist's choice in epicene pronouns.
Performs flexibly as a subject, an object, and a posses-
sive epicene; for it is declension-free.
For example:
To each hu own. (Archangul Foundation)

This new pronoun is promoted in a style consisting entirely of sentence fragments. But regardless, I fear that "The
Epicene hu" won't get much traction in English because
most language change occurs in a more grassroots manner.
Deluna's is not a natural evolution of language; it's just the
zany fabrication of a professor who probably doesn't even
seriously believe in it, uh, huself.

Permit me a prediction: By the year 2020, *they*, *them*,
and *their* will be accepted as pronouns used with singular
antecedents. The reason is that all other options (listed
below) fall short:

1. using a male pronoun is inaccurate and gender-biased,
   and using only female pronouns would have a similar
   liability;
2. *he/she*, *his/her* locutions are awkward, especially in
   speech;
3. newly contrived pronouns (*herm*, *hu*) are a bit too weird
   to usurp the more familiar pronouns we already have;
4. alternating pronouns (say, one paragraph with *her* and
   the next with *him*) is often confusing to readers;

5. using plural antecedents is acceptable in writing, but in speech, singulars often pop out prior to the use of the pronoun, thus forcing the speaker back to one of the other options.

Maybe eighteenth-century grammarian Lindley Murray, who whimsically outlawed the use of *they* with a singular antecedent (Curzan 872), will finally be put to rest.

Chapter 4

Punctuation, Part I—The Comma: Promiscuous Uses

Introduction: Punctuation Substitutes for Oral Emphases, Facial Expressions, and Body Language

When people speak, they consciously and subconsciously use an arsenal of effects to get their points across. They might emphasize certain words, pronounce others slowly or in an animated way, pause, use hand and facial gestures, insert filler phrases such as *you know* or *like*. In fact, body language and facial expression—extralinguistic communicative actions—account for an enormous portion of communication, perhaps more than we realize. Psychologist Paul Ekman contends, for example, that the forty-three facial muscles convey the majority of a person's emotional state and thus constitute a significant part of communication (Foreman).

When we write, though, we don't have the power to emphasize words in special ways or to slowly and carefully pronounce some and glide over others. We don't have hand gestures when we write, or the ability to smile or frown or give the side-eye. But we do have something that's invisible in speech. We have punctuation.

In the last hundred years or so in the United States, English punctuation has become quite standardized. There are ranges of acceptable usage (for example, some writers tend to use a large but acceptable number of commas, while others prefer to give fewer cues as to how their sentences should be read. I've been accused of overusing semicolons and dashes. Who, me?). In general, punctuation aids readers in understanding what you as a writer mean. You don't want to confuse your reader or force that reader back to reread, especially when the simple insertion of a comma might ease straightforward, relatively unambiguous communication. In fact, sometimes a sentence with a comma can mean one thing, yet without that comma can mean the exact opposite. In legal writing, millions of dollars can hinge on a comma, which makes that little mark potentially a keystroke of great value. Or as the T-shirt would have it,

"Let's eat, Grandma."

"Let's eat Grandma."

COMMAS SAVE LIVES

Some punctuation decisions are less a matter of choice than others. You should probably not, for example, join main clauses using just a comma: this error, a comma splice, which I rail against in at least four places here, violates the rules of standard English usage. It stigmatizes the writer and slows or confuses communication. (However, you may join two main clauses with just a comma plus a coordinating conjunction, or what I have termed an ABS OF NY word.) You should not use a semicolon to set off an appositive, or use a colon after an incomplete sentence.

Yet people do these things, and live to tell. Punctuational risks differ from risking one's life. There are quite a few "rules" to learn, but, as I did in the parts-of-speech chapters, I will here separate out "fundamentals" from "fine tuning" and "deep focus." While all are important, you ultimately need to decide what level of accuracy/ formality your audience expects, and adjust your usage accordingly.

Fundamentals

This chapter title uses the word *promiscuous* in the sense of *miscellaneous*. This is how Goold Brown (and others) used it in the nineteenth century, in his various grammar guides, such as *The Institutes of English Grammar* (1863). The comma can be put to a multitude of uses. Perhaps the all-purpose nature of this mark of punctuation makes it so difficult to get right and explains why it causes no end of confusion and heartache to students and editors alike. Like the sexually promiscuous, the comma has a bad reputation.

George Orwell, in his great dystopian novel, *1984*, has his protagonist, Winston Smith, working on a comma-related issue. After Smith has been tortured and brainwashed by the Party, he is assigned to work on a committee reviewing "something to do with the question of whether commas should be placed inside brackets, or outside" (242). Such work, which occasionally involved haggling and disputes, and "long memoranda which were never finished," evidently epitomizes a wasted life—pointless debates, trivial distinctions, meaningless consequences. This might be the standard view that most people take toward the comma. And Orwell, who had declared in "Politics and the English Language" that "correct grammar and syntax . . . are of no importance so long as one makes one's meaning clear" (99), conveys a contempt toward "correctness," though I feel compelled to point out that his *so long as* clause is a gigantic provision: yes, you can do anything you want, just so long as you make your meaning clear. Thus Orwell's declaration is suddenly a lot less sweeping inasmuch as it allows that not all "grammar and syntax" issues are as trivial as where to place a comma with respect to brackets.

I offer below thirteen fairly standard uses of the mark, and include only one "catchall" category (Use 1). As to whether the comma goes inside or outside of brackets—or parentheses, for that matter—I would recommend outside, if the bracketed or parenthetical words are part of an enclosing sentence; inside, if an entire sentence is parenthetical or bracketed. (On the other hand, you never want a comma directly preceding a parenthesis or bracket.)

The Thirteen Uses of the Comma

Use 1: Commas Mark a Natural Pause
and/or Prevent Misreading

I include the "natural pause" catchall since I suspect everyone's been taught it, and I want to build on that previous instruction: place a comma in sentences where there is a natural pause, where you hesitate ever so briefly while reading. It's not such a long pause as one during which you might take in a breath if you were reading aloud, but it's one that almost requires a breath. The trouble is that what's a "natural pause" for some won't be for others, so you might want to work with others to check your "naturalness." Two rows up from me right now on the train is a man who tows an oxygen cylinder behind him and breathes pure oxygen through a little plastic tube positioned beneath his nose. I note that his breath patterns differ from my twelve breaths per minute—his respiratory rate is close to twenty-five times a minute. Yours also might differ from mine, though perhaps not quite so much. These next three sentences use commas to denote natural pauses:

> A single file line of school children walked past a military checkpoint Sunday as a bomb-loaded truck veered toward them and exploded, killing 14 in a flash, as captured by a U.S. military security camera. ("World Watch: Afghanistan")

It is a parable about people who thought they could outwit competitors and market forces alike, and who behaved as though they were uniquely positioned to sidestep the disasters that had destroyed so many financial dreams before them. (O'Harrow and Dennis)

I saw a version when I was little, and thrilled to the sight of a disembodied hand writing on the wall. (Ross)

The commas are "optional" here, but the writers make good calls by including them.

In addition, use a comma where you need to have one in order to prevent misreading, as in the following (second comma):

Obesity surgery can reverse diabetes in teens, just as it does in adults, according to a small study. ("Study: Obesity Surgery")

Without that second comma, the sentence might mislead. It would seem that the surgery worked only for "adults according to a small study," or maybe adults following a protocol—perhaps those who somehow modified their behavior to accord with some study's suggestions. So the comma is needed.

Here are three examples of how a comma might have been inserted to prevent misreading (the first is from the *New Yorker*, the second from *New York*, and the final from *National Review*):

> ❓ An F.B.I. affidavit, seventy-six pages long, describes
> such activities as threatening to rescind eight million
> dollars in state funds for a children's hospital because
> an executive neglected to give him a campaign contribu-
> tion and trying to blackmail the Chicago *Tribune* into fir-
> ing editorial writers who had displeased him. (Hertzberg)

A comma might be useful after *contribution*, which would
indicate Blagojevich was behind the two separate incidents
being described.

Here is a difficult-to-understand sentence about the
then-president of the New School, Bob Kerrey:

> ❓ He's rankled segments of the faculty, who say he's
> out of touch with the 89-year-old institution's progres-
> sive roots and the students, several dozen of whom
> stormed his office to protest his endorsement of the
> Iraq War in 2002. ("Intelligencer: Old School")

Without a comma after *roots*, the sentence suggests that
Kerrey is out of touch with the students; what it's trying to
say, I think, is that Kerrey has rankled them, which is something quite different. If the writer wants to say Kerrey has
rankled the students, he needs a comma after *roots*; if he
wants to make it more clear that Kerrey is out of touch with
the students, he should insert a *with* before *the students*.

Here is another somewhat ambiguous sentence, which
would be a lot easier to understand with commas around
finally:

> ❓ Overspending, inflation, spiraling deficits, and finally
> severe fiscal retrenchment are the results. (O'Sullivan 20)

Without commas around *finally*, the sentence images up the notion of "finally severe fiscal retrenchment," a scenario that seems pretty scary, but one I can't quite envision for all that.

Use 2: Commas Can Be Used to Mark an Omission

Use a comma to mark an omission. Here, in "For Kurdish Girls, a Painful Ancient Ritual," the comma after *whimper* substitutes for the word *and*, making this barbaric scene of female genital mutilation happen very swiftly:

> [Seven-year-old] Sheelan began to whimper, then trem-
> ble, while the women pushed apart her legs and a mid-
> wife raised a stainless-steel razorblade in the air. "I do
> this in the name of Allah!" she intoned. (Paley)

Note here that there is no comma required after the exclamation point, which seems to be in contradiction with Use 13 below. When there are two possible punctuation marks, my suggestion is that you need use only the one that provides instruction on how the sentence might be read aloud—in this case, the exclamation point. Some writers call this the more "emphatic" punctuation mark.

Use 3: Commas Separate Items in a Series

Place a comma between coordinate adjectives and between items in a series, including after the item directly prior to the conjunction. In the antic "As If Things Weren't Bad Enough, Russian Professor Predicts End of U.S.," the list is correctly punctuated (note, too, that effective lists like this one place the most striking element last):

> Mr. Panarin posits, in brief, that mass immigration, economic decline, and moral degradation will trigger a civil war next fall and the collapse of the dollar. (Osborn)

R. Jeffrey Smith also precisely uses commas in his list:

> Current and former career officials at OSHA say that such sagas were a recurrent feature during the Bush administration, as political appointees ordered the withdrawal of dozens of workplace health regulations, slow-rolled others, and altered the reach of its warnings and rules in response to industry pressure.

Students used to be taught to omit the comma before the conjunction prior to the final element in the series. Now, however, most usage texts suggest putting in that comma. It's called the "Oxford comma" or "serial comma."

The Oxford comma serves a good purpose. Consider, for example, this sentence, from "Israel Pursues Strikes on Gaza; Toll Mounts and Outcry Swells":

> ❓ Israel said that among 30 or more targets destroyed Saturday and Sunday were the main security compound and prison in Gaza City known as the Saraya, metal workshops and Hamas military posts. (El-Khodary and Kershner)

Is *metal workshops and Hamas military posts* an appositive for (i.e., a restating of) *Saraya*? Or are these three distinct items in a series? I think it's three. But I'm not instantly sure. By inserting *known as* before *the Saraya*, the writers are attempting to clarify, but it doesn't help as much as a comma would. In speech, the way this sentence is spoken—maybe with a pause after *workshops*—would likely clarify. In writing, a comma after *workshops* is needed.

Sometimes, too, omitting the last (the serial) comma, invites a problem with sentence structure:

> ❓ The current system is arbitrary, inefficient and results in years of delay. ("Lawyers' Bills")

If the writer had introduced a comma after *inefficient*, the problem of the sentence might have emerged, namely, that it employs a nonparallel construction: "The current system is arbitrary." Fine. "The current system is . . . inefficient." OK so far. But, "The current system is . . . results in years of delay"? Maybe a better version would be "The current system is arbitrary, inefficient, and plagued by delays," or "The current system, arbitrary and inefficient, can generate unconscionably long delays."

Conventions of genre often defy grammar and logic. Newspapers, for example, traditionally omit the serial comma. If you are taking a journalism class, you should follow the conventions of journalism. However, in most other fields the serial comma is preferred in American usage.

Here is a non-12/29/08 example of how the serial comma

rule, when ignored, can generate confusion. In an article about Edward Kennedy, Jonathan Karp writes,

> **?** We subsequently met in Hyannis Port, Washington and Miami for a series of conversations that extended over days.

Maybe the writer assumes that everyone has heard of Hyannis Port, Massachusetts, but the punctuation makes it seem as though it's a city in Washington State. If three different locations are being named, though, the sentence needs to be revised.

Not only newspaper style (e.g., Associated Press and *New York Times*) but also British convention dictates omission of this serial comma. Still, I strongly recommend using the serial comma for the sake of clarity: it's too often confusing to omit it.

Consider the following, from a De Beers Family of Companies advertisement in the *New Yorker*. The sentence seems to be a list:

> **?** A diamond radiates warmth, light and unfailing beauty.

Many editors would accept this. However, I think that a comma after *light* would improve the sentence. Admittedly, the sentence works without that comma, with *light and unfailing* modifying *beauty*. But that interpretation doesn't really hold up. What is "light" beauty, after all? Isn't the sentence really saying that a diamond radiates three things, namely, "warmth," "light," and "unfailing beauty"? Let's make that clearer. A simple comma will do it.

Sometimes an omitted comma in a short list (two adjectives in the following) can change the meaning of a sentence, as in this *New Yorker* article about cell-phone novels.

> ❓ Its collection of Akutagawa stories, named for his classic short piece "The Spider's Thread," has horizontal blue-gray text and, for cover art, an image of a slender uniformed schoolgirl, lost in thought. (Goodyear 66)

Is the uniform slender or the schoolgirl slender? It seems to me likely that it's the latter, so the sentence should end, "an image of a slender, uniformed schoolgirl, lost in thought."

To test a sentence that includes a list of adjectives, you might try to insert *and* between them; if you can do so, and the sentence still makes sense, then commas would be acceptable instead of the *and*s. For example, we could talk about the "slender and uniformed schoolgirl" of the last sentence. The diamond sentence (in a rewritten version) could also make sense with the insertion of *and*s between its elements: "A diamond radiates warmth and light and unfailing beauty." But the following sentence fails this test:

> ❓ He has occupied the same, gracious apartment since 1945. (Nordlinger 47)

It doesn't sound right to say, "He has occupied the same and gracious apartment." By contrast, *large, gracious apartment* would work, as would *gracious, high-ceilinged apartment*, or something similar. But not *same, gracious apartment*.

Why not? The reason is that *same* modifies *gracious apartment*, not just *apartment*. The two adjectives (*same* and *gracious*) are not interchangeable here. Something sounds odd about "He occupied the gracious, same apartment since 1945," at least to my ear. "He occupied the same gracious apartment since 1945" seems to me preferable.

Here's another example of a similar kind of sentence. John Lahr, writing for the *New Yorker*, includes the following:

> ❓ He is trying to dramatize our psychic state, the perpetual, noodling back-and-forth between the conscious and unconscious mind. (115)

Let's put it to the test. *The perpetual and noodling back and forth* does not make sense. *Perpetual* modifies *noodling back and forth*, so no comma is required after the word. *Our psychic state* stands in apposition, by the way, to the whole phrase that follows it, so the first comma is a good example of Use 5 (below). What we probably should have, then, is this:

> He is trying to dramatize our psychic state, the perpetual noodling back-and-forth between the conscious and unconscious mind.

That seems to flow much more smoothly, at least for me.

Use 4: When Joining Main Clauses with "ABS OF NY" Words, Use the Comma

Use a comma in addition to *and*, *but*, *so*, *or*, *for*, *nor*, or *yet* (ABS OF NY words) to separate main clauses. Here's a good use of this structure:

> A man whose memoir about his experience during the Holocaust was to have been published in February has admitted that his story was embellished, and on Saturday evening his publisher canceled the release of the book. (Rich and Berger)

This could easily be two separate sentences, the first ending with *embellished*, and the second starting with *On Saturday*. Linking them with a comma and a coordinating conjunction implies a contiguity, a close cause-effect relationship. If you want a tighter connection, you could omit the coordinating conjunction and use a semicolon. To loosen up the cause-effect, just convert the single sentence into two.

This comma between main clauses is often omitted, but I think such an omission usually results in less than ideal clarity. Consider the following, the first from "Israel Strikes Gaza in 2nd Day of Attacks," and the second from "Time to Break Out the Big Guns," which is about how a moviemaker decided to use real soldiers, rather than actors, to make a war movie:

> ❓ In Sunday's air strikes, the high-rises of Gaza City shook and glass showered into the streets.

A comma after *shook* would help smooth reading, though some people would accept the sentence, since the second main clause is so short.

> ❓ But for the moment, they are stars and this is the climactic battle of next summer's sequel *Transformers: Revenge of the Fallen*.

The sentence needs two additional commas, after *stars* and after *sequel*. That second comma is Use 5.

These next examples seem more definitely in need of a comma before the *and* and the subsequent main clause:

> ❓ [Tom Cruise said,] "At one point, I thought she was going to ask me to marry her first and I put her off by changing the subject." ("Loose Talk")

> ❓ In this melancholy French drama, Philippe Claudel's direction is both probing and delicate and Kristin Scott Thomas's face keeps you searching for hints of her character's past. (Rev. of *I've Loved You So Long*)

> ❓ One look at the bill of fare taped to the window of Wilfie & Nell and Ms. U.G.—who reads menus the way Talmudic scholars read the Torah—was in a tizzy. (Raisfeld and Patronite 84)

This last example is especially difficult: I thought that maybe the establishment being alluded to was called "Wilfie &

Nell and Ms. U.G." Doesn't that sound like a good name for a Manhattan restaurant?

Use 5: Commas Separate Appositives

Use a comma with appositives. Again, an appositive is repetition, in different words, of a noun or noun phrase. It's usually a "nonessential," "nonrestrictive" element. To recall Dalgish's characterization of an appositive, it sets up a "non-assertive" equivalence between two nouns or noun phrases. An appositive includes extra information but is not needed to get across the main idea of the sentence, namely, what the subject is "verbing." In the following, I have marked with italics the two noun phrases in apposition:

> With his investment bank facing a near-certain failure, *Lehman Brothers Holdings Inc.'s chief executive officer, Richard Fuld Jr.*, placed yet another phone call to the man he thought could save him. (Craig et al.)

> *The Rev. Jeffrey Brown, executive director of the anti-crime Ten-Point Coalition in Boston*, said the spike in fatal shootings by and on black youths "bears out what I see on the streets every day." ("Black-on-Black Slays Rising")

Note that either the name or the person's title could be omitted and no sense would be lost—just some extra (though admittedly important) information. I should point out that in many newspapers and magazines, appositives frequently appear, since they allow writers to transmit information in a highly compressed form.

Here is a situation in which the writer has omitted two commas:

> ❓ There are many possible futures one can imagine for them, from becoming foundation-run nonprofits to relying on reader donations to that old standby the deep-pocketed patron. (Surowiecki)

After *donations*, a comma (Use 1) would probably help: it sounds, without one, as if the donations are being made to *that old standby*, which phrase should also be followed with a comma, since it stands in apposition to *the deep-pocketed patron*.

I should add that sometimes appositives can be essential, as when the information they supply is needed for the sake of clarity. If, for example, you have several brothers, you'd write, "My brother Bob is a surfer" (say). But if Bob is your only brother, you would use commas ("My brother, Bob, is a surfer"), since his name is not essential—he's your only brother; *my brother* and *Bob* are synonymous in this context.

Use 6: Commas Should Set off Other Nonrestrictive Elements

Use commas to separate out (i.e., "set off") other nonrestrictive or nonessential elements. In "Drillers Eye Oil Reserves off California Coast," Jane Kay sets off a relative clause:

> The Interior Department has moved to open some or all
> federal waters, which begin 3 miles from shore and are
> outside state control, for exploration as early as 2010.

Although this relative clause contains important facts, it is
"nonrestrictive" or "nonessential." Without it, the main
idea of the sentence, of the Interior Department's somewhat bold maneuver, would still be evident, namely, "The
Interior Department has moved to open some or all federal
waters for exploration as early as 2010." The facts that these
waters begin three miles offshore and are outside state control would be lost, but people who knew something about
federal waters would have known those facts anyway.

Sometimes, though, a "nonessential element" is slipped
into a sentence in a nonassertive way, but it actually functions as a sort of undercover operative. Deepak Chopra, in
"If Terrorism Is a Cancer, Treat It Like One," uses commas
to identify a nonessential element:

> Surveillance, within the bounds of civil liberties, is a
> fruitful tool for policing.

Without the commas, the sentence's meaning does not
change much:

> Surveillance within the bounds of civil liberties is a fruit-
> ful tool for policing.

I think that Chopra might have added commas to deemphasize the kind of scary notion of surveillance, as if he

were saying something like this: "Surveillance—I mean, rational, careful, selective surveillance, and of people and groups everyone would see as being dangerous, not of you and me of course!—is a fruitful tool for policing."

But the fact of the matter is that surveillance still is a pretty scary idea, and I'm not fully certain that "within the bounds of civil liberties" makes me feel all that much better about the concept of surveillance as a standard practice. Can, in fact, surveillance be done within those bounds? Isn't surveillance in direct contradiction with civil liberties? And has the insertion of commas around the phrase conveyed enough?

In sum, you need to decide which information in your sentence is "essential" to its meaning and what is nonessential or added only to provide context or background. For example, in the following two (made-up) sentences, a comma marks the difference between essential and nonessential information.

> The landlord hated students who had proven themselves to be slobs. [essential clause]

> The landlord hated students, who had proven themselves to be slobs. [nonessential clause]

Again, the comma marks the difference between two very different states of affairs. The first sentence reports how the landlord hated *only the slobby students*, which wouldn't be an unreasonable emotion to feel with respect to renters.

The second sentence, though, describes a landlord who hates *all students*. It gives a sort of reason for this feeling, but that's only extra information. The important information is in the initial four words.

Use 7: Commas Can Set Off Introductory Clauses and Phrases

Note the comma in Chopra's title above, "If Terrorism Is a Cancer, Treat It Like One." This title correctly uses a comma after a long (four-or-more-word) introductory element. Usually these are prepositional phrases, participial phrases, or participial or subordinate clauses. The following example is of an introductory prepositional phrase:

> Amid a sour economy, one business appears to be
> thriving as the year comes to a close: counterfeiting.
> (Leinwand)

And here are two subordinate clauses ("If . . . ,"), each followed by a comma. Steven Knobel remarks about WaMu,

> "If you were alive, they would give you a loan. Actually,
> I think if you were dead, they would still give you a loan."
> (Goodman and Morgenson)

This last sentence also includes Use 11, with a comma after a mild interjection, *Actually*.

Omitting the comma between a main clause and a subordinate clause can slow down reading, though making this omission does not usually distort sense, even if it takes some readers an extra moment to grasp the structure of the sentence. In "Explosives-Laden SUV Kills 14 Afghan School-children," the following appears. I would lobby for a comma in it after *camera*, though it's not wrong without one:

> ❓ The vehicle moves toward the security camera while the children walk in the opposite direction, nearly pass-ing the SUV, when the footage ends in a fiery blast. (Straziuso and Shah)

Some might argue that a comma before *while* might blunt the scary suddenness of the events, but I think the leisurely pace a comma establishes would increase the sentence's impact.

However, if a main clause starts a sentence and is fol-lowed by an *essential* subordinate clause, no comma should separate them. This would be the case if the sentence had read,

> The vehicle moves toward the security camera that was running through the whole episode.

The next example sentence, from a *Sports Illustrated* story about Michael Vick's fighting dogs, which he kept locked in cages when they weren't fighting, omits the comma after the introductory clause. This has the effect of initially mis-leading the reader:

> ❓ As far as they knew bad things happened when peo-ple came. (Gorant 76)

I first read *As far as they knew bad things* as the start of a sen-tence that was going to be about how those dogs certainly knew a lot of bad things. Of course, since the sentence is short, I easily reread it and got the actual sense. But I'm suggesting here that you strive for sentences that don't require your reader to reread to get the message, that don't spark initial confusion at all.

The following, from "The War on Terror Has Not Gone Away," includes the comma after a subordinate introductory clause, as well as illustrating Use 5 (commas with an appositive):

> While the attacks of 9/11 will never be forgotten, the consequences of 9/15, the date when Lehman Brothers declared bankruptcy, are now in the forefront. (Rosenbaum)

But this next sentence does not make quite enough sense as it stands; a comma should not intervene between a subordinating conjunction (*While*) and the clause it introduces:

> ❓ While, Pennington was effective once again Favre struggled. (O'Gorman)

The comma needs to be omitted after *While* and moved either before or after *once again*. This is a misplaced comma, rather than a "superfluous comma." (Admittedly these categories overlap. See the section on superfluous commas, below.) The sentence must include a comma, just not after the inital *while*.

Why this makes a difference is worth noting. Was Pennington once again effective, or did Favre once again struggle? Which of these two states of affairs is O'Gorman describing?

> While Pennington was effective, once again Favre struggled.
>
> OR
>
> While Pennington was effective once again, Favre struggled.

Yes, we know that Pennington was effective and Favre struggled. Fair enough. But the writer is trying to give us a little background here about these two quarterbacks' respective seasons, and his punctuation (not to mention his editor) isn't helping him out too much.

Use 8: Commas Should Be Used with "Interruptives"

Use a pair of commas with "interruptives"—expressions such as *on the other hand, for example, however,* or *though*— when they are used either transitionally or parenthetically. A sentence by R. Jeffrey Smith, quoted above (p. 113), shows *however* used this way. But if you'd rather not page back, this next sentence, from "The Beautiful Machine," demonstrates *though* used as an interruptive:

> At the end, though, the story of Financial Products is not about math and financial formulas. (O'Harrow and Dennis)

(To provide some context, O'Harrow and Dennis contend that the story is simply about greed.)

Use 9: Commas Are Used in Some "Conventional" Ways— in Dates, Titles, Degrees

Use commas before degrees and titles that follow a name. It is also conventional to use a comma to separate elements of dates, as in "Monday, December 29, 2008," and in elements of addresses. In the first sentence below, the last comma is used with a title (*associate burn director*, which is [correctly] not capitalized, I should point out, because it comes after the name); the sentence also includes comma Uses 1 (natural pause), 7 (with introductory element), and 13 (with *said*). In the second of the following pair, we have a sentence showing correct comma usage within an address:

> "That's why kids like Paige, if they don't get treated for burns right away, they can have disastrous consequences," said Ananth Murthy, associate burn director at Children's Hospital. (Kelly)

> Make a tax-deductible donation by writing a check or money order payable to "Children's Hospital" and mailing it to Washington Post Campaign, P.O. Box 17390, Baltimore, MD 21297–1390. (Kelly)

The convention is that no comma precedes the zip code. I'm not sure why. Perhaps a comma could be machine-misread as a numeral?

Use 10: Commas Can Be Used for Contrast and Emphasis

Use a comma for contrast and emphasis, and with "tag questions," even though you have probably noticed that those questions are often full sentences. The following ends with the tag question "isn't it?" which lends levity to the issued discussed:

> Mark Halperin, of *Time* magazine, one of the many usual or unusual suspects rounded up for the taped hour, says of [President George W.] Bush near the show's end, "He did not want this job as much as most people who seek it." That's sort of positive, isn't it? (Shales)

Tag questions in writing attempt to replicate speech patterns. They are somewhat out of place in formal writing. And in speech, they often denote an uncertainty or tentativeness.

The following sentence sets off the phrase *maybe even killing*, to give added emphasis:

> Environmentalists contend that the Navy's use of sonar is hurting, *maybe even killing*, whales. (Perry)

And in "Amid Gaza Violence, a New Task for Obama," the phrase *not less* (set off by commas) emphasizes a contrast:

> In Gaza and southern Israel, enraged citizens backed their respective governments and called for more, *not less*, violence. (Wolf and Stone)

Use 11: Commas Set Off Mild Interjections

Use a comma with mild interjections (like *alas*) and with *yes* and *no*. Here are two letters to the editor (the second comma in the longer example represents Use 1):

> Alas, maybe the CIA will continue to do "whatever it takes to make friends and influence people," regardless of how many people have to be hurt in the process. (Grose)

> No, schools are doing exactly what they are supposed to do. (Hwang)

Consider a version of the previous sentence that omits the comma:

> No schools are doing exactly what they are supposed to do.

Again, a comma's inclusion can provide one meaning and its mere omission the opposite one.

The rule is that a comma follows "mild" interjections" How about a less-mild word like *damn*? I will let you decide about this *National Review* sentence, though my recording it here clearly lets you know what I think it lacks:

> ❓ "Damn I wish I could be on your side on that one," Buckley wrote to Reagan in January 1988. (Hayward 43)

The sentence might be even better with an exclamation point after *Damn*.

Use 12: Commas Show Direct Address

Use a comma with words in direct address and after a letter salutation in an informal letter:

> I don't mind telling you, dear readers, that the day the
> Cardinals walk onto the field as the NFC's Super Bowl
> representatives will be the proudest day of my life. (Chad)

Dear readers and *you* are also in apposition.

Use 13: Use Commas to Represent Attributed Dialogue

Use a comma with *he said*, *she replied*, *Marv asked*, *Jana remarked*, *McKayla declared*, or similar constructions one uses when reproducing the spoken or written words of others. In "Obama's Tax Cuts Likely Soon," Philip Rucker quotes Obama senior advisor David Axelrod:

> "Look, we feel it's important that middle-class people
> get some relief now," Axelrod said on "Meet the Press."

(This example also includes Use 11 [comma after the mild interjection *Look*].)

Fine Tuning

Superfluous Commas

Avoid putting a comma between the subject and the verb except in the case where it's paired with another comma, which probably indicates that the early portion of the sentence contains a relative clause, an appositive, or a non-restrictive element of some kind. My advice is that if you have just one comma, then, check to see if it's needed—or if it's sufficient. (You might just need another.)

This following example, however, a headline index in *USA Today*, shows a pair of commas that could easily be eliminated:

> ❓ Six ways that television, and viewers, can change channels

While it may not be fair to use this as an example of questionable English usage—I mean, it's not really intended to be a regular sentence—I am doing so anyway, since even in a headline there is no good reason to insert commas between subject and verb. The writer might have used dashes or parentheses around *and viewers* (or omitted the commas).

Like O'Gorman's sentence above ("While, Pennington was effective . . ." in the section on Use 7), what follows is an example of a comma inserted too early in a sentence. Perhaps it remains there because of hasty editing. In "Latins Quiet about Madoff Losses," the authors write,

> ❓ Mr. Piedrahita, is a son-in-law of Walter Noel, founder of the Greenwich Group, which may have lost $7.5 billion it had invested with Mr. Madoff. (Córdoba, Regalado, and Millman)

No comma is needed after *Mr. Piedrahita*, as placing one there separates the subject from the verb. On the other hand, if we restructure, the sentence makes a bit more sense:

> Mr. Piedrahita's father-in-law is Walter Noel, founder of the Greenwich Group, which may have lost $7.5 billion it had invested with Mr. Madoff.

Commas before *That* and *Which*

Some writers maintain that one should never use *that* to introduce a nonessential element. Hence one should never have a comma before *that*. Some word processing programs even highlight as incorrect any comma before the word *that*. Well, generally, commas do not precede *that*. But sometimes they do. I'll start with an example of a questionable comma before *that*. In "Inventors Find Inspiration in Natural Phenomena," Jane Benyus is quoted as saying the following:

> ❓ "Preserving their habitats is really preserving the wellspring of ideas for the next industrial revolution, that gets us there with the minimum amount of energy, the minimum amount of toxins." (Eilperin)

That might be turned to *which*, but it's a quotation, so Eilperin couldn't make the change. It would also be confusing, since the *which* would refer to *industrial revolution*—not Benyus's point. So we'll have to forget *which* as a quick fix. I'd recommend using a semicolon or a period rather than a comma after *revolution*, which transforms the sentence effectively into one that's composed of two main clauses, the second starting with the subject *that*.

One significant difference between *that* and *which*, however, is that *that* can function as the subject of a sentence or main clause (as it does in Tim Goodman's article in which he claims, "But 25, that was fairly easy"). *Which* cannot, except in sentences just like this one. A sentence starting with *which* typically must rely on a previous full sentence. Consider, for example, the last paragraph in an article from the *National Review*. Assessing the Bush presidency, which was nearing its conclusion, the writer is quite critical of Bush:

> ❓ Which is why the best description of the Bush presidency was formulated almost 100 years ago by the great Canadian humorist Stephen Leacock: "He flung himself from the room, flung himself upon his horse and madly rode off in all directions." (O'Sullivan 20)

I think O'Sullivan should have connected this sentence to the last main clause in his previous paragraph, which derides George W. Bush's "impulses": "Almost always they prevail."

Why, though, given the relative simplicity of the grammatical "solution" to the problem, does O'Sullivan—a well-known professional writer—use *which* as the subject of a sentence, in fact as the first word in a paragraph? I think the answer to this has to do with style. He's arguing that Bush was somewhat out of control as a president; he was a creature, finally, of his impulses. Hence Bush failed to really respect conservative—or any—ideology. O'Sullivan sees this as a problem. He is a conservative writer who feels let down by a president he thinks was far too liberal and whose policies opened the door for a new president (Obama) who would be, by his lights, even worse. So O'Sullivan crafted his last paragraph to call attention to itself on a stylistic level. Just starting a sentence with *Which* does this.

This technique, called "foregrounding" by some linguists, is intended to shock the reader into some new insight. Here is how it's explained by Peter Childs and Roger Fowler:

> Foregrounding may be most readily identified with linguistic *deviation*: the violation of rules and conventions, by which a poet transcends the normal communicative resources of the language, and awakens readers by freeing them from the grooves of cliché expression, to a new perceptivity. (90)

I think it might be an exaggeration to call O'Sullivan a poet, but he relies here on a poetic device—a slight deformation of language—to call attention to his last paragraph, his last point. (Interestingly, just six months later, Mike Huckabee picks up the same Stephen Leacock quotation O'Sullivan had used and employs it in his morning "Huckabee Report" of June 29, 2009. But he uses it in reference to politicians on the other side of the aisle from Bush, namely, President Obama and Majority Leader Nancy Pelosi. I guess Leacock has something of an "all-purpose" quality.)

Back to *that* and *which*. Sometimes, *that* with no comma preceding it can generate a confusing sentence when the thing that the *that* refers to is a little ambiguous. Here is a sentence from an editorial, "Orszag's Health Warning," in the *Wall Street Journal*:

> **?** The insurance program for children that Democrats plan to expand in January will cost an extra $80 billion over the next 10 years.

I know many readers would accept this sentence unhesitatingly. But I ask the following: How do the Democrats "plan to expand" these children? I imagine inflation devices, or perhaps just a lot of sugar-filled treats. Maybe the sentence could be revised,

> The children's insurance program, which Democrats plan to expand in January, will cost an extra $80 billion over the next ten years.

In the following sentence, though, from an article about the financial meltdown, the *that* after a comma is correct:

> The hedges involved precisely calibrated transactions, including the purchase of Treasury bonds or other swaps, *that* brought a cash flow in almost direct proportion to the money going out. (O'Harrow and Dennis)

On the other hand, this next sentence needs a *that* without a comma (rather than a *which* with a comma), since the element set off is essential to the meaning of the sentence (or **restrictive**):

> ❓ It was also the kind of hustling play, which exemplifies the way TCA head coach Fred Falchi expects his team to play all the time. (Birch)

The description after the *which* is absolutely essential information because it specifies the "kind of hustling play" that "TCA head coach Fred Falchi expects his team to play all the time." Birch's *which*-clause is necessary for the meaning of the sentence. So a comma should not precede the *which*. (If he had wanted to keep *which*, however, that would have been acceptable, but he has to delete the comma.)

To repeat, *that* usually precedes elements that are essential to your sentence's meaning, while *which* typically introduces "nonessential" elements, and usually refers to the material directly before it.

Thus a sentence such as the following, from the *New Yorker*'s review of *Revolutionary Road*, might be somewhat confusing:

> ❓ There's a sourness, a relentlessness about the movie which borders on misanthropy. (Denby 117)

Is it the movie that "borders on misanthropy," which the construction seems to suggest, or do its "sourness" and "relentlessness" border on misanthropy? *Borders* agrees with a singular subject, which seems to point toward the idea that the movie borders on misanthropy. But I think Denby wants to suggest that the sourness and bitterness are the genuinely misanthropic elements. He might have tried something like this:

> The movie's relentlessness and sourness border on misanthropy.

> OR

> A relentlessness and sourness make the movie border on misanthropy.

Though the that/which distinction I outline here is strongly entrenched in formal U.S. usage, some linguists do not believe there is a significant difference between *that* and *which* as used in relative clauses. In their view, the words can be used interchangeably, except, perhaps, in the subject position or in certain expressions ("be that as it may," "any one of which").

Deep Focus

Omitting Commas in Short Sentences

When very short main clauses are joined, the conventional wisdom is that you may omit the comma. I disagree, since I think that the comma provides a useful pause, even in such cases:

> ❓ No one was injured but the lightning caused some superficial damage to the plane, spokesman Keoni Wagner said. ("Across the USA")

I would call this borderline, but it can be confusing. I first read it as saying the lightning was injured, an "absurd universe" moment.

Here, though, while the sentences are not short, omission of the comma between them is closer to acceptable. However, it's still not quite as good a sentence as it would be with a comma after *half hour*:

> ❓ The blaze was brought under control in around a half hour but heavy smoke claimed the lives of the seven victims. ("My 3 Dead Kids Are the Reason")

I recommend you use that comma. Such an inclusion would require the reader to pause, and that pause allows the reader time to process the events being described.

Remember, usually we want to write sentences that communicate our ideas. Most handbooks give the advice that you must lucidly convey these ideas—that's the goal. But sometimes it might be necessary to be less than fully direct and lucid. In fact, this situation emerges all the time. You need to make sure you have control over your own language to such an extent that you can be indirect, circuitous, and even sometimes obfuscatory if and when you want. It's when language gets away from us and obscures and confuses without our intending it to, that we find ourselves stymied, thwarted, and misunderstood. (I will leave it to your imagination as to when one might want to be obfuscatory—though I fear that this is not as infrequently as one would hope.)

Commas, Dashes, or Parentheses?

When do you use commas, when parentheses, and when **dashes** to set off an appositive or other nonessential element? Dashes underscore the element—emphasizing it—while parentheses have the opposite effect: they deemphasize the portion being set off. Commas are somewhere in between. Takeaway message? Punctuation can silently help you make your argument.

In an attempt to emphasize a detail, the following sentence uses dashes to set off a long relative clause. But I think the clause might be a bit too lengthy to set off in this way:

> Obama—who, since the election, has sent some pretty tough signals to the world with the national security team he has chosen—should harbor no illusions over Cuba. (Montaner)

If you're using dashes to emphasize an internal sentence element, that's fine, but if that element goes on for twenty-one words (as Montaner's does), its emphatic quality dissipates. I recognize, though, that many of you might disagree with me here, especially readers who take in words much more rapidly than I do.

Dashes are also a way to set off and clarify something in a sentence that already contains a comma. A *Washington Post* editorial writer emphasizes his or her point about a proposed increase in cigarette taxes:

> The proposal is long overdue, is eminently sensible—
> and is expected to wither in the House Finance Com-
> mittee. ("Mr. Kaine's Budget")

And Andrew Osborn slyly undercuts—via his use of a
dash and an emphasized phrase—the credibility of the
aforementioned Russian professor's prediction of the end
of the United States:

> Around the end of June 2010, or early July, he says, the
> U.S. will break into six pieces—with Alaska reverting to
> Russian control. (Osborn)

This structure makes us focus on the Alaska issue. Russians
have been angry about Alaska for a long time, and the emphasis on Alaska's return to Russia abruptly makes the professor's claims seem overall less scrupulous, scholarly, or
disinterested. It tips the professor's hand—he is just pan-
dering to mass sentiment in Russia.

Comma Splices Occasionally Acceptable

Sometimes, with two very short main clauses, you may use
a comma as a joining mechanism. For example, I think
most people would agree that this works as a sentence:

> You cannot filibuster, you cannot stall. ("The Kaizen Kraze")

On the other hand, the following two sentences seem less
acceptable. The first is about Pabst Blue Ribbon beer; the
second, about a sexless marriage:

❓ College kids are discovering it, retirees are rediscovering it. (Chad)

❓ I made my choice, now he has to make his. (Hax)

Each sentence contains two very separate ideas.

But of course this is not simple. Some teachers and editors accept comma splices if the second clause reverses a negation made in the first. Here are three more examples, the first from a letter to the editor published in the *Washington Post*, and the following two from articles in *USA Today*:

❓ Public safety, crime and violence aren't problems of race, they are problems that communities of any and all races must deal with. (Loge and Beckerman)

❓ And Apple didn't have to shell out for a big-name spokesperson, it just recast its PC and Mac ad characters and wrote a clever script. (Petrecca)

❓ "It's all being allocated on the basis of somebody's political pull or power," he [Steve Ellis, from Taxpayers for Common Sense] said. "It doesn't mean that money is wasted, it just means that if something good happens it's almost by accident instead of by design." (Fritze)

It seems to me that a semicolon would help us understand all of these sentences, but it is not absolutely necessary. Maybe. I think many writers avoid the semicolon because they don't quite understand its uses. And in newspapers, the use of a semicolon might be perceived as too academic or fussy. Still, I've labeled all of these as questionable, you probably noticed.

The following usages also press on the margins of acceptability. I would recommend against them, but I have put in square brackets the possible justification for letting each of these pass editorial muster. I use the question mark, though, since, after all, we do have a very good punctuation mark—the semicolon—that could more effectively join each pair of main clauses in the next four examples:

❓ "Let's face it, I had a primary, too—that was a factor." (Dilanian) [short main clauses; possibly "mild interjection" use of comma?]

❓ Forget what you've heard, believe what you read. (GMC) [short main clauses]

❓ "Watch your 6, the bad guys have you on their scope. . . .
It served their political agenda. Inflame the masses, get their votes." (Kings County Doc) [short main clauses]

❓ The worst outcome would be a ground assault, a la the one in Lebanon in 2006, that stirred anti-Israeli sentiment but stopped short of achieving its military goals. ("Israel's Gaza Defense")

This last example shows how using *that* after a comma, as the introduction to a nonessential clause, can be read as a comma splice, largely because *that* can serve as a sentence's subject. I would substitute *which* for *that*.

In general, as with the "acceptable fragment," the "acceptable comma splice" will likely meet with mixed reactions and results no matter what you do. Some editors, teachers, or readers would accept the previous sentences, but most would likely reject them all.

Punctuating a Series of Main Clauses within One Sentence

If you have more than two main clauses, you may connect these with commas and a coordinating conjunction. In the following example, Monica Hesse, discussing Tom Cruise, writes,

> **?** Cruise rambles, he cackles, he avoids proper nouns and he proclaims himself "the only one who can really help" at car accident scenes.

This actually takes the form of "main clause, main clause, main clause coordinating conjunction main clause." Unfortunately, Hesse omits the final, serial comma, as do most journalists. I'd include it, as it reinforces the parallel structure and makes the sentence slightly easier to process.

Chapter 5

Punctuation, Part II—The Colon, Semicolon, and More Mysteries of Punctuation

---

The Colon and Semicolon

The colon and semicolon are now used in fairly uncontroversial ways. Yet these punctuation marks have attained a kind of "don't try this at home" status: they seem sort of flashy and anguishedly rarefied. But they needn't be.

The Colon: Fundamentals

The colon is used to introduce things: a list, a longish quotation that you want to set off for some reason, or any element that you want to single out for special emphasis. It is also used after a salutation in a formal letter; in expressions of time; or at the end of a sentence, to set off an appositive for effect.

One thing to keep in mind about using the colon is that—except in time expressions or in a salutation—you should have a full sentence preceding a colon. Another way of expressing this idea is that you don't want to break up a sentence with a colon, for example placing a colon between the subject and the verb or between the verb and its object.

The following sentence, from *New York*, should probably use commas instead of colons:

> ❓ To be clear: D'Antoni only came here for the money. He could have had a better team in Chicago. But hey: Isn't that why we have the money? (Leitch)

Here is an example of a sentence fragment preceding a colon:

> ❓ Six schools from the Big 12 ranked among the nation's top 12 in total offense, but as Florida quarterback Tim Tebow was quick to point out after his team had earned the spot opposite Oklahoma in the BCS title game: He'd like to see what kind of stats *he* would put up against a Big 12 defense. (Beech)

Sports Illustrated's editors should have opted, I think, for a comma and lowercase "h" here, rather than a colon and a capital.

In addition—and here is another prohibition—you don't want to have more than one colon in a single sentence, unless one of those colons occurs in a time expression. Maybe I'm discovering why you shouldn't "try these at home."

Here is another common but questionable way that the colon is more and more often being used. The following is from "Food and Medical Supplies Grow Scarce on Besieged Gaza Strip":

? Because of the emergency, authorities had shut down the local silverware factory where he is employed. The reason: It was a non-essential business, and the Israeli government wanted to prevent gatherings of people from becoming targets of retaliatory rocket attacks from Hamas. (Raghavan and Abdel Kareem)

Using a colon after just a noun phrase makes your prose seem more like shorthand—not an ideal to be worked toward, though one our society seems to be embracing via text messaging, tweeting, and the like.

The Semicolon: Fundamentals

Earlier in 2008, the semicolon made the news: it appeared on a placard in the New York City subway. The *New York Times* ran a short piece on the usage, and the article's author, Sam Roberts, interviewed various language experts to get their response. Roberts's lead to the article captures a popular opinion about semicolons:

Semicolon sightings in the city are unusual, period, much less in exhortations drafted by committees of civil servants. In literature and journalism, not to mention in advertising, the semicolon has been largely jettisoned as a pretentious anachronism.

I'm not so sure. If it's been "largely jettisoned," why does it appear so often? And calling it "a pretentious anachronism" seems a bit much; actually the semicolon is a valuable mark of punctuation, though often misused and maligned.

Despite the apparent mystery surrounding its uses, the semicolon is employed in just two principal ways: first, it joins main clauses (full sentences), but only when those two clauses are closely linked for some reason (e.g., need for close contiguity, cause and effect, alternative explanations, important added information); and second, it serves to establish and separate elements in a list, when one or more of the list's elements have internal punctuation.

The two following sentences are examples of the first use. The authors employ the semicolon effectively in order to shorten the pause that might occur with two separate sentences:

> In the end, our fates and futures as humans and wild animals are not separate; they are inextricably linked. (Eilperin)

> The fatalities included 22 children younger than 16; more than 235 children were wounded, he said. (Raghavan and Abdel Kareem)

This next sentence successfully uses a colon and also exemplifies the second use of a semicolon, namely, separating elements in a list, when internal punctuation appears in one or more of the elements:

> Over the years, Dr. [Samuel P.] Huntington probed a number of the overarching issues of the modern world:

matters of war, peace, social progress and international development; the place of the military in a repub-
lic; tensions between democratic forms and social
order; the upheavals of the 1960s; and even the very
nature and distinctiveness of the United States.
(Holley and Weil)

But in the following, the author seems to have sacrificed
clarity for an intermittent respecting of the rule, and at
one point has used a semicolon rather than a comma. The
list ends up seeming haphazard and random:

> ❓ In addition to Dosso's children Ramere Dosso, 8;
> Mariam Dosso, 6; and Zyhire Wright-Teah, 1; the other
> victims were Henry Gbokoloi, 54, and siblings Vivian
> Teah, 26; Elliott Teah, 23, and Jennifer Teah, 17. ("My 3
> Dead Kids Are the Reason")

It's a sad, tedious task piecing through this list, but I would
suggest a revision something like the following:

> Among the victims were Dosso's children: Ramere
> Dosso, 8; Mariam Dosso, 6; and Zyhire Wright-Teah, 1.
> Other victims included Henry Gbokoloi, 54; and siblings
> Vivian Teah, 26; Elliott Teah, 23; and Jennifer Teah, 17.

Because semicolon use troubles so many writers, I will
present a few other problematic uses of the semicolon.
The first is from an article that appeared in nydailynews.
com. No semicolon is needed here, just a simple comma.

> ❓ That translates to 2.8 mpg for regular buses; 3.2 for hybrids. (Reich)

A similar problem emerges here, in a sentence from the *New Yorker*:

> ❓ Like Richter, Dumas confronts the problems head on by hewing, in paint, to the arbitrary givens of a photograph; in her case, photographs that she has found or has taken herself (usually Polaroids of people close to her). (Schjeldahl 113)

Again, just a comma would suffice. However, a colon or an em dash would also work.

Something seems awry in the following, from "In Our Pages 100, 75 & 50 Years Ago: '1908: Earthquake Devastates Italy.'" But it's slightly comforting to discover that journalists a century ago seemed to have as much trouble with semicolons as we do.

> ❓ A brief telegram brought from Sicily to the mainland by the gunboat Spica to a certain extent confirmed the fears, and stated that half the houses in the town had been destroyed; that there were hundreds, perhaps a thousand persons killed, and it was necessary for 3,000 men to be at once dispatched to clear away the ruins and bury the bodies.

There are a few ways to revise this, but I think the best way would simply be to omit the comma after *fears* and replace the comma after *killed* with a semicolon. In the service of parallel structure, I would also insert a *that* before *it was necessary*.

What follows is a pair of long lists that similarly flout the "rules" of semicolon usage. The first is from "Barack Obama Can Crack Cuba Open—but Only after Fidel Castro Dies," and the second from an article entitled "Boom in Australia Goes Bust in Record Time as Global Showdown Hits":

> ❓ Raúl [Castro] has three objectives: to gain access to soft credit so he can import American goods; to attract hundreds of thousands of American tourists, and to gain the release of five of the 14 Cuban spies captured in 1991 by the FBI. (Montaner)

> ❓ We're likely to go into the macro crisis first as debt growth plummets; then a housing crisis as the newly unemployed are unable to maintain their mortgages; and finally a credit crunch where the banks' solvency doesn't look so hot anymore. (Wiseman)

Neither of these requires any semicolons; instead, commas would have been acceptable. Semicolons are needed in a long list only if one or more elements of that list have internal punctuation.

Here are a couple of borderline-correct usages, ones in which the authors are fundamentally staking out their own punctuational terrain, and almost getting away with it. The first, from the *New Yorker*, is a list including one item with internal punctuation (commas). Yet the author has decided against using semicolons. Is the sentence clear enough? You decide:

> ❓ Still, some of the music is strong and catchy, the motley cast, with its less-than-perfect voices and bad accents, is charming, and the set—a huge, spare room in an old Brooklyn church—is grand in an aptly shabby way. (Rev. of *London Cries*)

Perhaps the idea was that since the sentence structure so carefully maintains its parallelism, the use of semicolons would have been otiose. I think I'd have used them. Call me pretentious and anachronistic if you like.

On the other hand, maybe this next example represents overcorrecting. While the elements of the list are lengthy, none contains any internal punctuation. So perhaps this *New York* writer does not need to use semicolons, only commas:

> ❓ They cast themselves as adoring specialists who keep massaging their relationships with a few compos-ers; self-abnegating fundamentalists who consider the score infallible and performance a matter of correct ex-ecution; cautious scholars who derive each interpretive decision from rigorous analysis; or flamboyant icono-clasts who treat a piece of music as putty to be molded by their personalities. (Davidson)

Some style guides claim that semicolons set off main elements either in a list containing one or more elements that have internal punctuation, or in a list that has long or complex elements. However, I find myself on the side of those guides that avoid as perhaps too imprecise the "long or complex" qualification, and maintain simply that if internal punctuation (commas or dashes) is used in an element or more than one element of a list, then semicolons are required. If not, use commas.

USA Today's masthead includes the following sentences, neither of which accords with standard semicolon usage (in square brackets, I have included suggested revisions):

▨ All advertising published in USA TODAY is subject to the current rate card; copies ["are" should be included here] available from the advertising department.

▨ USA TODAY is a member of the Associated Press and Gannett News Service; ["the newspaper" should be inserted here] subscribes to Reuters and other services.

The *Wall Street Journal* conveys the same information about advertising, using punctuation in a standard way:

All advertising published in *The Wall Street Journal* is subject to the applicable rate card, copies of which are available from the Advertising Services Department.

Fine Tuning: Semicolons to Mark Pauses

Not long ago, English teachers taught students that a semicolon was used for a pause longer than that of a comma but not as sharp or definite as that of a colon or period. This usage survives in constructions such as the following, which I am marking as questionable:

> ❓ Conservative Islam has been growing all over the region; in Jordan, Egypt, Lebanon, and even within Israel's Arab community. (Picow)

In this example, the semicolon cannot really be replaced with a comma (which might make the list confusing). However, a colon or an em dash would probably be better.

You can use the semicolon in a sentence that's in the "main clause, coordinating conjunction main clause" format, provided that the main clauses are long. Here is how *New Yorker* writer Darryl Pinckney uses it:

> In the earliest entries, the lists included William Faulkner, Nathanael West, and Sherwood Anderson; and in the early sixties she did take note of a list of metropolitan writers (Bellow, Ellison, Grace Paley). (108)

Using a comma after *Sherwood Anderson* here could be confusing, I think; Pinckney makes a good choice in using the semicolon. Some, though, would opt for a comma.

When people have their writing "corrected," they usually discover that their long, complicated sentences receive the most correction and criticism. So they resort to—guess what?—writing short, simple sentences. This is called the "my puppy syndrome": "My puppy is cute. He has a long tail. He wags it a lot. I love my puppy." All of these are accurate sentences—but not ones at the adult level. Please don't give up on long sentences. It's just that as you increase your sentence length and complexity, you also need to increase your vigilance and the care you take to revise.

The Apostrophe

The apostrophe is being used less and less, and at the same time with less and less accuracy. Some people refer to it as a "high comma" or "comma above the line." (I'm not making this up.) This shows how people use the familiar to describe the unfamiliar. I expect apostrophes will soon disappear from our language and vocabulary, but probably not in our lifetime, hence the necessity of including the following section.

The Apostrophe: Fundamentals

As you might expect, the apostrophe's use is not entirely regular. The standard uses are in contractions and in noun possessives.

Contractions

Apostrophes are used to form a contraction. An apostrophe indicates the missing letter: *it's* (*it is* or *it has*), *doesn't* (*does not*), *can't* (*cannot*). Sometimes this involves a modification of the original complete words, as when *will not* shortens to *won't*.

N.B. *IT'S* MEANS *IT IS* OR *IT HAS*. *IT'S* IS **NOT**
THE POSSESSIVE FORM OF "IT"! (EVEN THOUGH IT
MIGHT SEEM TO BE).

Misusing *it's* is a particularly bad error. Editors watch for it—so it's not surprising that I couldn't find any examples of it in the December 29 writing I examined. Among non-professional writers, though, it's very common.

A Method of Determining Placement
of the Apostrophe in Possessives

People often ask me how to figure out where an apostrophe or an apostrophe + "s" should be placed. Here is what I suggest. This may seem complicated, but isn't, really. (I know that's what everyone says right before introducing an incredibly complex or impossibly difficult notion or system, but really, this isn't so hard; it just takes some space to explain. And I will try to reinforce how the method is applied in practice when I comment on some of the example sentences that follow.)

Start with the sentence in question, the one in which possession is indicated in some way, such as the following headline:

No Easy Indian Response to Pakistan's Troop Shift (Sengupta)

Is the apostrophe correct? There seems to be something like possession being described. Here's the two-step procedure you need to employ:

Step 1: Find the base (the nonpossessive or "uninflected") form of the noun. You can find this by modifying the sentence in such a way that it does not require a noun doing any possessing. Usually you just import a *belonging to* or *of* phrase.

No Easy Indian Response to Troop Shift of Pakistan

Such an operation reveals the base form of the noun: *Pakistan*.

Step 2. Determine whether the noun is singular or plural. *Pakistan* is singular. Insert that base form back into the original sentence.

No Easy Indian Response to Pakistan Troop Shift

Interestingly, *Pakistan* is acceptable, functioning adjectivally. But maybe you want to emphasize the possessive element here. If so, using the following guidelines, add the required element:

- If the base form of the noun ends in "s" and it is singular, add an apostrophe + "s."
- If the noun ends in "s" and it is plural, add only an apostrophe.
- If the noun, singular or plural, ends in anything other than "s," add an apostrophe + "s."

Pakistan fits into the third category. It's a noun ending in a letter other than "s" and therefore needs an apostrophe + "s": "Pakistan's troop shift."

Using this procedure not only helps place the apostrophe but also sometimes helps uncover the meaning of a sentence. Consider this headline:

❓ Left's Witch Hunt Should Be Halted. (Kondracke)

Is the apostrophe correct? We don't usually see *Left* in the possessive form. But let's follow the procedure outlined above. We can locate the base form by rewriting the sentence in one of the two following ways:

Witch hunt of the Left should be halted.

Witch hunt belonging to the Left should be halted.

The first suggests that the Left is being hunted—or maybe the opposite; the second implies that the Left "owns" a witch hunt, which seems unlikely. So what does it mean?

Kondracke's editor has invented a titillating headline that can be read more than one way: either the Left is engaged in a witch hunt, or it's the subject of a witch hunt. Thus people who are either pro- or anti-Left should be drawn to reading the editorial.

I can't recommend building such ambiguity into your sentences. The headline "Witch Hunt by Left Should Be Halted" would be a better option, since that in fact is what the editorial is about.

Singular Noun Possessives

To form the possessive of a singular noun, add apostrophe + "s": *dog's, father's, man's, telephone's.* If two nouns are linked, indicating joint possession (or joint sponsorship, as in the following), use just one apostrophe:

> Mexicans and Americans should question whether Felipe Calderón and President Bush's "war on drugs" is worth it. (Newman)

On the other hand, the following sentence does not indicate "joint possession," so possession probably needs to be shown by apostrophes with both names:

> ❷ According to other fund managers, wealthy Brazilians invested in Mr. Madoff or Fairfield's funds via private banks, including Safra and UBS. (Córdoba, Regalado, and Millman)

The reason I say "probably," though, is that it's not entirely clear what proportion of Fairfield's funds were in fact

Madoff's funds. There was some separation of the two enterprises—enough, I think, to warrant two apostrophes. But it's a close call.

Names Ending in "s"

Names ending in "s" cause something of a problem. Some styles (e.g., MLA and *Chicago*, for example) require these to take an apostrophe + "s"—*Charles's, James's, Ross's*. Some styles require just an apostrophe.

My recommendation is that, to indicate possession, use an apostrophe + "s" for all names, even those ending in "s," including those that end in an "eez" sound (*Xerxes's, Demosthenes's*); those that look like plural nouns (*Rivers's*); and biblical names, such as *Moses's* and *Jesus's*. This seems to be the direction we are going, as it's a move toward greater consistency.

But regardless of how you choose to solve this problem, check first the style manual for your discipline, and then try to be consistent within a given essay: if you use *Charles's* in one place, you don't want to use *Charles'* in another, even if your discipline's style guide allows for both.

Plural Noun Possessives

To form the possessive of a plural noun, add only an apostrophe, as in *two friends' wishes, three lionesses' cubs, eight families' houses, ten battalions' firepower*. Irregular plural forms (ones that don't end in "s") are handled the same way as singular nouns: *children's, women's, media's*.

Plural possessive proves troublesome for many writers. In the single issue of *New York* magazine that I looked at, I found four sentences that used plural possessive with the apostrophe in the wrong place. Three examples come from the same article.

> ❓ It's 1955: Frank works in a mindless job at the business-machine company that ground down his dad, and puts drunken moves on a chubby secretary; April stays home in Connecticut with two kids and cleans and stares at patios of other peoples' houses and feels her creativity and optimism leaching out of her. (Edelstein 90)

> ❓ In *Bug* he played (to the hilt) a delusional paranoiac, but his John has a different vibe—acid, wires humming, ripping off other peoples' scabs to keep from ripping into his own. (Edelstein 90)

To offer my suggested revision of these two examples, I would recommend "other people's houses," that is, the houses of other people, and "other people's scabs." (I know that the "houses of other peoples" and "the scabs of other peoples" are remote possibilities—the plural "peoples" exists, as in "the peoples of the ancient world"—but it seems to me highly unlikely that these are the concepts Edelstein is trying to communicate.) In fact, I think he just needs an editor to help out with apostrophe use. Here is another of his sentences:

❓ Well, she [Kate Winslet] could force anyone into the moment. In *Revolutionary Road*, her emotions are too big for her face; she's such an elastic actress, so in tune with her characters' feelings, that her features seem to expand or contract in every scene. (Edelstein 90)

I think that Edelstein is talking about only the single character Winslet portrayed in *Revolutionary Road*; hence it should be "her character's feelings," that is, the feelings of this one character.

Plural possessive is actually quite knotty, since we do use an "s" to indicate plural and an apostrophe + "s" to show possession. Thus having plurality and possession taking place at once can lead to confusion. Here is another sentence from *New York*:

❓ New York is full of monuments to guy's egos: Ever hear of Rockefeller Center? (Pressler)

Pressler probably is referring to *guy* in the plural, and wants to use plural possessive: *guys'* would be the form needed. The monuments are to the egos of guys.

The sports pages often show problems with plural possessives, since the names of most teams are plural: the Mets, the Yankees, the Giants, the Royals. Thus when one wants to create a possessive form, that is, when one wants to put a team's name in what is sometimes called the "genitive case," the apostrophe needs to go after the "s": the *Mets'* great season, the *Yankees'* lost glory. Here, though, on the last page of *Sports Illustrated*, the editors throw us a curve:

> It might have been more helpful to African-American coaches as a whole, for instance, if Ty Willingham had stayed at Stanford, where he was exceeding the *Cardinal's* relatively modest expectations, but instead he left for Notre Dame, where one good season and two sub-par ones earned him a quick pink slip. (Taylor)

One might ask, which Cardinal's expectations would have been exceeded by Willingham's leaving Stanford for Notre Dame? But actually, Stanford calls its teams "The Cardinal," not "The Cardinals," so Phil Taylor's usage is correct, which fact might be lost on non–sports fans.

The Apostrophe: Fine Tuning

Pronouns That Take Apostrophes

Some pronouns take an apostrophe to signal possession (*one's*, *somebody's*, *nobody's*); others—already structured to show possession—do not: *his, hers, ours, yours, theirs, its*.

Expressions of Time or Duration

Expressions of duration used adjectivally are formed as if they were possessives, as in *a day's drive, an hour's wait, a year's time*. Garner refers to this as the "idiomatic possessive" (647). It's sort of counterintuitive, since the day doesn't "own" the drive, the hour doesn't "own" the wait, and the year doesn't "own" the time.

Not All Words Ending in "s" Require the Apostrophe

Generally, you do not need an apostrophe to indicate a plural. This incorrect construction is seen sometimes in signs: "Apple's—fifty cents each." It is sometimes called the greengrocer's apostrophe, though I'm not myself endorsing this expression (some greengrocers are, after all, very well educated). And here is one generated by a professional writer. All that's needed is plural, not plural possessive:

> ❓ Fear of lawsuits prompts doctors' to overprescribe diagnostic tests. ("Lawyers' Bills")

Here is one from a reader—odds are, also not a greengrocer:

> ❓ Well, Hamas was warned. I guess they found out that the Israeli's were not bluffing. (Downwithracism)

While generally an apostrophe is not used in the formation of a plural, see the "Deep Focus" section below.

Contractions in Formal Writing

In formal writing, it is best to avoid using a great number of contractions. Some of your teachers or professors might altogether prohibit contracted forms, but if you find this out early enough in a semester, you can put drop/add to good use. Such professors' prohibition is too sweeping. I recommend using a contraction when the noncontracted form sounds awkward or stilted.

The Apostrophe: Deep Focus

An Obscure Use of the Apostrophe

Some words take *only* an apostrophe: *for conscience' sake, for righteousness' sake, for goodness' sake*. The rule is definitely an "endangered species," neither widely known nor often respected, but for conscience' sake I have included it.

Apostrophes to Indicate Plural

One additional confusing element with apostrophes concerns such expressions as "Mind your p's and q's" or "I received all A's and B's on my report card." Both show correct usage of an apostrophe indicating a plural. Dates and numbers (1930s, fours, 8s and 9s), do not require an apostrophe. There seems a certain inconsistency in advice— some writers suggesting that apostrophes should never be used to indicate plurals, some taking the more pragmatic approach that I follow here. *The Chicago Manual of Style*, 16th edition, puts it this way:

> Capital letters used as words, numerals used as nouns, and abbreviations usually form the plural by adding s. To aid comprehension, lowercase letters form the plural with an apostrophe and an s. (353)

I can add to this that while the "usually" seems like something of a weasel word, it suggests to me there is some leeway in terms of how this rule should be applied. Just the same, try to be consistent in your practice, at least within a given document (e.g., don't refer to the "1930's" in one place and the "1930s" in another).

The Dash

Dashes: Fundamentals

One-en, One-em, or Hyphen?

Some styles make a distinction between a hyphen (-), a slightly longer "en dash" (–), and a still lengthier "em dash" (—). All of these have separate and surprisingly complex usages. Again, follow whatever guidelines are conventional in your field, but if you don't know what these are, here is a simple suggestion: make sure you don't use a hyphen interchangeably with an em dash. This is the most common mistake—and it generates a lot of rereading and confusion.

A hyphen is used in various compound word formations: *high-flying*" *S-s-s-surprise!* (to indicate stuttering); a "suspensory usage" (*a fourteen- to sixteen-line poem*); in compounds like *pre-Enlightenment thought*; and in words that, without the hyphen, would include an awkward repetition of a vowel (such as *co-opt*). It's also used if closing up the words undoes or distorts your meaning (*re-create* and *pro-creation* differ markedly from *recreate* and *procreation*).

Editors and dictionaries now usually close up two-word phrases, making them just one word, unless the words are used adjectivally and can stand alone. Here are a few examples: *bumblebee, chickpea, crybaby, leapfrog, logjam, lowlife, pigeonhole, waterborne* (Rabinovitch). On the way in are words like *fundraiser* and *ebook*, I believe. (As I said, it's complex.) For example, in "When Hedge Funders Are Sent Home, Careful Tending Is in Order," the following sentence correctly hyphenates *home-office*:

> Mr. Madigan also found that many of his new home-office clients don't want any old Gmail account.
> (Dominus)

Home and *office* can stand alone; *home-office* is being used as an adjective, not a noun; therefore the hyphenated form is correct.

Purdue's OWL website (Conrey and Stolley) is an excellent resource for grammatical issues. I excerpt the following from their "rules" for hyphenation:

1. Use a hyphen to join two or more words serving as a single adjective before a noun:

> chocolate-covered peanuts
> well-known author

However, when compound modifiers come after a noun, they are not hyphenated:

> The peanuts were chocolate covered.
> The author was well known.

2. Use a hyphen with compound numbers:

   forty-six
   sixty-three

3. Use a hyphen to avoid confusion or an awkward combination of letters:

   re-sign a petition (vs. resign from a job)
   semi-independent (but semiconscious)
   shell-like (but childlike)

4. Use a hyphen with the prefixes ex- (meaning former), self-, all-; with the suffix -elect; between a prefix and a capitalized word; and with figures or letters:

ex-husband	mayor-elect
self-assured	anti-American
mid-September	T-shirt
all-inclusive	mid-1980s

The writer Nicholson Baker all but despairs of the "rules" regarding the use of hyphens. He writes, "Truly, American copy-editing has fallen into a state of demoralized confusion over hyphenated and unhyphenated compounds—or at least *I am* demoralized and confused" (9). No need to be demoralized: there are thousands of cases, so just consult the dictionary when in doubt; it will help you resolve 90 percent of the cases. (Sadly, that does leave one case in ten still problematic.)

The em dash is used, as I suggest above, when—for effect or emphasis—you want to set off some element of a sentence.

Though the em dash calls for a deft writer's hand, its use is simple in comparison with that of the en dash. To explain en dash use I must defer to Garner, who captures some of its difficulty in the following:

> The *en-dash*, which is half as wide as an *em-dash*, is distinct (in print) from the *hyphen*. It joins pairs or groups of words to show a range, and also indicates movement or tension (rather than cooperation or unity). It is often equivalent to *to* or *versus*. (679)

In the following sentence, *billion-dollar* has a hyphen, but an en dash should be used in *Iran–Iraq*:

> ❓ In exchange, France agreed to restore diplomatic relations with Iran, which had been strained over the Iran-Iraq war, and paid off the last segment of a billion-dollar dispute over a nuclear energy project with Iran. (Derschau)

The Chicago Manual of Style (which, incidentally, doesn't endorse the "*to* or *versus*" use) goes on for almost two pages about the en dash. Newspapers almost never use en dashes at all (which is why Derschau doesn't use one). The *MLA Style Manual and Guide to Scholarly Publishing* altogether withholds explanation of the en dash but itself uses that dash on several occasions. Apparently the publisher of the MLA guide uses *Chicago* style.

The Quotation Mark

The Quotation Mark: Fundamentals

In general, I recommend that you follow the rules set out in various handbooks, such as *MLA Style Manual and Guide to Scholarly Publishing* or *The Chicago Manual of Style*. What follows is a brief condensation of MLA's guidelines.

Dialogue

When representing dialogue, you need to start a new paragraph with each change of speaker.

If one speaker continues for more than a single paragraph, you should not put an end quotation mark at the close of each paragraph. However, you must open each new paragraph (of that speaker's words) with quotation marks. When the speaker finally finishes, then a closing quotation mark is used. This punctuation might seem strange, I know, but represents the conventional usage.

Avoiding Plagiarism in the Epoch of the Post-Original (TEPO)

When you quote a source, you must indicate that the words you use are not your own. You may do this either by inserting quotation marks around the words being quoted or by setting off a passage from the main body of your writing. You also need to make clear whose work you are quoting, by using either internal reference form, or a footnote or endnote. If you don't, you could be accused of plagiarism.

In February 2010, German wunderkind author Helene Hegemann, when accused of plagiarism, said, "There is no such thing as originality, just authenticity" (Kulish). Indeed, we may have entered what I term the "Epoch of the Post-Original" (**TEPO**) where all ideas are on the Internet, and everything's a mash-up, and it's all up for grabs. But that's not in fact the case. You still need to be aware that if you use, without attribution, others' words or ideas, you can be accused of plagiarism, of cheating. In some contexts that could even result in lawsuits involving "fair use," copyright laws, and the U.S. Constitution, which discusses the matter in Article I, Section VIII.8.

Keep in mind that there are many electronic programs, such as turnitin.com, that scan the Internet and their own database for matches to word strings in your work. So make sure to include the quotation marks.

Again, if the quotation is more than four lines (approximately forty words), you must set it off from the rest of your text, indenting ten spaces (one inch) from your left text margin. A "ragged" (i.e., not justified, not squared-off) right margin should remain the same as the right text margin of the body of your paper. The set-off passage does not need quotation marks, unless it includes a mixture of dialogue and narration, in which case you use the same quotation marks as used in the text being quoted. The setting off itself indicates that the passage is a quoted one. Note that MLA's guidelines differ from Chicago's here; the *Chicago Manual* allows for much more quotation to be included within the (nonindented, non-set-off) text proper. And your professor, teacher, or editor might give specifications for the treatment of quotations that vary somewhat from either guide.

Introducing a Quotation

Usually when introducing a quotation, you should use a colon or a comma, a colon being used after a full sentence. But if the quotation closely joins the syntax of your sentence, no punctuation is needed. In an article from the *New York Times*, Raúl Esparza, a costar of *Speed the Plow*, discusses a new actor, Norbert Leo Butz, who was recently added to the cast:

> What Mr. Butz contributes is "a theater actor's ability to tell a story well, to play in the ensemble," he added. (Itzkoff)

No comma or other punctuation is needed after "What Mr. Butz contributes is." But in this next sentence, which I introduce using author and source, a comma is correctly included:

> As Tom Polansek writes in the *Wall Street Journal*, "Wheat produced in Ukraine and Russia is generally of lower quality than U.S. wheat."

Note that I am using a "signal phrase" at the beginning of this example sentence. In it, I indicate the source of the quoted material and give its writer the authority that the *Wall Street Journal* lends him. When quoting from sources, make sure that you use signal phrases, unless your audience is completely familiar with the person or source you are quoting. Your audience has to know whom you are quoting and why he or she is important, why his or her words deserve repetition.

Internal Reference Form

To indicate (internally, without a footnote or endnote) a page number for a quoted source, you should place some identifying information in parentheses after the quotation. In MLA form, this is typically just the page number, unless the name of the author hasn't already been made clear. In *Chicago* style, though, you can indicate additional information such as the author, year of publication, and page number as well.

Why do editors, teachers, and professors insist on *exact* bibliographic form? Why does the information always have to go in just the right sequence, especially if all that necessary information is included somewhere or another? There are three main reasons:

1. using the same sequence and format helps assure that all information is indeed present;
2. using correct-for-your-discipline form makes a silent argument for your credibility (and not using it makes the opposite argument);

3. using a field's or discipline's form (MLA, APA, *Chi-cago*) reinforces the fact that you are a member of that community.

Punctuation in and around Quoted Material

Periods and commas go inside quotation marks, except when parenthetical references are being used. (The British system differs, by the way: in it, periods and commas go outside the quotation marks.) Semicolons and colons go outside. Exclamation points and question marks go either inside or outside, depending on the sentence (if the quotation itself is an exclamation or question, then the punctuation goes inside the quotation marks; if the enclosing sentence is an exclamation or question, then the punctuation goes outside the quotation marks).

I often teach placement of punctuation with quoted materials, yet only about 5 percent of my students get it. I suppose, in some dartboard target of important things, punctuation of quotations is either on the very edge or, maybe, on the wall. It's one of many small details to attend to—ones I'm arguing that do ultimately matter. Here is a shorthand version of the possibilities, using a quotation from Jim Holt. Numbers 6, 8, 12, and 13 work on the premise that the quoted sentence is an exclamation or a question:

1. Simple punctuation at end of a quoted sentence:
   "But philosophy isn't just talk."

2. Punctuating a quotation that continues on into the surrounding sentence:

   "But philosophy isn't just talk," Holt maintains.

   [or, when quoted material does not require a comma]
   "But philosophy isn't just talk" and pointless palaver, according to Holt.

3. Quotation that will introduce something else, using a colon:

   "But philosophy isn't just talk": hence the problem.

4. Quotation that will be joined to another main clause, using a semicolon:

   "But philosophy isn't just talk"; it's something else altogether.

5. Quotation embedded in a sentence that is an exclamation:

   Don't believe Holt when he says, "But philosophy isn't just talk"!

6. A quoted exclamation:

   "But philosophy isn't just talk!"

7. Quotation embedded in a sentence that is a question:

   Why would Holt maintain, "But philosophy isn't just talk"?

8. A quoted question:

   "But philosophy isn't just talk?"

9. Quoted sentence, including page reference:
   "But philosophy isn't just talk" (72).

10. Quoted sentence embedded in a sentence that is an exclamation, and including page reference:
    Don't believe Holt when he says, "But philosophy isn't just talk"! (72).

11. Quoted sentence embedded in a sentence that is a question, and including page reference:
    Why would Holt maintain, "But philosophy isn't just talk"? (72).

12. Quoted exclamation, including page reference:
    "But philosophy isn't just talk!" (72).

13. Quoted question, including page reference:
    "But philosophy isn't just talk?" (72).

14. Quoted sentence including name of author and page reference:
    "But philosophy isn't just talk" (Holt 72).

15. Set-off block quotation, including author and page reference:
    But philosophy isn't just talk. (Holt 72)

16. Set-off block quotation, including author's name:
    But philosophy isn't just talk. (Holt)

Note that in 10–13 above, you have what amounts to double punctuation. Please note too that in the case of set-off block quotations, simple sentences are handled the same way as questions or exclamations, and, oddly, there is no punctuation after the parenthetical reference.

The Quotation: Fine Tuning

Modifying Quoted Material

Use square brackets [like these] to show where you as an author have modified the original or inserted some new material, such as a capitalization or a word needed to make the quotation flow better and/or to explain its context. If you omit a section of material in a passage you are quoting, use an ellipsis (...):

> For now, businesses are hunkering down. Anglo-Australian mining giant Rio Tinto just announced plans to slash 14,000 of its 112,000 jobs. Drill Technics . . . has cut its drilling crew to 15 from 32. [Mining equipment manufacturer Leigh] Davies has laid off 15 of his 27 workers. (Wiseman)

If there is an ellipsis already in the original, MLA (but not other forms) allows you to put your own ellipsis in square brackets, like this [. . .]. In keyboarding your work, intersperse the dots with spaces.

Quotation Marks, Italics, and Underlining

Use quotation marks around titles of certain genres of writing and of portions of books. Quotation marks should be used with short stories, poems, short plays, article titles, or single episodes in a TV series. Italicizing should be used for stand-alone physical or virtual entireties: titles of novels, full-length plays, book-length poems; TV series and movie titles; titles of magazines, journals, or newspapers; names of ships or spaceships; foreign words unfamiliar to American readers, and names of websites.

The Quotation: Deep Focus

Special Uses of Words

Use quotation marks if you wish to call attention to a special use of a word:

> As financial markets crumbled, terms such as "bailout," "credit crunch," "subprime mortgage securities" and even "credit default swaps" became commonplace. (Petrecca)

> Insurance firms will soon be allowed to diversify by investing directly in infrastructure projects for the first time on a consistent basis, the industry regulator has said. But this is deregulation Chinese-style, so "allowed" doesn't quite explain it. "Encouraged" is the word policy makers are using. (Peaple)

Single or Double Quotation Marks?

Use double quotation marks as the first indication of quoted material or of words not your own (or "special"), then single quotation marks if you need to quote inside a quotation. If you need to go another level (i.e., a quotation inside of a quotation inside of a quotation), switch back to double marks. The next two sentences provide interesting examples. Um Shadi al-Bardaweel, a resident of Gaza, reports,

> "After each air strike, my sons ask me, 'Why are we targeted? Will they arrest us? Will they come after us?' I tell them not to panic. We are far away from the shelling. But then, tonight the bombing reached our doorsteps." (Raghavan and Abdel Kareem)

And in an unsigned editorial, another example of quotation within quotation emerges:

> Mr. Abbas yesterday said, "We talked to them [Hamas] and we told them 'please, we ask you, do not end the truce. Let the truce continue and not stop' so that we could have avoided what happened." ("Israel's Gaza Defense")

The British system reverses this, using single quotation marks as the first option.

End Punctuation and Combining Sentences

End Punctuation: Fundamentals

The period, exclamation point, or question mark ends sentences.

A question mark ends a direct question, not an indirect question. You do not need a question mark when you write, "She wondered what she was going to do" or "He asked himself how the machine worked." A question mark would be necessary, though, for something like, "He asked himself, 'How does this machine work?'"

Here is an example of what happens when a writer fails to abide by this particular use of the question mark:

> ❓ For all its faults, how a tiny country like Cuba can have socialized health care is amazing? (Yeshua)

I think Yeshua means something like the following:

> Isn't it amazing that a tiny country like Cuba, with all its faults, can have socialized health care?

A simple period would have been fine. And to continue about periods, "Mr.," "Mrs.," "Ms.," and "Dr." all require a period in American English but not British.

End Punctuation: Fine Tuning

Varieties of Sentence Structure

Some sentences are long, others short, and the rest somewhere in between. Some are tangled, complex, difficult-to-follow, while many are simple and straightforward. Often a sentence includes several subsentences (or "embedded" sentences), which is fine, just so long as they are correctly connected and punctuated in such a way that your reader knows what you are doing. What follows are several examples of the basic ways that two sentences may be legitimately welded into one.

The December 22/29 *New Yorker* includes a previously unpublished article written by Mark Twain in 1905. It is called "The Privilege of the Grave" and concludes with a wonderfully self-referential confession:

> Sometimes my feelings are so hot that I have to take to the pen and pour them out on paper to keep them from setting me afire inside; then all that ink and labor are wasted, because I can't print the result. I have just finished an article of this kind, and it satisfies me entirely. (51)

It is interesting to pull this apart and reveal how many clauses in this two-sentence passage could be separate sentences:

> Sometimes my feelings are so hot.

> I have to take the pen and pour them out on paper.

> Then all that ink and labor are wasted.

> I can't print the result.

> I have just finished an article of this kind.

> It satisfies me entirely.

But a couple of these main clauses have words in front of them that make them dependent, meaning that they have to be attached to another, independent, separate sentence:

> . . . *that* I have to take to the pen and pour them out on paper to keep them from setting me afire inside.

> . . . *because* I can't print the result.

The first dependent clause does not have a comma before it; the second does.

This leads me to emphasize the important distinction between restrictive and nonrestrictive sentence elements. The first clause of the pair above, which opens with *that*, is restrictive, which means that it's needed for Twain's enclosing sentence to make sense—it's essential to the meaning; it's the actual point Twain is making. The second clause, introduced with *because*, is nonrestrictive: it adds to the meaning, but isn't absolutely essential to the main idea of the sentence. It's just going on to say why he has wasted paper and ink. Since it is nonrestrictive, it's introduced with a comma. He could easily have introduced it with *since* or *inasmuch as*.

And while they require some skill to put together, sentences such as Twain's have considerable power. Here's what they would look like without being joined in some way to one another:

> Sometimes my feelings are so hot. I have to take to the pen. I have to pour them out on paper. This keeps them

> from setting me afire inside. Then all that ink and labor
> are wasted. I can't print the result. I have just finished
> an article of this kind. It satisfies me entirely.

Something gets lost here, don't you think? The paragraph just doesn't quite hang together, since all the clauses have an equivalent weight. Using subordinators and relative clauses helps to guide the reader toward a greater understanding.

To remind you again, a restrictive element delimits, controls, and *is necessary to the meaning of a sentence*—is an essential element of the sentence's idea. A nonrestrictive element is parenthetical, providing supplementary material. Usually restrictive elements should *not* be set off with commas, while nonrestrictive elements should be.

It is sometimes puzzling, of course, to determine what is essential or restrictive and what is not. Consider the following:

> He was afraid to touch the burner that he knew was hot.

> He was afraid to touch the burner, which he knew was hot.

The first sentence suggests that there was probably more than one burner, inasmuch as the *that he knew was hot* distinguishes it from a non-hot burner. The second sentence implies that there was only one burner in question. In these two sentences, too, because of the use of *the* before *burner*, we can infer that the implied audience knows the physical situation (burners hot or cold in the first sentence, just one

hot one in the second). So again, as you put sentences together, even deciding which elements are restrictive or nonrestrictive, you must be mindful of your audience—of what
you think they know about the situation you're describing
or commenting on.

Moving around parts of a sentence, modifying punctuation, and trying out various meanings, you discover right
away that English is a remarkably malleable language, its
component parts subtle. What I want to do here is take a
sentence from Lauren Collins's "Getting and Spending:
Brown Baggers," a short essay from the *New Yorker*'s "Talk
of the Town" section, and show how that sentence might
be structured in a variety of ways. The sentence is from
about the middle of the piece; it's neither part of the conclusion nor an opening gambit:

> Shopping bags with rhinestones, or shopping bags
> treated to look like patent leather, are not in favor right
> now; recyclable ones, and those made in natural fibers,
> are.

KEY

[MC]: a main clause—that is, a full sentence, with a
noun phrase and a verb phrase
[cc]: a coordinating conjunction
[rSC]: a restrictive subordinate clause
[nrSC]: a nonrestrictive subordinate clause

---

1. [MC], [cc] [MC]. "Shopping bags with rhinestones, or shopping bags treated to look like patent leather, are not in favor right now, but recyclable ones, and those made in natural fibers, are." *[This is called a compound sentence, since it has two independent clauses.]*

2. [MC]. [MC]. "Shopping bags with rhinestones, or shopping bags treated to look like patent leather, are not in favor right now. Recyclable ones, and those made in natural fibers, are." *[Here we have two independent sentences, the connection between them not specified; this construction just places them side by side.]*

3. [MC]. [MC]. [MC]. "Shopping bags with rhinestones, or shopping bags treated to look like patent leather, are not in favor right now. Recyclable ones are. Those made in natural fibers are too." *[Sometimes using short sentences works quite well, as in this example.]*

4. [MC]; [MC]. "Shopping bags with rhinestones, or shopping bags treated to look like patent leather, are not in favor right now; recyclable ones, and those made in natural fibers, are." *[The original version. The semicolon implies a tight connection between the two sentences, emphasizing the fake-vs.-natural contrast.]*

5. [MC], [nrSC]. "Shopping bags with rhinestones, or shopping bags treated to look like patent leather, are not in favor right now, while recyclable ones, and those made in natural fibers, are." *[This sentence also works*

*well, though perhaps Collins opted for the use of the semi-
colon (as in 4 above), since omitting it loads up the sentence with too many commas and pauses. It seems to me
that this version might also be OK without commas after*
ones *and* fibers.*]*

? 5A. [MC][nrSC]. "Shopping bags with rhinestones, or
shopping bags treated to look like patent leather, are
not in favor right now because recyclable ones, and
those made in natural fibers, are." *[This would sound
better with a comma before* because. The Chicago Manual of Style *recommends that if you have doubts, put the
comma in. In this case, I'd agree. Note that not all subordinating words are created equal. Some, such as* because
*rarely require a preceding comma, since usually the two
clauses it joins are closely linked. Other subordinators are
less predictable. See 7 below.]*

6. [nrSC], [MC]. "Although shopping bags with rhinestones, or shopping bags treated to look like patent
leather, are not in favor right now, recyclable ones, and
those made in natural fibers, are." *[This shifts the emphasis to the rhinestones and patent leather, and it suddenly makes their loss somehow poignant.]*

? 6A. [nrSC] [MC]. "Although shopping bags with rhinestones, or shopping bags treated to look like patent
leather, are not in favor right now recyclable ones, and
those made in natural fibers, are." *[When you start with*

*a nonrestrictive clause, you pretty much always need to
have the comma. If you leave it out, the results are mixed.
Here, there just seems to be an omitted comma.]*

7. [MC] [rSC]. "Shopping bags with rhinestones, or
shopping bags treated to look like patent leather, are
not in favor right now since recyclable ones, and those
made in natural fibers, are." *[Making the second clause
restrictive—with no comma—implies a cause-effect: now
that we have all these natural or recyclable products, we
can abandon the rhinestones and pleather stuff.]*

? 8. [rSC], [MC]. "Because shopping bags with rhinestones, or shopping bags treated to look like patent
leather, are not in favor right now, recyclable ones, and
those made in natural fibers, are." *[Note that a comma
has to be used here, even though the opening clause is restrictive. The cause-effect does not quite work.]*

? 8A. [rSC] [MC]. "Inasmuch as shopping bags with
rhinestones, or shopping bags treated to look like patent leather, are not in favor right now recyclable ones,
and those made in natural fibers, are." *[This needs a
comma before* recyclable. *See the* Chicago Manual's *suggestion in 5A above. The sentence also suffers from the
same problem that afflicts the previous version. Again, the
cause-effect seems somehow forced, possibly nonsensical.]*

9. [MC]. "Shopping bags with rhinestones or treated
to look like patent leather—variants not in favor right

now—have given way to recyclable ones and those made in natural fibers." *[This has a certain dramatic impact.]*

10. [MC], [MC], [cc] [MC]. "Shopping bags with rhinestones are not in favor right now, shopping bags treated to look like patent leather are not popular either, but recyclable ones and those made in natural fibers, are." *[AP style would omit the comma before the* and.*]*

The meaning changes ever so subtly in each of these variants.

The Run-On: Comma Splice and Fused Sentence

Important tip: In any sort of formal writing you should *not* join these sentences in the following ways, both of which are types of **run-on sentences**.

❋ 11. [MC], [MC]. "Shopping bags with rhinestones, or shopping bags treated to look like patent leather, are not in favor right now, recyclable ones, and those made in natural fibers, are." *[This is called a comma splice, and should be avoided. Here, you can see that the sentence is hard to process in this form; you have to pause and go back, I think, to recognize that* recyclable ones *is going to start a new idea.]*

Here is an anecdote about comma splices: One of my friends went to a prestigious college, and, full of eagerness, he laboriously composed his first English paper, on Henry James's novel *The Portrait of a Lady*. When the teacher returned the graded paper, it included the final comment, "brilliant and well-written: full of insights. Excellent work. F." That was confusing. My friend went to speak with the professor, who again praised the paper. "But isn't 'F' a low grade?" he asked. "Oh yes," said the professor. It's a failing paper." "But why did I fail, if it's brilliant?" "Well, it is brilliant." She shrugged, took a drag on her long, thin cigarette. "But it has a comma splice." My friend asked, "What's a comma splice?" (He has now published six books and teaches at an Ivy League university.)

> ✱ 12. [MC] [MC]. "Shopping bags with rhinestones, or shopping bags treated to look like patent leather, are not in favor right now recyclable ones, and those made in natural fibers, are." *[This is called a fused sentence, and also should be avoided.]*

To reiterate some ideas from above, run-ons smash two (or more) sentences together, often leaving readers confused about what's going on, and sowing within them doubts as to the writer's competence. Often these sentences require one or two rereadings. Here is an example from the *New York Times*'s "Arts, Briefly" column:

> ❓ Alluding to possible criticisms regarding censorship, Mr. Burnham said, "This is not a campaign against free speech, far from it, it is simply there is a wider public interest at stake when it involves harm to other people." (Bloom)

There should be a break—either a period or a semicolon—before or after *far from it*. The writer could have inserted this quite easily into the oral language he is quoting. In transcribing speech, you have all the control over the punctuation, since few (sane) people say aloud their commas, periods, and semicolons. Once again, when joining full sentences (main clauses), unless you use ABS OF NY words or subordinators, you need to take especial care, and probably should figure out how to incorporate the semicolon into your punctuational repertoire.

Conjunctive adverbs, such as *however*, *therefore*, *thus*, *consequently*, *hence*, *otherwise* do not function in the same way as the ABS OF NY words. If you opt for a conjunctive adverb, you should probably use a semicolon to break the sentence, as the next structure category demonstrates:

13. [MC]; [conjunctive adverb], [MC]. "Shopping bags with rhinestones, or shopping bags treated to look like patent leather, are not in favor right now; however, recyclable ones, and those made in natural fibers, are."
[Some handbooks cite the use of a semicolon prior to a conjunctive adverb as a totally separate use of that mark. I don't do so because not all conjunctive adverbs are preceded by a semicolon: "Shopping bags with rhinestones, or shopping bags treated to look like patent leather, however much in favor in years past, have given way to the increased popularity of recyclable ones, and those made in natural fibers."]

And here is a final structure possibility:

14. [MC], [MC], [MC]. "Shopping bags with rhinestones or treated to look like patent leather have fallen out of favor, shopping bags made of recyclable material are gaining ground, shopping bags made of natural fibers really are completely the rage." *[This is OK, though it seems to me less than fully natural. I think it might be improved with a coordinating conjunction, such as* but *prior to the last main clause. But you can decide.]*

This example of [MC], [MC], [MC] comes from a *Washington Post* interview with Stefan Jacoby, a Volkswagen executive:

"We needed a new start, we needed to be closer to our customers, we also needed to streamline our own organization and to build up a very talented team." (Lazo)

In his discussion of these kinds of sentences, Frederick Crews, writing in the *Random House Handbook*, remarks, "By omitting *and* before the last clause, the writer brings out the rapidity and urgency of the three actions. This is a rare case of an acceptable comma splice" (254). Not only does this fit into the I-wish-I-had-said-it-myself category; it also gives an example of how grammatical constructions support, aid and abet—and even help create—your sentence's meaning and message.

Chapter 6

Diction: Sentences as Clockwork

On the Interconnectedness of Words

In English, as in most languages, sentences serve to communicate ideas. Sentences include many working parts, which I have been discussing in (I hope not boring or too exhaustive) detail, but let me point out a very significant feature of these parts. They often must be put together with the same kind of care that a watchmaker must use.

How does a watchmaker think? Here a watchmaker-writer gives some sense of an internal monologue he goes through when he disassembles a watch: "I am now removing the bridge that holds the chronograph wheel and minutes runner in place. Removal of the hammer comes next, and now the chronograph wheel and minutes runner can be lifted out" (Kelly 225). There's a similar detailed balance and interconnectedness within and between sentences. As you look at them, try to take them apart—as the watchmaker does the watch—and think of how they should be reassembled, of how each part depends on the others, and of how the entirety will function.

Of course, we toss off sentences, hear them all the time, read them on computer screens and in newspapers, magazines, books. Language proliferates and surrounds us, and the world seems to run on and on, more or less functionally, despite the miscellaneous quality of our linguistically created and mediated reality ...

So what's with the sentence maker as watchmaker?

I'm suggesting a couple of things here. First, sentences can have remarkable detail and complexity. They have the potential to be as complex, intricate, and effectual as well-maintained watches. Second, the world runs—yes—but (ahem) not always all that well. Finally—and maybe this goes without saying—there is really only one way to assemble a watch, and a limited number of parts, usually fewer than a hundred. Language is by contrast much more complex, and in English there are at least a quarter of a million words, though some estimates are as high as a million words.

The big difference, of course, between sentences and watches is that broken watches won't run or keep the correct time. You know right away if you have been careless with your timepiece or your watchmaker has made a mistake. With sentences, the results are less immediately apparent. But they are still important—important for one's ideas to run, to go, to reach others in an exact, timely way.

Here's an author's depiction of language that doesn't quite work: it breaks down logically. In A. A. Milne's classic children's novel *The House at Pooh Corner*, Pooh is not fully conscious of what he's doing in a poem he constructs, and I think Milne is using him as an example of verbal carelessness. Pooh's friend Piglet notes that Tigger (another companion) is small but "seems big":

> Pooh was thoughtful when he heard this, and then he murmured to himself:
>
>> But whatever his weight in pounds, shillings, and ounces,
>> He always seems bigger because of his bounces.
>
> "And that's the whole poem," he said. "Do you like it, Piglet?"
>
> "All except the shillings," said Piglet. "I don't think they ought to be there."
>
> "They wanted to come in after the pounds," explained Pooh, "so I let them. It is the best way to write poetry, letting things come."
>
> "Oh, I didn't know," said Piglet. (196–97)

Pooh, in constructing his poem, fails to recognize that *pounds and ounces* refers to weight, while *pounds and shillings* refers to currency—and that he shouldn't really be mixing the two. While on a grammatical level his poem is acceptable, it doesn't make sense semantically (i.e., in terms of meaning). His idea of "letting things come" has something to recommend it, but he needs to recognize that not all the things that he lets come make complete sense.

In his 1946 essay "Politics and the English Language" (without alluding to Pooh, Piglet, et al.), George Orwell explains the thought process that many people use when putting together sentences:

> In prose, the worst thing one can do with words is sur-
> render to them. When you think of something abstract
> [as Pooh does, thinking of weight] you are more inclined
> to use words from the start, and unless you make a con-
> scious effort to prevent it, the existing dialect will come
> rushing in and do the job for you, at the expense of blur-
> ring or even changing your meaning. Probably it is better
> to put off using words as long as possible and get one's
> meaning as clear as one can through pictures or sensa-
> tions. Afterwards one can choose—not simply *accept*—
> the phrases that will best cover the meaning, and then
> switch round and decide what impression one's words
> are likely to make on another person. This last effort of
> the mind cuts out all stale or mixed images, all prefabri-
> cated phrases, needless repetitions, and humbug and
> vagueness generally. (99–100)

The problem that Milne and Orwell see is simply this: we are so surrounded by language, especially by language used poorly or mindlessly, that we often end up letting it slip into our brains without consciously thinking about what it means. Pooh, for example, knows the phrases *pounds and shillings* and *pounds and ounces*—and these have merged, without his really knowing it, into the phrase *pounds, shillings, and ounces*. The problem, though, is that phrase makes no sense, which fact Piglet notices. Your goal needs to be generating language that makes sense.

Fundamentals

Parallel Structure and Mixed Constructions

English sentences usually rely on certain kinds of patterned repetitions. Many sentence structures include, for example, interchangeable parts, such as ones in lists or other kinds of repeating structures. When setting up a sentence of some complexity, you need to make sure that its interchangeable parts are genuinely interchangeable.

The trouble is that not all sentences that are "correct" make sense, because some portion of a list (say, as in Pooh's poem) does not quite fit in with the others. Sometimes an element does not fit logically; at other times it could fit, but it's not in the proper tense or form. Some people might argue that the second category is only a subcategory of the first.

Repeated elements, such as forms of a verb or the nouns or noun phrases that make up lists, always require quite a lot of attention. For example, if you have a sentence that starts a list using a particular verb tense, it needs to continue in that same tense. In the following example sentence, Anita K. Rosenberg, in "Acrophobia: Soar Subject, New Perspective," starts off in the conditional and correctly maintains the same form throughout:

> Squashed in the back seat between my two older broth-
> ers, I would *hunker* down with Cherry Ames or Nancy
> Drew, *slip* my coat up to my eyebrows and *try* to hide my
> growing terror.

The initial part of the sentence establishes the sentence
structure that Rosenberg uses in the remaining portion. "I
would hunker . . . [I would] slip my coat up . . . [I would] . . .
try to hide."

If you switch the form or structure midway, you will
end up with what's called a **mixed construction**. Try to
avoid such situations as the following, a sentence that
starts off well, establishing an organizing structure, but
that breaks down:

> ❓ "The legacy of the Bush administration has been one
> of dismal inaction . . . like turning a ketchup bottle up-
> side down, banging the bottom of the container, and
> nothing comes out." (Robert Harrison, qtd. in R. J. Smith)

This leaves us with the verbal equivalent of an empty
ketchup bottle. Rather than "and nothing comes out," Har-
rison might have said, "and getting nothing out," maintaining the parallelism of a gerund-based structure. (In his
defense, this is spoken English.)

Here is another parallel structure confusion. Rob
Stein's December 29 story, "Premarital Abstinence Pledges
Ineffective, Study Finds," describes a study of young peo-
ple who took a "pledge of abstinence":

❓ By 2001, [Professor Janet E.] Rosenbaum found, 82 percent of those who had taken a pledge had retracted their promises, and there was no significant difference in the proportion of students in both groups who had engaged in any type of sexual activity, including giving or receiving oral sex, vaginal intercourse, the age at which they first had sex, or their number of sexual partners.

I'll leave you to momentarily untangle this lust-based enumeration, but it seems to have three elements that are not quite parallel: percentage of "active" students, age at first sexual encounter, and number of partners. Stein suggests that along these three lines the two groups studied (those who pledged to abstain and those who did not) were all but identical. (So much for teenage pledges.) Here is a possible rewrite:

By 2001, [Professor Janet E.] Rosenbaum found, 82 percent of those who had taken a pledge had retracted their promises, and in both groups—those who pledged abstinence and those who did not—the same percentage of students engaged in sexual activity (oral or genital intercourse), the average number of sex partners was identical, and the age of first sexual activity was the same.

Stein's sentence is quite complex, so in some ways the break in parallelism is understandable. Less forgivable, though, are parallelism issues in very short sentences. Here is one from *Us*:

❷ Also banished were her signature entourage, flashy Bentley convertible and who can forget those mink eyelashes. (O'Leary 45)

So were the mink eyelashes banished? I'd like to know.

The most common mixed construction is probably "The reason is . . . because. . . ." In the following, a blogger quotes Paul Watson:

❷ The *reason* the whalers have not been charged is simply *because* they have the money and the power to circumvent the law and to bully other countries into not opposing them. (starburd)

The reason already implies *because*. This sentence should probably be something like the following:

Whalers have not been charged because they have the money and power to circumvent the law and bully other countries into not opposing them.

This next example comes from *Sports Illustrated*:

❷ One of the reasons these guys have moved the ball so well is because they held on to it better than anyone in the country, committing nine turnovers, a Division I-A low. ("BCS Preview" 35)

Just omitting *one of the reasons* and *is* considerably improves this sentence. Here's my modified version:

These guys have moved the ball so well because they held on to it better than anyone in the country, committing only nine turnovers, a Division I-A low.

The next example is a slightly different kind of mixed construction, one involving the incorrect form of a word:

> ❓ In three decades in public office, [Edolphus] Towns, the former Brooklyn deputy borough president, *has developed a personality that contrasts markedly with Waxman*, the California liberal who is known for his work on consumer-friendly legislation such as the Clean Air Act, crusades against tobacco and headline-making investigations. (Dilanian)

This should read, "developed a personality that contrasts markedly with that of Waxman" or "with Waxman's," since a personality can "contrast markedly with" another personality, not with an entire person.

If your word processing program highlights a word or sentence as being possibly incorrect, you should probably check to see if the program is right: every now and again it is. But it's usually wrong. These programs should improve over the course of time. But right now, don't automatically accept each suggestion. Check. I recently received an essay a student had written for my class. He had me listed as Professor Frank Coffin. Autocorrect: Kiss of Death.

Keep in mind that a sentence can be correct in terms of word order and structure but still be in need of revision.

The sentence also has to make sense. For example, the store proprietor who devised the sign I quote below might consider rewording it. Robert Graves and Alan Hodge encountered this in front of a butcher shop:

"Family, Pork, and General Butcher" (140)

This seems to cry out for revision. I'll leave it for you to cut up and reassemble.

Confused Words

Words are the component parts of sentences, and you need to make sure that each one you choose is in fact the right one. According to a recent study by Andrea and Karen Lunsford, the most commonly marked error in college students' papers is "wrong word" (784). Many wrong words occur in our daily newspapers. For example, here the writer confuses *defuse* (i.e., "disarm," "render not dangerous") with *diffuse* (dispersed, spread out):

✳ Dramatically, "Bone by Bone" is defuse; it would have benefited from a Mallory surrogate. (Maslin)

And the following, from "13 Children Killed in Afghan Bombing," confuses *donate* with *detonate*:

✳ The attack came a day after the police acting on intelligence located a suicide car bomber as he tried to enter the city of Kandahar, said Matiullah Qait,

> provincial chief of Kandahar. He donated his bomb at a
> security checkpoint west of the city, killing three police-
> men and one civilian. (Elick)

I suppose in some ironic way terrorists do "donate" their
bombs, but I don't think this is what Adam B. Elick is
getting at here. It seems likely that he and those who edited his *International Herald Tribune* article just overlooked
a mistake. Or they were blithely accepting autocorrect.

Sometimes these errors are subtle. For example, I object to this use of *galvanize*, which means to stimulate or
excite as if by electric shock (or to plate a metal, say, in
order to strengthen or rustproof it):

> ❓ Websites such as SavePolaroid.com have popped
> up, where fans have galvanized to try to save the cam-
> era. (Marshall, "On Deadline")

I think we just need the word *organized*, but truth be told,
I'm seeing *galvanize* used this way more and more. (Many
linguists would object to the use, too, of *galvanize* without
a direct object.)

In a similar structure, that is, one that catches readers
unawares, Thomas Frank seems not to have considered the
literal meaning of the word *support*, so that his sentence
about the border fence images up a funny picture:

> ❓ Some residents quietly support the fence, saying it
> will make their city safer and improve conditions. (Frank,
> "Tensions")

One imagines residents going out every day to take a turn at the fence, holding it up (quietly) against the wind and rain.

Here is another problem with confused words, a perhaps more subtle one. It also involves dismemberment. In "Israel Pounds Gaza Again, Signals More on the Way," the following sentence appears:

> ❓ A witness reported seeing dozens of bodies with limbs severed and heads decapitated from a Sunday attack at a Hamas police station. (Coker and Levinson)

"Heads" cannot be "decapitated"; *decapitate* means "to remove the head." "Seeing dozens of headless and limbless bodies" might be a better way to describe the awful scene.

You don't want to make such mistakes. They undermine your credibility. *Defuse/diffuse* and *donate/detonate* are occasionally mixed up, but typically writers make even more basic and glaring errors. I thought it would be useful to provide a very brief list of some often-confused English words. I could make this list several hundred pages long (see the books I've listed by Garner and also Bremner), but I've decided to limit it to what I perceive as the most stigmatizing yet commonplace confusions. The asterisk indicates something awry; in this list, words with asterisks are not actual words in English, but malapropisms.

You need to *search* your written work in an effort to discover errors. Especially make sure that key words (*diffuse, detonate*) are correct, and that your word processing program has not incorrectly "autocorrected" something.

In the list of confused words below I include *alot*, but Word autocorrected that to *a lot*, which isn't what I want. It wasn't until the third or fourth read-through that I caught it, which makes me want to encourage you to share your written work with others you trust, in hopes that they also will carefully search your work for errors, inconsistencies, or other problems.

The first part of the list consists of words that are homonyms, words that sound the same but have different meanings. No one notices homonym errors in speech. The second (shorter) part consists of confused words that emerge as glaring errors in both writing and speech. Again, this list is exponentially expandable.

SOME COMMONLY CONFUSED WORDS

I Homonyms

affect/effect
✱ *alot/a lot*
complement/compliment
do/due
its/it's/ ✱ *its'*
led/lead
principle/principal
there/their/they're
then/than
too/to/two

II Nonhomonyms

amount/number **(less/fewer)**
imply/infer
lay/lie/lie
like/as

Confused Words—Homonyms

affect/effect

Affect, usually a verb, means "to have an impact on," "to influence," or "to impact" (a less attractive but now widely accepted form). *Effect* is usually a noun, meaning "result." These words are so hard to use correctly that in a newsroom where my wife once worked as an editor, a sign was put up: "Do Not Use 'Affect' or 'Effect.'" I guess, as Charles Schulz's Linus points out, "No problem is so big or so complicated that it can't be run away from" (Schulz).

> **Memory trick** → You might remember the distinction by recalling that Affect usually means "hAs an impAct on; Effect means "rEsult."

(Less often, *to effect* can be a verb too, though, which makes things more challenging. It means "to cause." And *affect* can function as a verb meaning "to pretend." As a noun it also exists. It means "emotionality," but this usage is rare and usually confined to social science writing.)

	Noun	Verb
affect	rare: used mostly in psychology: visible manifestation of mood *She could tell by his blank affect that he was still in shock.*	usual: to influence or have an effect on *His enthusiastic attitude affected them positively.*

	Noun	Verb
effect	usual: outcome, result *The effect of her studying was a good grade.*	relatively rare: to bring about *The teacher effected changes in the curriculum.*

Here are some correct examples.

Affect as verb:

That can be one of the first signs of an age-related hearing loss—a more general problem that can creep in during middle age and *affects* one-third of adults ages 65 to 75. (Ritter)

Effect as noun:

The acoustics of the church enhanced the *effect* so that everything could be heard, including the slightest defects, of which there were very, very few. (Campbell)

Effect as verb:

Of course if Obama had talked about an end to Jewish settlement building on Arab land—the only actual "building" that is going on in the conflict—relations with Hamas as well as the Palestinian Authority, justice for both sides in the conflict, along with security for Palestinians as well as Israelis, then he might actually *effect* a little change. (Fisk)

❏ **alot/a lot**

A lot, meaning "a considerable amount," is always two words. It is frequently written (incorrectly) as just one.

> **Memory trick** → *A lot* is as separate as a lot on which one might build a house.

Here, from the *Daily News*, is a headline:

> ❏ Clean Air Buses in the City: Eco-Friendly Hybrid and Natural Gas Vehicles Make Up *Alot* of Fleet (Reich)

This is inexcusable, even in a tabloid, I fear.

complement/compliment

Complement means to "match" or "go with." *Compliment* is a noun that refers to a nice thing one might say about someone. It's also the verb, meaning to say something that is a compliment. Here are two effective usages, the first from *Sports Illustrated* and the second from the *New Yorker*:

> Kaman is redundant in L.A.—the Clippers would still have a nice high-low combo in Marcus Camby and Zach Randolph—but he rebounds, blocks shots and has a low-post game that would *complement* jump-shooting power forward Yi Jianlian. (Thomsen)

> The blogosphere, much of which piggybacks on traditional journalism's content, has magnified the reach of newspapers, and although papers now face far more scrutiny, this is a kind of backhanded *compliment* to their continued relevance. (Surowiecki)

do/due

Do means to accomplish or make. *Due* comes in phrases such as *due to* or *the book is due soon*. Some writers prohibit using *due to* in an adverbial phrase ("The man ran due to fear"), and say it should be used only as a synonym for "attributable to." I believe that's too strong of an injunction, but I admire its level of rigor. Just make sure that *do* and *due* remain distinct. Here are two correct usages:

> Israeli Hospital Moves into Bomb Shelter *due* to Missile Strike Fears. ("Israeli Hospital")

> *Due* to Wall Street woes and tight-fisted tourists, the amount of money spent could easily be down 30%. (Hill)

its/it's/✖ its'

As I note above, *it's* provides particular problems for writers. It looks like a possessive form. It's not. It's a contracted form of *it is* or *it has*. *Its'* does not exist in English, unless we are talking about multiple entities named *It*: "The Its' genders were unspecified." I admit that this is an unlikely scenario. Three correct uses follow:

> *It's* the Laptop, by a Nose. (Williams)

> In the case of the Federal Reserve, the money comes from *its* authority to print dollars from thin air.
> (P. Goodman)

And from "Hamas Credo Led It to End Cease-Fire,"

Its secular rival, Fatah, sits on the sidelines, marginal to the violence unfolding in Gaza, from which Hamas effectively expelled it at gunpoint in the summer of 2007. (Farrell)

led/lead

Lead is an element (atomic symbol Pb). Pronounced precisely the same way, *led* is the past tense of the verb *to lead* (this infinitive form, *to lead*, is pronounced "leed"). Make sure you don't make the following gaffe, confusing the past tense with the element. In "Black Sea Region Wheat Exports Surge," Tom Polansek writes,

> ✳ In 2008, favorable weather *lead* to bumper crops in Ukraine and Russia, where production is expected to climb nearly 28% from last year to a record 63 million metric tons, according to the Agriculture Department.

principle/principal

Principle is typically a noun and *principal* an adjective.

> **Memory trick (1)** → Remember that the one with the "a" (principal) is the adjective. It does form into a noun, though, and the word it modifies is omitted, in such contexts as the "principal administrator of a school," the "principal actor in a play," or a "principal amount of money," where all three can be shortened to *principal*. (You probably heard the mnemonic that the way to recall how to spell *principal* of a school is that he is "a prince of a pal." It always struck me as curiously self-promotional

for schools to teach that mnemonic, and it ends up confusing students more than helping them, since it reinforces the idea of *principal* as a noun, when usually it's
an adjective.)

Memory trick (2) → *Principle* is a "rule," the spelling of
which you can remember by recalling that they both end
in *-le*.

Here is a line from the *New Yorker*'s masthead:

PRINCIPAL OFFICE: The Condé Nast Building, 4 Times
Square, New York, NY 10036. (118)

their/there/they're

Most people who make this error recognize what's wrong
when it's pointed out to them. Two things to keep in mind,
though, are that *their* violates the "i before e" spelling rule, and
that word processing programs will not flag or autocorrect
there/their/they're errors. Yet such errors tend to be glaring.

then/than

Than is a comparative word, as in *greater than . . . , smaller
than . . . , happier than. . . .* Three correct examples follow
the "memory trick."

Memory trick → You can remember this by the "a" in
th*A*n and comp*A*rison. Th*E*n implies n*E*xt. Note the "e" repetition of th*E*n and n*E*xt.

For now, Barack Obama's response to the deteriorating
situation in Gaza, where Israeli airstrikes appear to

have killed almost 300, is to point out that he doesn't take office for more *than* three weeks. (Schone)

That overly convenient term popped up more than 1,160 times in Chicago Sun-Times news stories and editorials in 2008—more *than* three times a day, on average—and no doubt found its way into official police reports many more times *than* that. (" 'Gang-related' Killings Much More Than That")

"The whole concept that one person in the story would lead to another, and *then* it would all end with her, was not something any of us anticipated." (Ellen McDonnell, qtd. by Clifford)

too/to/two

Actually I have had college seniors ask me the difference between *to* and *too*. *To* is the preposition, usually implying a directionality, as in *going to the store*, or the "particle" in infinitive forms (*to succeed, to be*). *Too* is an adverb meaning "extremely" or "excessively." It also can mean "as well" or "also." *Two* is the numeral 2, spelled out.

Memory trick → In *too*, there's an extra "o," which might seem "too much."

Confused Words—Nonhomonyms

If you confuse these in speech, some people will notice. Even more people will notice nonhomonym confusions in writing.

amount/number

Amount is used in reference to quantity that cannot easily be counted or divided up into small parts. *Number* refers to quantities that are countable. Some people give the advice that *amount* refers to quantities that don't end in an "s," while *number* refers to ones that do (though this doesn't work for irregular plurals, like "people" in the third example below). These words are rarely confused by professional writers but rarely used correctly by nonprofessionals. Here are three correct examples:

> An analysis of how the money has been used over the past decade shows that a disproportionate *amount* goes upstate. (Belson)

> The Washington area, with a large *number* of recent college graduates who frequent the social networking site, is also a hotbed of foreclosures. (Shapira)

> Homeland security secretary Michael Chertoff said in a Dec. 19 speech that there's been "a collapse in the *number* of people who come across the border illegally." (Frank, "Fewer Caught")

But here's a *Wall Street Journal* sentence that I find puzzling. In "Palestinians Need Israel to Win," the following appears:

> ❓ The left's victory, though, remained largely theoretical: The right won the practical argument that no

amount of concessions would grant international legitimacy to Israel's right to defend itself. (Oren and Halevi)

What's interesting working with actual sentences, I note, is
that often they do not give us pure and simple paradigm
examples. *No amount of concessions* violates the rule (*amount*
shouldn't be used for countable items or, typically, for
things that end in "s"), but in this situation, it seems to
work. *No amount* works better than *no number* perhaps because *concessions* is best seen as an entirety, which entirety is
reinforced by the negation, *no*. *No number*, in fact, seems to
be an awkward construction in most situations.

But *no amount of concessions* is only slightly better than
no number of concessions. I would probably avoid the construction altogether and rephrase the sentences in the following way:

The left's victory, though, remained largely theoretical.
The right won the practical argument that no matter how
many concessions Israel made, its right to defend itself
would never be granted international legitimacy.

Amount and *number* have an interesting parallel pair of
words in *less* and *fewer*. *Less* is applied to noncountable
items (less courage, less hope, less hassle), while *fewer* ap-
plies to countable things ("Express Lane: 10 Items or
Fewer"). How often, though, do we see the following?

❓ Express Lane: 10 Items or Less.

imply/infer

Imply means to subtly suggest. *Infer* means to "read into" or "deduce" something. "The *implier* is the pitcher; the *inferer* is the catcher" (Theodore Bernstein, qtd. by Bremner 200). Here are two correct examples:

> I read elsewhere that the Ford Fusion hybrid will run only on its electric motor at speeds of 47 mph or lower. That means you can avoid using gas for a long time if you drive with a close eye on city speed limits. Uh, until the battery charge runs down, which will take a few seconds to at best a minute or two. You *infer* that you can run all day at less than 47 mph without the engine coming on. (Spencer)

> On Nov. 13, Treasury's Paulson told NPR that he believed the banking system had been "stabilized," and he *implied* that there was no major institution likely to present a problem that would shock regulators. ("2008 Memories")

lay/lie/lie

I present the principal parts of these three verbs below. *To lay* means "to set" or "to place." *To lie* is to lie down. The same infinitive verb form means "to tell an untruth."

Writing in *Teaching English in the Two-Year College*, Mark Blaauw-Hara has an interesting remark about the problem with *lay* vs. *lie*:

> If a student has grown up with everyone around him
> using "lay" when they should use "lie," the rule for dif-
> ferentiating between them seems incredibly abstract
> and slippery, and the only reinforcement comes in
> school; when he goes back home, his father will still tell
> the dog to "go lay down"—and when even the dog un-
> derstands what is meant, who can blame the student
> for continuing to confuse the two . . . ? (169)

After laughing, I realized that usually our audience is
more sophisticated than the average pooch.

Two things work against changing the way you speak
and write. First, "bandwidth" poses a problem. So much is
going on in our culture. How does anyone find time to
worry about, say, the use of a semicolon, especially if
you've happily lived eighteen or twenty-five or forty years
without this knowledge? And that leads to my second
"working against you" element. In America it is very hard
to change your social class, but it's perhaps even more difficult to change your "language class"—though the two
do seem to be linked. Language class, like social class, has
been created, supported, and encouraged by what you do
and with whom you spend your time—by your occupa-
tion and society.

Here are two nydailynews.com stories reporting on vi-
olent incidents. The first example is correct. The second
should use *lie* rather than *lay*:

Capone wriggled free but *lay* still until, after 3–1/2 hours, the crooks finally left her home in the early hours of Christmas Eve. (Pearson, Burke, and Gendar)

❊ There was a lot of fluid coming out of his nose. His mother told me he was having trouble breathing and he wanted to *lay* down on the floor. (Durkin, Sandoval, and Goldsmith)

	Present	Past	Participle
To lie (down)	lie	lay	(had) lain
To lay (or set)	lay	laid	(had) laid
To lie (or fib)	lie	lied	(had) lied

These relatively simple, often encountered words are rarely used correctly; not only are they irregular, but using them correctly sometimes even sounds funny. Consider *lay* vs. *lie*: when was the last time you said, "I had lain down for an hour"? But that's the correct form. Using the correct forms will single you out as a person very careful with his or her speech—or maybe as someone who talks funny: a stuffy pedant. Again, you need to decide what persona you want to convey, and what you think your reader or listener is apt to expect or likely to notice.

like/as

These are very commonly confused words. *Like* and *as* are used differently. *Like* introduces a noun or noun phrase. *As* introduces a clause. All of these example sentences use *like* instead of *as*; I've put suggested revisions in square brackets:

■ *Like* [As] they had for years, the two families—one in the city of Torreon in Mexico, the other in Covina—called each other late Christmas Eve on the radio. ("Covina Shooting")

■ Whatever your motive, attacking nations is usually bad for you. Dangerous even when you're a big powerful country attacking a weaker nation, *like* [as was] Nazi Germany when it invaded Poland in 1939. (Steinberg)

■ "It would be 'disheartening' if stocks start 2009 like [as] they did in 2008, when the S+P Index slid 6.1%," says Paul Hickey of Bespoke Investment Group. (Shell)

■ This fall, dad of six Brad Pitt dished details—like [such as] Shiloh wants to be called "John" and Maddox and Pax often sit in the time-out chair—to Oprah Winfrey. (Agresti 58)

■ If 9/11 ultimately revealed America's self-imposed constraints, November 4 is already understood as a comprehensive repudiation even of that qualified resolve. Like [As] I said: For America's enemies, that's useful to know. (Steyn, "Happy" 52)

It is very common to use *like* instead of *as*. But that still does not make it "correct," at least to academic audiences, who might say, along with Hamlet, "Ay, madam, it is common" (act 1, scene 2).

Little changes can make a big difference. Think of all those TV shows about "makeovers": a Botox injection here, some hair dye and styling, a quick peel to smooth those acne bumps, a diet to lose some baby fat, some sexy clothes, and—voilà! The average-looking man or woman suddenly, amazingly, transforms. The same thing can happen to your sentences. They can be enormously improved via many small changes. (And the opposite is also true: lots of little errors tend to add up, pile on, and ultimately undermine your work's meaning and authority.) One difference between makeovers and sentences, though, is that changing a sentence's appearance often changes its very essence.

A Brief Note on the Use of Capital Letters

Capitalization does not usually cause a great number of difficulties beyond the grade school level. Names (proper nouns, as they are called) are capitalized, as are titles of people (if mentioned prior to their name), key words of books or film titles, and the like. Conventions vary somewhat in the matter of which words of titles get capitalized. Usually, it's the first word of the title, the first word of the subtitle, and all following words except for articles, prepositions, and conjunctions.

The first word of a sentence needs to be capitalized. But what if the first word of a sentence is the name of a person or entity that does not use capital letters, such as *bell hooks*, *e. e. cummings*, or the navigation system known as *nüvi*? These need to be capitalized, if they appear as the first word in a sentence. The caption from this Garmin advertisement is "wrong," then, though advertisements have no real responsibility to display accurate use of language. In fact, sometimes inaccurate usage catches the attention of readers—another example of "foregrounding." Perhaps this is the rationale for the following:

❋ nüvi routes drivers around the trouble spots, saving time, fuel, and frustration.

I have noticed that some usage guides say *e. e. cummings*, if it begins a sentence, should be *E. E. Cummings*, but it seems to me that *E. e. cummings* would be the proper form. Just the same, since there is disagreement and confusion, why not just reword the sentence? "The poet, e. e. cummings, wrote some. . . ." English is a fabulously malleable language, and while sometimes that very malleability is annoying, it also can be used to one's benefit.

Slang and Trite Expressions

How do you recognize slang and triteness? Ideally you have to ask yourself, "Have I expressed this idea in an original way—or am I borrowing something that's not ultimately worthy of repetition? Can I say this in a fresher, more striking manner? Are there other words I might use?"

Sometimes the message you send, especially in slang or with metaphoric language, is inadvertent—something you really don't want to send, but that your audience receives. For example, a couple of weeks ago, a waiter who served me and my friends dinner stopped by late in our meal and asked, "How we doin', folks?" He paused, since we did not immediately answer, and then said, "Still pickin'?" What message was this waiter inadvertently sending? What kind of animals (or people) "pick" at their food? Am I just oversensitive? OK, I am. But you as a speaker should think about the person in your audience who might be similarly oversensitive—especially if you're looking to get a tip. (Old vultures pick at food.)

Using quotation marks around vulgar slang expressions does not justify their use. Of course if you are quoting something that is vulgar slang, you will need to put quotation marks around the entire quotation.

> ❓ For almost all of the 20th century, the United States played the "our S.O.B." card throughout Latin America, and the results were dreadful. (Montaner)

On the other hand, slang sometimes works. On my train, a conductor announces, "Put baggage in the overhead racks. This is a rush hour train. Don't hog up the seats." Now I had never heard that last expression, but I knew, as did almost all the other passengers, I suspect, exactly what was being conveyed. And when I was shoveling the snow from my driveway, a snowplow stopped, and the driver said to me, "You know, a plow's coming through here soon that will slush this off," I also got the message, despite never having heard that particular slang usage before. The plow was going to push the slush off the road and—guess where?—back into the driveway I had just shoveled. And indeed it did slush off my driveway.

It's fairly clear that formal writing does not exactly replicate speech, with its many pauses, circumlocutions, redundancies, and self-interruptions—not to mention its frequent use of vernacular language. And keep in mind that even if something sounds right, it may not necessarily be correct when put into writing.

Sometimes, too, words will be understandable within a given context, but if the context isn't clear, the words make no sense. A man in my extended family, S. K., who once worked in airport security, saw a couple (actually his elderly parents-in-law) coming toward a screening point. He took aside the man who was going to screen them. "Take care of this couple," he said, meaning, "Let them through easily, without hassle." Hours later, he found his in-laws waiting in a holding cage. "I said, 'take care of them'!" he exclaimed to his fellow worker. "Oh," was the reply, "I thought you meant TAKE CARE of them!" Evidently, the two men were working with different contexts in mind: for one, the context was "suspicious people here—screen them very thoroughly"; for the other, "I know these people—make their screening easy and painless." These are very different ways of "taking care" of people.

Mixed Metaphors

Like slang, metaphoric language occasionally has the effect of blocking your meaning. The following, for example, initially confused me:

> **?** But beyond the question of price, growing numbers of customers are looking for Champagnes off the tracks that have been beaten by the most famous houses. (Schmid)

Tracks beaten by houses? Champagne? I for some reason hear the sound of bottles breaking and glass being crunched beneath the railroad car wheels. You need to be cautious in how you use metaphors. Here's another example of metaphoric excess:

> **?** Compounding the recessionary gloom, trade is being choked by the credit crunch, which is drying up routine export financing. (Lynch)

Can "crunches" "choke" things and at the same time "dry them up"? And we need to bear in mind that all this compounds "gloom." It sounds like a sad state of affairs, I know, but the metaphors are distractingly discordant, and their clash unintentionally amusing.

A mixed metaphor also clouds the meaning of the following sentence—one we've looked at before—from "Amid Gaza Violence, a New Task for Obama," by Richard Wolf and Andrea Stone:

❓ Enter Obama, who in 22 days will walk into the Oval Office and assume the mantle of Middle East peacemaker played with little success by U.S. presidents for decades.

It seems to me also that the sentence might be revised—can a "mantle" that's been "assumed" be "played with little success"? Literally, "mantles" are worn. As I offered on p. 125, I again recommend the following:

Enter Obama, who in 22 days will walk into the Oval Office and assume a role that for decades has been played with little success by U.S. presidents: Middle East peacemaker.

One more example of a mixed metaphor in reference to President Obama comes from the *National Review*:

❓ The question, then, is whether Obama's cherished infrastructure agenda can be ramped up quickly enough to calm the economic seas of the next twelve to 18 months, which may be dark and stormy. Obama's platoons of bureaucrats-in-waiting are desperately seeking projects that are "shovel-ready." ("The Week" 16)

There are a few too many metaphors fighting in this passage, I fear.

Nancy Gibbs, in a "Commentary" for *Time*, also mixes her metaphors:

❓ They are part of a moral diet that we need to attend to, especially now when so many forces conspire to pull us further apart.

A "moral diet" doesn't really work that well with the metaphor of forces conspiring "to pull us further apart."

Perhaps the best way to end this mini-section on mixed metaphors is with a quotation from Joel Madden, which is reproduced in *Us*. He is referring to what it's like to share parenting with Nicole Richie:

❓ "You've got to work as a team, but she runs the ship." ("Loose Talk")

Crews, not teams, typically run ships.

A Microconclusion

Agnes Denes's 1975 eulogy/prose poem, "Human Dust," reads in part,

He was an artist. He died of a heart attack. He was born fifty years ago. . . . He was unhappy and lonely more often than not, achieved 1/10,000 of his dreams, managed to get his opinions across 184 times and was misunderstood 3,800 times when it mattered. (282)

While this life might be typical, it's also sad, isn't it? It's sad that the man was unhappy, that he died at an early age, and that he achieved so few of his dreams. But what really moves me about this piece is that its artist/hero so often was misunderstood *when it mattered*—3,800 times, in fact, which works out to 76 times a year, or once every 4.8 days.

I believe a fundamental human desire is to be understood by others. People want confidence that their words convey and fully embody their thoughts, feelings, and ideas. And often people fear that they are not succeeding. They fear their language will prove inadequate to the task, because English itself brims with all kinds of rules and difficulties, subtleties and nuances, traps and complexities: even on the sentence level—or on the level of spelling— it's hard to get it all exactly right.

Problems of all kinds emerge when people are misunderstood or ignored—not listened to, not validated— because their language fails to command respect, its errors stigmatizing and distracting, its phraseology or sense incomprehensible. "Unemployed and Isolated by Language Barrier, Killer Showed Hints of Frustration": so reads a subheadline for an article in the April 5, 2009, *New York Times*. And many people interviewed about the subject of this article, who killed thirteen people in Binghamton, New York, before killing himself, mentioned the killer's frustration about—what?—not knowing English: "He felt that he was degraded because of his inability to speak English," one man noted (Rivera and Schweber A28). Admittedly this is an unusual situation, but one wonders to what extent it exists for many other speakers of English, native and nonnative alike.

Language use matters. I've suggested that often misusage affects, for example, your clarity, your ability to clearly communicate your ideas. If that's the case, you want to rephrase and make your point with more lucidity. I've also claimed that misusages or certain verbal choices stigmatize you as a writer or speaker. To an extent you are your language.

There is another reason that usage matters, one that I have not alluded to specifically but which has perhaps been inherent throughout: improving your language and making it more precise will also spark creativity. When you revise your writing to make it more exact, more in accord with conventions, more "correct," new relationships, new areas of exploration or inquiry, and even new ideas will, amazingly, come to light—ones implicit in what you had written, but only lurking, invisible in the margins. It resembles the situation where the poet turns free verse into a "traditional form," with a regular rhyme scheme, say, and a metrical pattern: putting your work through the filter of standard English can purify your ideas—and often help you create new ones. This doesn't always happen, but when it does, the revision seems at once profound and natural. You also need to pay attention to those speakers and writers who lack communication skills. Why bother? you might ask. Well, if you're paying attention to them, trying to figure out their language, asking for rephrases and clarification, listening closely not to judge but to understand, you essentially bring them into the discourse. Maybe society at large ignores or writes off people who are less than fully articulate. But that's a mistake. Communication is a two-way street. You can improve overall communication not just by working on your own language but also by helping others refine and clarify what they're trying to get across. In addition, knowing how the language works and is structured may help you to avoid misunderstandings, mistakes, and even quarrels that occur when speakers and writers lack sufficient clarity and exactness. Language matters because its careful use makes society work more smoothly.

And to narrow this down to something more personal, you yourself want to be heard. I am reminded of the 1967 Harlan Ellison story "I Have No Mouth and I Must Scream." The cover of a collection this appeared in depicts a man who has a huge, funnel-shaped ear, but below his nose, nothing—just a long, smooth chin. He can hear a lot but can utter no sound. No mouth. Using correct and precise language not only gives you a mouth, but it allows you to voice ideas more articulately than you could by screaming. Giving everyone a voice is the start—no, more: a prerequisite—for a better, even a more moral, culture.

Some of these sentences I've recorded here were agonizing for me to read and transcribe. I am still haunted by the family in Philadelphia who lost all their children in a fire, by Sheelan Anwar Omer's screams of pain as she was genitally mutilated, by the story of the bomb-laden SUV that blew up fourteen Afghan schoolchildren. How can one worry about language use, about correct English, in the face of such indelible horror, of such destruction of human lives? It seems somehow remote and heartless to be sitting in my comfortable middle-class home, to be browsing newspaper accounts of atrocities and anguishes, of lost dreams and lost lives, of death and war and devastation, coolly recording sample sentences to offer in a book about English usage. To borrow and slightly modify a line from David Mamet, "We got baby seals dying in Alaska, and we're"—and here's my change—"and we're worried about commas?"

Well, I'm worried. What I have recently noticed is that we find ourselves reading so much miscellaneous, unprofessional, and bizarre material—especially online—that our verbal environment has radically transformed over the last decade or so. "It is this deep blankness is the real thing strange," William Empson observes in his poem "Let It Go," almost as if he had anticipated the deep but also curiously "blank" Internet culture of this new millennium. And yet, this blankness is also a clutter: the language that appears on our screens is often a confusing, oddly-pieced-together mixture of slang, jargon, misusages, and difficult words. The model of writing is no model really at all, just a farrago of verbal artifacts, often ones that plagiarize one another, and almost always ones whose sense is hard to discern.

I urge you to look for another model. As you reflect on and compose, as you polish your sentences, as you imagine an audience of interested others, another need will soon surface: you will want to communicate with precision, with accuracy, with power. My guess is that you'll find yourself drawn to the writing that uses language correctly, forcefully, and elegantly, for only that writing will speak at your own level of intensity and purpose. Certain usage patterns will always characterize careful thinkers and influential writers, and you yourself need to discover and define what these usage patterns are—and emulate them.

Language shapes, even creates, experience. Putting something into words brings it into existence. And to articulate something often gives birth to some new voice, new perception, or new idea. Hence, as language describes a world we already know, it also creates a future. In fact, it finally comes down to this: we must be mindful—thoughtful— terrifyingly aware—of the future we create as we write and speak. It's a universe we all must inhabit, and that we will leave to our children, our children's children, and to all who come after us, after December 29, 2008. We need to create a world where others listen, where we each have a mouth, where what we say compels interest and attention—maybe even attentiveness—and where we will be understood—especially when it matters.

Appendix I

Fifteen Myths of Digital-Age English

---

1. *In the age of the tweet, short and concise is always the best.*

   True, true, short messages are often the best. But not always. Sometimes one needs to go on at some length. Sometimes it is necessary to provide a context, especially if one is trying to communicate more than just minimal information. And sometimes the very brevity or terseness of a tweet makes it impossible to understand.

2. *My word processing program doesn't let me change margins, spacing, or other aspects of format.*

   Most word processing programs can be set up to accommodate any standard style; however, you need to use the program's capabilities and not always accept default settings. In Microsoft Word, for example, many writers allow the program its silly default—to put an extra line space between paragraphs of the same format. This should be unselected as a default off the "paragraph" menu.

3. *My word processing program will highlight and automatically fix any errors I make.*

These automatic correction programs are notoriously unreliable, as they often "fix" writing that is in fact correct. For example, at first I thought one of my students had subject-verb agreement problems; then I noted that the program tried to get me to introduce such errors into my own work. You, not the program, are the mind behind the words. Don't rely on your program to fix everything. Let it check—but you check too.

4. *"Logical punctuation" is the best option in most situations.*

This idea usually refers to putting punctuation either inside or outside of quotation marks. The logicality of doing so or not doing so has been questioned by many. It's probably best to follow conventions of a given style, unless you are not working within any particular field. In that case, you can invent new rules; just don't expect others to understand or follow them.

5. *People don't really read anymore; they merely "scan a page for information."*

Gary Shteyngart brings up this idea in his 2011 novel *Super Sad True Love Story*. It's interesting and has some truth to it: I agree that many people don't read with a lot of care or seek to understand and internalize the written ideas they encounter. But some do. Think of that "some" as your audience. At the same time, consider the needs of an audience that just "scans the page." Ask yourself, "Does this page I've just written include information worth scanning?"

6. *Anyone can publish written material nowadays, so what's the value of Standard Written English?*

   With the Internet, it's true that anyone can publish now. And many self-publishing options are open to any writer seeking to get work in print. Simply publishing something is now less a guarantee of its excellence or importance than it once was, but if you strive to have your work read—by more than family and friends—it will have to respect some standard forms and conventions. Or to put it another way, no matter what your publishing goals, if you want people to read your work, you will have to write with a high level of competence and lucidity.

7. *People are much less precise and exact than they used to be, now that they have computers to rely on.*

   This is clearly not the case in all situations. In fact, people must be much more careful now with details such as spelling, especially when entering passwords or usernames. In many digital contexts, attentiveness to language accuracy is obligatory. If you are inattentive, you often can't even use the computer or the program. If you don't respect the syntax of a program, it just won't run.

8. *"Talking street" is what most people want to do anyway.*

   I think that most people have to use multiple forms of English. They might speak one way to their family, one way to their friends, one way on their jobs, and another way, perhaps, when they need to write a paper for a college course they are taking. People can and should become multilingual.

9. *Most grammatical stuff is of minor importance—kind of too boring and persnickety to bother with.*

   I agree that there are more important things in the world, but I have been making the argument throughout this book that in fact these "minor" matters do seem to make a difference to some people—and a major difference to a small minority. And writ large, they make a big difference in our society. Admittedly, there is a persnickety quality to some of the material, but isn't specialization all about being persnickety?

10. *Someone else can "wordsmith" my ideas; I just generate them.*

    The line between the idea and the expression of it is very fine; that is, how you say something is often inextricable from what you say. You need to take charge of not just coming up with a basic idea or notion but also of how that idea gets expressed. If you have a stake in how an idea exists in its final form, you should take great care with its exact verbal formulation.

11. *Since so many "styles" (MLA, APA, Chicago . . .) are available and used by various specialties, it's pointless to worry about this kind of superficial overlay.*

There are a lot of forms and styles, to be sure. But you need to find the form that's conventional in your professional field and use that. If you don't, you almost automatically label yourself an "outsider" to that field, or perhaps even an interloper. And sometimes, just abiding by the conventions of a style gains you credibility in and of itself, allows entrée into a field.

12. *There's no possibility of an original idea anymore: it's all been said.*

One certainly feels as though this might be possible, considering the ever-expanding scope of the Internet and the existence of over seven billion human minds on the planet. However, each of us has his or her own individual experience—which is unique. And out of that, I feel, originality can emerge. You must really want that originality to emerge, though, and resist succumbing to the pressure of the multitude to simply conform to what's standard, acceptable, predictable, dull.

13. *If something is published on the Internet, it's true.*

I know that no one really believes this. But I want to emphasize that a great deal of material on the Internet is simply false—posted by people who are not reliable, well-informed, or even honest. Much Internet material that claims to be true is in fact only a form of advertising. And finally, do keep in mind that almost anyone can create websites and post content, whether they are sane or insane, children or adults, good or evil, informed or misinformed.

14. *The Internet is a total latrine.*

A few years ago, I heard a well-known public intellectual give a talk for which this was the thesis. And there are certainly many things on the Internet and about the Internet that bear out such a judgment. However, there are also some amazing things, which prompt me to say that the Internet is the greatest accumulation of information and knowledge in the history of humankind. But you need to learn how to use it efficiently and effectively, and sort the good from the bad.

15. *I can cut and paste my way through any college paper assignment.*

There are many opportunities to create what looks like your own work—cutting and pasting here, autosummarizing there, adding a few transitional sentences, and mashing it all together. I don't recommend this kind of work; it doesn't really benefit you to create it. You want to write papers of your own, ones that express your own ideas and that use your own language. The cut-and-pasters are ultimately sacrificing their humanity, as they become people of the machine. And when they're caught, the penalties can be severe.

Appendix II

Using This Book to Teach College Writing: A Microguide

What follows are some suggestions for how to use this book in class—either as a main text or as a supplementary one. I use the book in a freshman-level writing course, one that focuses on argumentative writing, but it's designed for use in any class in which students need to complete writing assignments. I'm ultimately arguing in this book (and in this appendix) that any course requiring the writing of papers should be not only about the "subject matter" of that course, but also about language—how to use it accurately, how to use it effectively, and how to determine what's most appropriate within a given writing/speaking situation.

Teaching Grammar Is Difficult

Teaching grammar is usually arduous and, for students and teacher alike, dull. If that's the situation, little learning takes place. I therefore recommend here a somewhat different-from-usual way of approaching grammar instruction. Usually, students must read a section in a "handbook" and then complete some exercises that reinforce the skill or point being described. These exercises might be handed in, graded as "problem sets," or gone over, aloud, in class. I am not including any exercises in this handbook, and I in fact reject this pedagogy altogether. It's not just that it's boring. It also isn't sufficiently student centered. By casting the teacher in the role of the supreme expert (often armed with an answer key), it all but assures you of replicating the quintessentially boring, one-room-schoolhouse classroom: it generally rewards students who have already mastered the material, but fails to help students who never understood and still don't understand the grammatical principle or concept. It allows students to fall asleep, physically or mentally. It makes grammar rote.

And it doesn't work. Far too often, I have graded problem sets that students complete perfectly only to be dismayed that the papers those same students turn in contain the very grammatical errors that they had had no trouble correcting in handbook exercises. Why is there no carryover? I think the answer is that when students work through exercises on commas, they focus on commas, say; but when they must generate their own work, the challenges of doing so are so much greater than those associated with correcting ten comma-problem sentences that commas get ignored, along with many other "basic" problems.

Grammar instruction should be a regular, ongoing feature of the writing course—an epicenter—not just something rote, not just something reserved for students who have failed to demonstrate mastery of it. I am urging you to design a course that regularly requires students to read this text yet also to look beyond this text for additional examples of grammatical issues and problems. In short, you're trying to make your students much more language sensitive. In-class activities should allow students to share what they have discovered and to write about it both in class and at home. The goal, to a large extent, is to make grammar instruction dynamic and exciting, to show how closely it connects with students' lives outside the classroom, and how it helped shape their lives up to the point they entered your class.

Reading *One Day in the Life of the English Language*

In assigning readings in this book, you have several options. Students can read the text through, over the course of the semester, perhaps, and you can discuss the various issues and set assignments for each section. This is probably the most typical way the book will be used, and I think it works this way.

Another option is to have students read all the "Fundamentals" sections first, then the "Fine Tuning" sections, and then, finally, the "Deep Focus" sections. This has the advantage of laying down all the basic principles and terminology first off (in "Fundamentals"), knowledge of which will be helpful when they further explore the nuances and complexities of language use and "correctness" that the "Fine Tuning" and "Deep Focus" sections explore.

Whatever sequence you use, I would strongly recommend that you spread out the reading of this book over a relatively long period of time. In a "beta test" version of this book, I tried using it in an upper-level English course called "Naked English: Baring the Secrets of the English Language." I had one week—in a supercompressed three-week session—to present formal English using my text. (Two other professors, both linguists, team-taught this course with me, and they each had a week to present other aspects of the language's "secrets.") The result was not encouraging for me. Despite the fact that this text is quite short, the students just did not "get" this book. It proved far too dense and difficult to be digested in such a short span of time. Since the example sentences are "real-world" sentences, they don't always simply and readily elucidate a given grammatical principle. Sometimes, too, they will exemplify more than one problem, which also presents a challenge. So I don't recommend using this text in compressed courses, or squeezing it into a small fragment of a semester.

In-Class Activities

I recommend that you build in some portion of class time, perhaps half of one day's meeting every week, for the discussion of grammar. In addition, I also recommend that you assign some homework assignments (i.e., papers) about grammar issues. (If language is an epicenter of the course, students should probably write about it.)

In-class activities might focus on grammatical issues, and these activities should connect with whatever reading has been assigned. Before getting to an in-class activity, however, you as the teacher might want to highlight certain aspects of the assigned reading. You might have your own interpretation of an issue, or might disagree with some aspect of my explanation—or think a sentence I've labeled as questionable is in fact OK or flat-out wrong. The example sentences allow for and encourage debate.

I try to start the discussion by asking questions of the class, questions—and here is the key—that I myself don't know the answers to. I try to draw students into my own perplexities. If I only ask questions for which there are easy, obvious answers, ones that I clearly know, my whole class morphs into a kind of "test" to see who has read the material, and suddenly, then, it's no longer a discussion. Also, asking questions that one really has evinces a genuineness that urges discussion forward. Some of these questions can be "unanswerable," as in debatable, ones, while others might be "unaskable" ones, that is, questions that stretch the bounds of propriety, maybe even of logic. At the same time, you can now and then just have a conversation with the students, so that your discourse with them has a multilayered vibrancy.

But class time should probably be used for more than lecture and discussion. I also urge you to get students to write some of their own responses and ideas. I employ the use of "streamwriting." This is related to Peter Elbow's concept of "freewriting," but I modify the terminology because the writing isn't really "free"—there are multiple constraints—and because "streamwriting" carries the idea of an ongoing flow of ink and idea. At any rate, these two practices share the following: having students, in class, generate ideas in longhand. (I avoid the use of laptops and other electronic devices here.) After "gathering" ideas for a minute or so, the students simply write—without cease, without going back to revise—for five to ten minutes. If someone cannot think of what to say, she/he should write, "I can't think of what to say," or some variant, which activity quickly becomes boring and drives the writer into engaging with the idea or with the problem of not being able to engage with the idea. The teacher should write along with the students, and this basically requires that the questions asked (I call these "rainmakers") be interesting ones to the teacher as well. And then, after a short period of time, the teacher asks the students to put down their pens and share what they have written, though with two provisos: first, they must actually read what they have written (they haven't been writing "talking points" but in fact a script, nor can they ad-lib their way through this); and second, they cannot offer any disclaimers about the value of what they have written. The teacher should read as well, perhaps toward the middle of the readings, so that his or her writing is not seen as the first or as the final word.

As the reading aloud progresses, discussion might ensue. (Note here that everyone, even the shy, uncertain student, is given both a space in which to talk and a script.) Listeners should be encouraged to ask questions, or to ask for sections to be reread, or simply to comment on the ideas being brought up.

In short, then, follow these guidelines:

- Provide a rainmaker that has some vitality for you, is something you would find interesting to explore in writing.
- Give everyone a minute or so to "gather" ideas before writing.
- Have students write without outlining or notes, without pause, without revision.
- Join the students in this activity. Model it.
- Stop everyone at the same time. (Probably best to time the whole activity.)
- Ask for volunteers to read aloud, or go around the room.
- Make sure people read what they have written rather than discuss it or use it as talking points.
- Do not allow anyone to offer a disclaimer ("This is terrible, but here goes . . ."), since this undermines the whole practice.
- Also read what you have written, but don't read first or last.

Here are some rainmakers for streamwrites or topics for discussion. Some of the following, you will note, will require considerably more time (or space) than others, whether you use them as topics or as rainmakers:

1. Find something in the reading that you disagree with and explain why.
2. Find an example you think is of acceptable English, yet gets a question mark. Defend it.
3. Do you have a "grammar horror story" that you would like to share? When have you been "hurt" by your grammar difficulty or use?
4. In your experience, how have texting, tweeting, and the Web had an impact on your usage? Changed usage overall?
5. Find something that's new and surprising to you in a chapter section and discuss it.
6. Take today's newspaper and look for examples of a given type of problem. Present it. (You will need to provide students with copies of the day's newspaper. It might, incidentally, be better to start with a tabloid rather than a broadsheet.)
7. Transform one of the book's (or the section's) "questionable" sentences into a better version of it.
8. If your dog understands your English ("Lay down!"), how can it be wrong?
9. Any other "commonly confused words" that you have trouble with? What are they, and why do you find them troublesome?
10. *It's* means "it is" or "it has." But it doesn't always work. Why do you think we can say, "It is what it is," but not "It is what it's" or "It's what it's"?

11. How do you respond to obvious misusages or errors in the English you see on social networking sites?

12. What do you think about in terms of usage when you post on Facebook or in blogs?

13. Leave the classroom to "collect" on campus or on the street language that you've never encountered before. Come back with a report as to its "correctness" or "appropriateness."

14. Read appendix I. Can you add a "myth" of your own? Or perhaps you disagree that one of these is a myth and would like to argue that it's actually true.

In addition to having students write about or discuss questions such as these, I recommend that you have them work (in class) with one another's drafts and papers, reading through them, noting any problems and also noting down the section of the text that might help the writers address the problem. This in-class activity gets students rereading and editing, activities that they need to do much more with their own work. Sometimes, to facilitate this activity, students might separate out and number the sentences of a paragraph. Then they might examine more easily each sentence in isolation. Here is an example of the first stage of this activity.

1. In addition to having students write about or discuss questions such as these, I recommend that you have them work (in class) with one another's drafts and

papers, perhaps going through them, noting any problems and also noting down the section of the text that might help the writers address the problem.

2. This in-class activity gets students rereading and editing, activities that they need to do much more with their own work.
3. Sometimes, to facilitate this activity, students might separate out and number the sentences of a paragraph.
4. Then they might examine more easily each sentence in isolation.
5. Here is an example of the first stage of this activity.

The general idea is to get students to look at the language of the writing that they encounter, and try to put their own writing into the "not-me" category—and then critically appraise it.

Outside-of-Class Writing Assignments

All of the following might start off either as discussion questions or as rainmakers for streamwrites. But I present them here as possible paper topics. Probably it's best to assign a mix of short and long papers, defining those terms as you see fit. I recommend assigning three or four papers. However many you assign, though, these papers need to involve students in issues of language study that connect to their own abilities and experiences. I usually assign a large number of papers, since I don't advocate the use of "blue book exams," and I since think students genuinely need to practice formal English. This tends to keep my classes small but my workload heavy.

I know that such a recommendation is not likely to be greeted with great enthusiasm, but here is another: you should complete your own assignments and "turn them in" to your students. Such a practice ensures that you have generated topics you find worthy of a paper, and it also lets you experience some of the specific pressures that your students feel in the course. Then, too, it will acquaint you with the readily available (especially the online) material relevant to the topic, material that your students might be accessing. Such knowledge will be helpful during grading, I might add.

You have the choice of handing out your papers in class or posting them on an intranet site like Blackboard. My method is to post the first few papers prior to the due date, so students have a "model"; for the middle portion of the term I bring my paper, in multiple hardcopy, to class on its due date, and read it aloud; for the final few weeks, I simply post it on Blackboard by the due date. For each assignment I ask a few students to read their papers aloud, giving everyone a chance to do so over the course of the semester.

Here are some possible topics for short papers:

1. Is "formal" English dying?
2. Are the new pronouns being proposed either suitable or necessary? Look at the issue of "gender-biased"

language, and argue for a solution to the problem—or that there is no real problem at all.

3. Explore the idea of "language class." Does this actually exist? What are the classes? How do they relate to social class? Can one change one's "language class" any more easily than one's social class? If, alternatively, you don't believe "language class" exists, explain why you think this.

4. Is the subjunctive mood dead? It's used so infrequently—perhaps it's a relic? Explore.

5. In what ways, if any, does rhetorical proficiency connect to worldly, material success?

6. Is the apostrophe a mark of punctuation that needs to be ushered out of our language? Why or why not?

7. Find some examples of language use or misuse that really affect something important, and explore how they work. (What about the comma that can have a million dollars hinged on it?)

8. Look at one of the major themes or recurring threads of *One Day in the Life*, and argue against the author's position on it. Alternatively, add some new complexity to his argument, some nuance or context that reinforces what he is advocating:

   - The Oxford comma
   - Possessive before gerund
   - The "absurd universe" notion
   - The insistence that correct usage "matters" enormously

Longer papers might examine issues such as the following:

1. Do the revisions that this book makes to the writers', reporters', and speakers' sentences, while perhaps more "correct," really make much difference after all? Isn't Orwell's dictum true, that grammar does not matter, unless it affects communication?

2. Are there really different "grammars" to speech and writing? One of my students said this to me: "But Professor, I ain't got no time to do the research." I suggested that he revise that sentence, even if it was only spoken, even though he was not graded on his speech, and even as we both completely understood what he meant. Do you agree or disagree?

3. When I was looking to buy a new car, the salesman at Volvo asked me what I did for a living. I told him I taught college English. He responded that he was always bad at English, and that "grammar was just for girls." Examine this assertion.

4. Concerning the discovery of "errors" in published material, one might ask, "Why are examples of thus-and-such so prevalent?" or "Why is this element of usage so very difficult to master?" Another question might be, "Why do native speakers of English, or nonnative but very fluent English speakers, continue to make certain 'mistakes' in English?" And further, "Why is it that those mistakes emerge in the edited writing of professional writers?" This naturally leads to the question

"Perhaps this particular 'rule' is ceasing to be observed?"
Your topic, then, is as follows: Who arbitrates "correctness"? Can we trust that entity?

5. What troubling aspect of language use do you wish
   this book had covered? Write a new section (or subsec-
   tion) of the book, using examples from language you
   find in current newspapers or magazines.

6. Explore the problems (or explain the organization) of
   a word processing program that would check for
   grammar problems. What are the major challenges?
   Why have people not so far been able to create a truly
   effective version of such a program?

7. Take a grammar problem from your own past and describe and explore it. Why was it a problem? Why did
   you change? (For my part, I used to say, "I are not."
   That was in the first grade.)

8. Do some research on a grammar issue that might be a
   "flashpoint" in the near, middle, or distant future in
   the United States. What will be at stake? What conclusions do you offer for us—for people who have not
   yet encountered it?

9. A college president I once met (in the course of an interview for a job I was not offered) contended that all
   students should just memorize William Sabin's *Gregg
   Reference Manual*, an extremely detailed, even exhaustive handbook of standard grammar. How good an
   idea is this? Why would a college president advocate
   for it? What does his doing so imply?

10. *Star Wars'* Yoda has had an impact on language use. Can you think of any other characters from fiction or film who have had a similar impact? What kinds of conclusions are you able to draw—that is, what is it about these characters' use of language that makes for its specialness or widespread popularity?

11. Is there an ethics to language use? Do some research on this issue. Look for where it is problematic and complex. With language use, what is "at stake" in terms of ethical standards? Are there relevant historical situations that you might examine to develop your argument?

12. Have you ever been in a situation where you felt, "I had no voice but I must scream"? Describe it. Why did you feel voiceless? And what did you want to scream about? To what extent, in fact, was it your own voicelessness?

Of course, these "long paper" topics could well be topics for the short papers, and vice versa—or they might work as questions to start a discussion or as rainmakers for stream-writes. My suggestion is that in writing about these issues, confronting grammar use head-on, and thinking about their individual relationship to language, students will become more self-conscious and effective users of English. Grammar shouldn't be viewed as just something that stigmatizes them or makes them feel helpless and ineffectual. You want to devise writing activities that emphasize how students have some control over the language we all use, and drive home the idea that grammar and usage are not simply arbitrary and apodictic intellectual constructs mandated by a surrounding culture. We want students to see grammar as something about which there is debate—a debate we'd like to invite them to participate in. Merely involving themselves in this debate will move them toward greater mastery.

So what I am finally arguing is that you can improve your students' grammar and language use. These are not fixed or fated. Do keep in mind that in order to get your students to change, you'll have to rewire their brains' circuits, initially breaking some down. Students will have to unlearn. It seems to be a little like bodybuilding: with each day's exercise, muscle tissue is broken down. But when that tissue builds back up (and this causes soreness, I know), it's larger, leaner, stronger. This works with grammar too—though probably it's less physiologically apparent, except maybe to neuroscientists. Your writing course will break down familiar patterns. This might hurt a bit, but not to worry. As your students rebuild, they will become more powerful users of the language—better able to generate and communicate their ideas. And they will appreciate (eventually) your helping them toward the formation of a new self.

Fifty Key Terms

A Microglossary

ABS OF NY: The coordinating conjunctions, namely, *and*, *but*, *so*, *or*, *for*, *nor*, *yet*. Sometimes the mnemonic used is FANBOYS. (Of the 5,040 possible permutations of the seven letters, I found ABS OF NY to be the most memorable.)

actant: A term invented by Bruno LaTour, and referring to the subject or object—the participants—in a sentence.

adjective: Adjectives give specificity, add information and vividness to your sentences. They modify (shape, narrow, sharpen, color, animate, limit) the meaning of a noun or pronoun—or of another adjective. A group of words can "function adjectivally." As mentioned in the text above, verb forms, known as participles, sometimes function as adjectives. Some typical forms of adjectives include "comparatives" (ending in *-er* or preceded by "more") and "superlatives" (ending in *-est* or preceded by "most").

adverb: A word that modifies verbs, other adverbs, or adjectives. Adverbs answer the questions "When?" "In what way?" "Where?" "How?" as well as other essential questions. They are hard to identify by how they look, and they can appear in various places in sentences. Adverbs can modify single words, phrases, or whole sentences. Often they can be identified by the *-ly* ending, though not all words ending in *-ly* are adverbs, and there are many adverbs that do not end in *-ly*. *Folly*, for example, is a noun, and *well* is often an adverb.

antecedent: The word or group of words that a pronoun replaces. Usually, but not always, the antecedent precedes the pronoun.

appositive: Repetition, using different wording and providing additional information, of a noun or noun phrase.

article: *A, an, the. A* and *an* are indefinite articles; *the* is the definite article, perhaps so named because it usually tends to delimit the meaning of the noun following it; it attempts to differentiate the noun following it from a group or class of other things like it. Sometimes called "determiners" (q.v.).

clause: A group of words containing a noun or noun phrase and a verb or verb phrase. A clause can be a full sentence (called a "main clause"), yet at other times it needs to be attached to a full sentence—the case with relative clauses or subordinate clauses, for example.

comma splice: An "incorrect" usage, to be avoided, in which two main clauses are joined with just a comma (rather than with a comma plus a coordinating conjunction, or with a semicolon). Sometimes comma splices are acceptable, as with short main clauses; if the second main clause reverses the negative meaning of the first; in "tag" questions; or when more than two main clauses form a series or list within a sentence.

conjunction: A word that joins two parts of a sentence. See entry for ABS OF NY, above.

conjunctive adverb: *However, therefore, consequently, thus,* and several other words are known as conjunctive adverbs. These join together parts of a sentence, but they usually require use of a semicolon (or a coordinating conjunction and a comma) to make that joining a legitimate (i.e., grammatical) one.

dash: Two major types of dash appear in print: the em dash (—), which typically marks a pause in a sentence, with the intent of emphasizing what is to follow it (often these are used in pairs); and the en dash (–), which is half as wide as the one-em, and which is used to mark a series (as in *pages 1–22*), or to indicate "versus" or "to," as in *the Iran–Iraq war*. Both of these are to be distinguished from the hyphen (-), which is used in certain words, often adjectival formations, or to divide words at the end of a line (a rarity in word processing nowadays, since most programs do not allow for word division).

determiners: Determiners include articles (*a*, *an*, *the*); quantifiers, such as *some*, *many*, *a lot*; demonstrative adjectives such as *this*, *these*, or *those*; and possessives, such as *my*, *your*, *her*, *our*, or *their*. They are placed before nouns, with the intent and effect of narrowing and specifying some detail about that noun. They have a fundamentally adjectival function, i.e., they modify the noun following them.

fused sentence: A type of "run-on" sentence, one that does not have any punctuation between two main, or independent, clauses.

gender-biased language: Language that—though referring to persons of either gender—uses pronouns that refer to only one (usually male). This has been identified as a problem only since about 1980. Today's usage handbooks almost unanimously agree that English as it had been taught had a gender bias, which may well have contributed to discriminatory beliefs, behavior, and/or thought.

gerund: A verb form ending in *-ing* that functions as a noun: *Seeing is believing*, for example, opens and closes with a gerund. Usually if a noun or pronoun precedes a gerund, that noun or pronoun should be in the possessive form, provided that it would be in that form for a nongerund noun.

imperative (mood): The command form of a verb. Note that verbs change somewhat when they're used as commands; in addition, the word order of their enclosing sentence also changes from typical word order.

indefinite pronoun: A class of pronoun: *each, everyone, everybody, no one, none, anyone, anybody, someone,* and *somebody.* Usually these take singular verbs, but occasionally, as when *none* means "not any," they can take a plural verb form.

indicative (mood): The verbs used in most speech and writing are in the "indicative" mood. It is used to tell stories, and to express ideas, facts, opinions, and judgments. Questions are usually in the indicative mood. Contrast "imperative" and "subjunctive," two other "moods" of verb.

infinitive: The basic form of a verb, in English usually preceded by the particle *to*: *to go, to eat, to run, to drive.*

interjection: An exclamatory word or group of words.

interruptive: Within a sentence, this is a word used to make the reader pause, and it usually appears when the writer wants to emphasize a contrast. "She wanted, however, to accept the article, even though it wasn't quite to the topic." *However* functions here as an interruptive.

main clause: A full sentence, including subject and predicate. It can stand on its own or, alternatively, can be part of another sentence.

misplaced modifier: A modifier is a word or group of words that attempts to limit, narrow, specify, color, shade, energize, complicate, or make vivid another word or word group. Typical modifiers are adjectives or adverbs. Misplaced modifiers are ones that can confuse the reader, since they apparently modify some element that renders the sentence absurd or nonsensical. ("With a husband and five children, her washing machine was going all the time" is a famous one. Did the washing machine have a husband and five children?) Most readers can ultimately sort out the correct meaning, but I argue throughout that understanding comes only after a distracting detour into an "absurd universe"—a detour that detracts from the writer's credibility or message.

mixed construction: An erroneous kind of sentence construction in which the writer starts out with one type of sentence and shifts midway. The most common example of this is "The reason is . . . because." *Reason* implies *because*; putting in the *because* as much as suggests that *The reason* that preceded it is unnecessary or is being ignored. "The reason is that . . ." is the correct form.

nonrestrictive (clause): A clause that adds something to a sentence but does not restrict or limit the meaning of the major part of the sentence. It is sometimes called a "nonessential" clause, since its information is not really "essential." Often these clauses open with *which*, or might be parenthetical in nature.

noun: A word referring to a person, place, or thing. Keep in mind that verb forms ending in *-ing* can be used as nouns. These are called gerunds.

object pronoun: A pronoun that is in the sentence position of receiving the action of the subject.

parallel structure: A phrase used to refer to the correct way of setting up sentences that have multiple elements: for example, if the first element of a list is a gerund, the others should be too. If the first main clause is structured subject-verb-object, the next should be as well. In the entry on indicative mood, I had first written, "It is used to express ideas, opinions, judgments, and stories." This is an example of a nonparallel structure: *express* fits with *idea, opinions, judgments*. But it doesn't work with *stories*. We don't usually say that someone can "express" "stories." So I revised.

participle: Form of a verb, ending with *-ed* in the past and *-ing* in the present, which is used as a modifier (usually adjectivally).

perfective (verb forms): Verb forms that use the "auxiliary" forms of *to have*: present perfect ("I have learned . . ."), past perfect ("I had learned . . ."), and future perfect ("I will have learned . . ."). The present perfect denotes actions that started in the past and continue up to the present or that are still continuing in the present; the past perfect denotes actions that started in the past and were completed in the past; and the future perfect indicates actions that will be completed in the future. (Other perfective forms include ones using "modals" such as *would, should, could, might, must,* and *may*.)

possessive pronoun: *My, mine, your, yours, his, her, hers, its, their, theirs, our, ours*.

predicate: The main verb of a sentence, the predicate performs the action of the subject (Jim *ran*), expresses that subject's state of being (Zuleima *is talented*), or reports something that's happening to that subject (It all *happened* at once).

preposition: Small word usually denoting placement or physical relationship of some kind: words such as *about, above, across, after, against, along, among, around, as, before, behind, below, beneath, between, beyond, by, concerning, despite, down, during, except, for, from, in, into, like, near, of, off, on, onto, out, outside, over, through, to, toward, under, until, up, with, according to, along with, apart from, as for, because of, by means of, except for, in back of, in case of, on top of, outside of*.

prepositional phrase: A group of words introduced by and including a preposition.

pronoun: A pronoun substitutes for a noun, noun phrase, or sometimes another pronoun.

pronoun case: The form of a pronoun—possessive, object, subject. See the individual entries for each of these. Pronoun case must be carefully attended to in formal writing. Errors in case emerge as a feature of slang ("Me and him went to get some gas"), which is acceptable in some contexts.

reflexive pronoun: A class of pronoun: *myself, yourself, himself, herself, itself, ourselves, yourselves, themselves*. Such a word emphasizes a noun or pronoun, or it can indicate that the receiver and doer of an action are the same entity.

relative pronoun: A class of pronoun: *who, whom, that, which*, and *where. Why* can also be used as a relative pronoun. These introduce a relative (adjective) clause. They relate and link one portion of a sentence to another. Sometimes the link is absolutely essential to meaning; at other times, the link is less crucial, with the material in the nonessential relative clause being only background or explanatory.

restrictive (clause): A clause that is tightly tied to the noun it's connected to, such that it is essential to the meaning of a sentence. (Also called an "essential clause.") Often introduced with *that* ("The car that I like is the blue one"), but *which* is becoming more and more acceptable as a way to introduce them. Some writers and teachers can't accept *which* when it's used this way, though.

run-on sentence: Fused sentence or comma splice. See entries above.

SALUTE: Stand-Alone Linguistic Unit of Thought or Expression—also known as a main clause or sentence. Note that I am not contending that this is a "complete thought," as it's often taught.

sentence fragment: A non-SALUTE, the fragment is usually not acceptable in formal written English. It lacks either subject or verb. In order to avoid being a fragment, a group of words requires a subject, predicate, and tense.

split infinitive: The insertion of a word (usually an adverb) between the particle *to* and the base verb form, as in *to boldly go*. Traditionally prohibited by Strunk and White (and others), but actually acceptable and often preferable to the "unsplit" variant.

subject: That which does the action of a sentence (or the central focus of being, if the verb is not one of action).

subject pronoun: *I*, *you*, *he*, *she*, *it*, *they*. These are in the nominative case, and they can be used as subjects of a sentence.

subject-verb agreement: An important grammatical principle, subject-verb agreement refers to the relationship between subject and verb. The verb form (singular, plural, first, second, third person) must match ("agree with") the subject in terms of both number and person.

subjunctive (mood): The "what if" mood of English verbs, used in contrary-to-fact statements ("If I were a rich man. . . .") or in clauses that are preceded by another clause with a verb such as *ask*, *demand*, *request*, *guess*, *recommend*, or similar words. The only words that change from the usual verb forms are present-tense, third-person singular; and *to be*. (Present-tense third-person subjunctive is formed by eliminating the "s" or "es" ["I recommend that he *discuss* . . ."]. For *to be* verbs, the present subjunctive is *be*, and the past subjunctive is *were*.)

TEPO (The Epoch of the Post-Original): I suggest that this is the very epoch we now inhabit, during which time the impression prevails that everything has been already thought, written, and—for the most part—put online. Many people feel that they have no hope to make an original contribution in this epoch, so they confine themselves to patching together material that others have written. I argue that this view is wrongheaded.

verb: A word of action or denoting an ongoing state (as in being or having). Verbs embody and depict events taking place, incidents occurring, states of mind, states of being. They show, as if filmically, what happens, is happening, happened, will happen, could happen, would happen.

Works Cited

General Sources

Archangul Foundation. "The Epicene Hu." Bookmark. N.d.

Baker, Nicholson. "Survival of the Fittest." *Best American Essays, 1994*. Ed. Tracy Kidder. Boston: Houghton, 1994.

Blaauw-Hara, Mark. "Why Our Students Need Instruction in Grammar, and How We Should Go about It." *Teaching English in the Two-Year College* 34.2 (2006): 165–78.

Bremner, John B. *Words on Words: A Dictionary for Writers and Others Who Care about Words*. New York: Columbia University Press, 1980.

Brown, Goold. *The Institutes of English Grammar*. New York: William Wood, 1863.

Browne, Alix. "The Happiness Project." *T: The New York Times Style Magazine* December 2, 2012: 111–14.

Carroll, Lewis. *Alice's Adventures in Wonderland*. Boston: Lee and Shepard, 1869.

Carson, Anne. *Autobiography of Red: A Novel in Verse*. New York: Vintage, 1999.

Celce-Murcia, Marianne, and Diane Larsen-Freeman. *The Grammar Book: An ESL/EFL Teacher's Course*. 2nd ed. Boston: Heinle & Heinle, 1999.

The Chicago Manual of Style. 16th ed. Chicago: University of Chicago Press, 2010.

Childs, Peter, and Roger Fowler. *The Routledge Dictionary of Literary Terms*. London: Routledge, 2006.

Chomsky, Noam. *Syntactic Structures*. The Hague: Mouton, 1969.

Cioffi, Frank L. *The Imaginative Argument: A Practical Manifesto for Writers*. Princeton: Princeton University Press, 2005.

Conan Doyle, Sir Arthur. *Sherlock Holmes: The Adventures, Memoirs, Return, His Last Bow & The Case-Book. The Complete Short Stories*. London: John Murray, 1928.

Conrey, Sean M., and Karl Stolley. "Hyphen Use." *Online Writing Lab.* June 7, 2013. https://owl.english.purdue.edu/owl/resource/576/01/.

Crews, Frederick. *The Random House Handbook*. 5th ed. New York: Random, 1987.

Curzan, Anne. "Says Who? Teaching and Questioning the Rules of Grammar." *PMLA* 124.3 (2009): 870–79.

Dalgish, Gerard. "Garden Path Sentences (from Various Sources)." 2014. TS.

———. "The Syntax and Semantics of the Morpheme *ni* in Kivunjo (Chaga)." *Studies in African Linguistics* 10.1 (1979): 47–63.

Davis, Lydia. "Foucault and Pencil." *The Next American Essay*. Ed. John D'Agata. St. Paul: Graywolf, 2003. 333–36.

Denes, Agnes. "Human Dust." *TriQuarterly* 20 (1985): 282–83.

Eisinger, Jesse. "The Fall Guy." *New York Times Magazine* May 4, 2014: 34+.

Elbow, Peter. *Writing without Teachers*. New York: Oxford University Press, 1973.

Ellison, Harlan. *I Have No Mouth and I Must Scream*. New York: Pyramid, 1967.

Empson, William. *The Complete Poems of William Empson*. Gainesville: University of Florida Press, 2001.

"EU Launches Probe to Find Truth about Russia-Georgia War." *DW: Deutsche Welle* December 2, 2008. www.dw.de /eu-launches-probe-to-find-truth-behind-georgia-russia -war/a-3842828.

Foreman, Judy. "The 43 Facial Muscles That Reveal Even the Most Fleeting Emotions." *New York Times* August 5, 2003.

Garner, Bryan A. *Garner's Modern American Usage*. 3rd ed. New York: Oxford University Press, 2009.

Gladwell, Malcolm. *Blink: The Power of Thinking without Thinking*. New York: Back Bay. 2007

Graff, Gerald. "Forum: Reply." *Profession 2008*. 259–62.

Graves, Robert, and Alan Hodge. *The Reader over Your Shoulder: A Handbook for Writers of English Prose*. 2nd ed. New York: Random House, 1979.

Haberman, Clyde. "Subjects and Verbs as Evil Plots." *New York Times*. January 14, 2011: A19.

Hagy, Chad. "How to Talk Like Yoda." January 27, 2010. http:// www.ehow.com/how_2112707_talk-like-yoda.html.

Huckabee, Mike. June 29, 2009. Radio.mikehuckabee.com.

Huddleston, Rodney, and Geoffrey K. Pullum. *The Cambridge Grammar of the English Language*. Cambridge: Cambridge University Press, 2002.

"J.C." [pseud.] "NB: Let's Do Luncheon." *Times Literary Supplement* January 9, 2009.

Jespersen, Otto. *Essentials of English Grammar*. Tuscaloosa: University of Alabama Press, 1965.

Karp, Jonathan. "Lion in Winter." *New York Times Magazine* December 23, 2009: 56.

Kelly, Harold C. *Watch Repair*. Peoria, IL: Chas. A. Bennett, 1957.

Kulish, Nicholas. "Not Plagiarism but Mixing and Matching, Says Best-Selling German Author, 17." *New York Times* February 12, 2010: A6.

"The Last Word: The Lecturers' Dictionary." *WOE: Writing on the Edge* 18.1 (2007): 99–100.

Lunsford, Andrea A., and Karen J. Lunsford. "'Mistakes Are a Fact of Life': A National Comparative Study. *College Composition and Communication* 59.4 (2008): 781–806.

Mamet, David. *"Sexual Perversity in Chicago" and "The Duck Variations."* New York: Grove, 1978.

Mason, Wyatt. "Smarter Than You Think." Rev. of *Although of Course You End Up Becoming Yourself: A Road Trip with David Foster Wallace*. *New York Review of Books* July 15, 2010: 12–15.

Medina, Jennifer. "Warning: The Literary Canon Could Make Students Squirm." *New York Times* May 18, 2014, late ed.: 1+.

Milne, A. A. *The Complete Tales of Winnie-the-Pooh*. New York: Dutton, 1994.

MLA Style Manual and Guide to Scholarly Publishing. 3rd ed. New York, MLA, 2008.

"My Big Break: To Mike Birbiglia's Parents, It's OK If Your

Son Sticks to Comedy." *All Things Considered*. National Public Radio. WNYC. March 23, 2014. Radio.

NASA Science News. "Biggest Full Moon of Year." December 9, 2008. science.nasa.gov/science-news/science-at-nasa/2008/09dec_fullmoon/.

Noguchi, Rei R. *Grammar and the Teaching of Writing: Limits and Possibilities*. Urbana, IL: NCTE, 1991.

"Oftenest." Wiktionary. en.wiktionary.org/oftenest.

Orwell, George. *1984*. New York: New American Library, 1961.

———. "Politics and the English Language." *Shooting an Elephant and Other Essays*. London: Secker and Warburg, 1950. 84–101.

Pinker, Steven. "Oaf of Office." *New York Times* January 22, 2009.

Quirk, Randolph, Sidney Greenbaum, Jan Svartvik, and Geoffrey Leech. *A Comprehensive Grammar of the English Language*. London: Longman, 1985.

Rabinovitch, Simon. "Thousands of Hyphens Perish as English Marches On." September 21, 2007. http://www.reuters.com/article/2007/09/21/us-britain-hyphen-idUSHAR15384620070921.

Raimes, Ann, with Maria Jerskey. *Keys for Writers*. 6th ed. Boston: Wadsworth, Cengage, 2011.

"Respected Poet and Leader Amiri Baraka Dies at 79: 'We Want Poems That Kill.'" January 10, 2014. kulturekritic.com/2014/01/men/respected-poet-leader-amiri-baraka-dies-79/.

Rivera, Ray, and Nate Schweber. "Before Killings, Hints of Plans and Grievance." *New York Times* April 5, 2009: 1+.

Roberts, Sam. "Celebrating the Semicolon in a Most Unlikely Location." February 18, 2008. nytimes.com/2008/02/18/ny region/18semicolon.html?_r=0.

Ross, John Robert. "The Category Squish: Endstation Hauptwort." *Papers from the Eighth Regional Meeting Chicago Linguistic Society, April 14–16, 1972*. Chicago Linguistic Society. 316–28.

Sabin, William. *Gregg Reference Manual*. 10th ed. New York: McGraw-Hill, 2004.

Schulz, Charles. *The Complete Peanuts, 1959–62*. New York: Norton, 2005.

Shor, Ira. "Who Won the Culture Wars?" Lecture. CUNY Graduate Center, New York. October 23, 2009.

Shteyngart, Gary. *Super Sad True Love Story*. New York: Random House, 2011.

Sloane, David E. E. "A Sentence Is Not a Complete Thought: X-Word Grammar." *English Language Teaching* 2.2 (June 2009). www.ccsenet.org/journal/index.php/elt/article/view /2354.

Span, Paula. "Tea, Two Sugars, and Death: Cafe Groups Ponder the End." *New York Times* June 17, 2013, late ed.: 1+.

Strunk, William, Jr., and E. B. White. *The Elements of Style*. 4th ed. New York: Longman, 1999.

Swift, Jonathan. *Gulliver's Travels*. www.gutenberg.org/ebooks /829.

"Taking You Back in Time: What Happened in 2008." *The People History*. www.thepeoplehistory.com.

"Timelines of History." www.timelines.ws.

Truss, Lynne. *Eats, Shoots & Leaves: The Zero Tolerance Approach to Punctuation*. New York: Penguin, 2004.

Wittgenstein, Ludwig. *Tractatus Logico-Philosophicus*. www.gutenberg.org/ebooks/5740.

Yankovic, Weird Al. *Word Crimes*. Video. 2014.

Zimmer, Ben. "On Language: Skxawng!" *New York Times Magazine* December 5, 2009: 20.

December 29, 2008, Examples

N.B. *New York* is dated December 22/29; *New Yorker*, December 22/29; *Time*, December 29/January 5; all other magazines, newspapers, and websites carry the December 29, 2008 date.

"Across the USA: Hawaii." *USA Today*.

Agresti, Aimee. "Flip-flopper: Brad Pitt Then & Now." *Us*: 58–59.

Alderman, Liz. "Paulson, Bernanke and Trichet Walk into a Bar . . ." *International Herald Tribune*.

American Airlines. Advertisement. *USA Today*.

Anderson, Sam. "Wake Up, Little Susie." Rev. of Susan Sontag, *Reborn: Journals and Notebooks, 1947–1963*. *New York*: 100–102

Arango, Tim. "Online Piracy Menaces Pro Sports." *New York Times*.

"Auctions and Antiques." *New Yorker*: 36.

"BCS Preview: Is the Gator Defense Immovable?" *Sports Illustrated*: 34–38.

Bechtel, Mark. "The Year in Sports: 2008: Farewell." *Sports Illustrated*: 55–70.

Beech, Mark. "Something to Prove." *Sports Illustrated*: 38.

Belson, Ken. "Obscure Fee Pays for Efficient-Energy Projects." *New York Times*.

Birch, Red. "TCA Overwhelms Steinert in Semis." *Trentonian*.

BklynAli [pseud.]. "Voice of the People for Dec. 29, 2008." ny dailynews.com.

"Black-on-Black Slays Rising among Teens." *Trentonian*.

Blair, Tony. "#3: Nicolas Sarkozy." *Time*: 90.

Bloom, Julie. "Arts, Briefly." *New York Times*.

"Body News." *Us*: 52.

Bolaño, Roberto. "Meeting with Enrique Lihn." Trans. Chris Andrews. *New Yorker*: 78–81.

Boswell, Thomas. "On the Season's Final Day, Campbell Finds Himself in a Rush." *Washington Post*.

Boucher, Geoff. "Even for Neil Gaiman, 'The Sandman' Is a Singular Dream."latimes.com.

Bowles, Scott. "'Marley' Runs ahead of Pitt, Cruise and Sandler." *USA Today*.

Brawndo [pseud.]. "No. 33." *New York*: 57.

Breznican, Anthony. "Time to Break Out the Big Guns." *USA Today*.

Broad, William J. "Soviets Stole Bomb Idea from U.S., Book Says." *New York Times*.

Bronner, Ethan. "A Stark Show of Power Calculated to Instill Fear." *International Herald Tribune*.

"Brown Sees Obama as Inspiration for Britain: Prime Minister Seeks Trans-Atlantic Pact." Reuters. *International Herald-Tribune*.

Campbell, R. M. "A Top-Notch Performance by Tudor Choir." seattlepi.com.

Canon. Advertisement. *Time*: 8–9.

Caputo, Pat. "Lions Should Pray for Parcells." *Trentonian*.

Carter, Kelley L. "They're over 'The Hills' and on Their Own." *USA Today*.

Chad, Norman. "Greatness for the Destined." *Washington Post*.

Chopra, Deepak. "If Terrorism Is a Cancer, Treat It Like One." sfgate.com.

Cieply, Michael. "Star-Filled Year-End Releases Draw Well." *New York Times*.

———. "When Megahit Means Just Average." *International Herald Tribune*.

Clifford, Stephanie. "An NPR Reporter Becomes the News." *New York Times*.

Coker, Margaret, and Charles Levinson. "Israel Pounds Gaza Again, Signals More on the Way." *Wall Street Journal*.

Collins, Lauren. "Getting and Spending: Brown Baggers." *New Yorker*.

Córdoba, José de, Antonio Regalado, and Joel Millman. "Latins Quiet about Madoff Losses." *Wall Street Journal*.

"Covina Shooting Ripples through Extended Family in Mexico." latimes.com.

Craig, Susanne, Jeffrey McCracken, Aaron Lucchetti, and Kate Kelly. "The Weekend That Wall Street Died." *Wall Street Journal*.

Davidson, Justin. "Classical Music: The Young Old Master." *New York*: 103.

De Beers Family of Companies. Advertisement. *New Yorker*: 9.

Denby, David. "A Better Life." Rev. of *Revolutionary Road, Gran Torino,* and *The Class. New Yorker*: 116–18.

Derschau, Verena von. "Pardon of Jailed Official Angers Sarkozy's Foes." *International Herald Tribune*.

Dilanian, Ken. "N.Y.'s Towns Set to Chair Key Panel." *USA Today*.

Dillon, Sam, and Antonio Betancourt. "Mexican Officer Accused of Working with Cartels." *New York Times*.

Dominus, Susan. "When Hedge Funders Are Sent Home, Careful Tending Is in Order." *New York Times*.

Downwithracism [pseud.]. Reader comment. nydailynews.com.

Durkin, Erin, Edgar Sandoval, and Samuel Goldsmith. "Accused Killer of 10-Year-Old Son Allegedly Admits Long-term Abuse." nydailynews.com.

Edelstein, David. "The Culture Pages: Hollywood Movie Blow-out." *New York*: 89–94.

Eilperin, Juliet. "Inventors Find Inspiration in Natural Phenomena." *Washington Post*.

Elick, Adam B. "13 Children Killed in Afghan Bombing." *International Herald Tribune*.

El-Khodary, Taghreed, and Isabel Kershner. "Israel Pursues Strikes on Gaza; Toll Mounts and Outcry Swells." *International Herald Tribune*.

Farrell, Stephen. "Hamas Credo Led It to End Cease-Fire." ny times.com.

Fields, Gary J. "Murders of Black Teens Are Up 39% since 2000–01." *Wall Street Journal*.

"'Firm and Patient.'" Editorial. *New York Times*.

Fisk, Robert. "How Can Anyone Believe There Is 'Progress' in the Middle East?" seattlepi.com.

"Ft. Dix Jihad Was No Prank." Editorial. *Trentonian*.

Frank, Thomas. "Fewer Caught Sneaking into USA." *USA Today*.

———. Tensions Up with Border Fence." *USA Today*.

Freeman, James. "The Ingredients of His Success." Review of *1,000 Dollars and an Idea* by Sam Wyly. *Wall Street Journal*.

Freeman, Jan. "Beware of Grammarians Who Rule by Whim." *International Herald Tribune*.

Freydkin, Donna "Keri Russell Shares Work-Time, Home-Time Stories." *USA Today*.

Fritze, John. "Groups Send Wish Lists for Economic Bill." *USA Today*.

Fuller, Thomas. "Mumbai's Torment Captured Click by Click." *International Herald Tribune*.

"'Gang-related' Killings Much More Than That." suntimes.com.

Garmin. Advertisement. *USA Today*.

Ghosh, Bobby. "Briefing: The Moment: 12/14/08: Baghdad." *Time*: 21.

Gibbs, Nancy. "Commentary." *Time*: 32.

———. "#4 Sarah Palin." *Time*: 92–94.

GMC. Advertisement. *USA Today*.

Going Nowhere [pseud.]. "Stuck on the Bridge." Letter to Editor. "BackTalk." *Trentonian*.

Goodman, Peter S. "Print Cash Today and Fret Later." *International Herald Tribune*.

Goodman, Peter S., and Gretchen Morgenson. "A Relentless Push to Approve Loans: At Washington Mutual, the Policy Seemed to Be: Don't Ask, Just Sell." *International Herald Tribune*.

Goodman, Tim. "And Then There Was One—'Mad Men.'" sfgate.com.

Goodstein, Laurie. "In America to Do a Job, an African Priest Also Finds a Home." *New York Times*.

———. "India, an Exporter of Priests, May Keep Them." nytimes.com.

Goodyear, Dana. "Letter from Japan: I ♥ Novels." *New Yorker*: 62–68.

Gorant, Jim. "Happy New Year." *Sports Illustrated*: 72–77.

Grillo, Ioan. "Postcard: Culiacán." *Time*: 13.

Grose, Jared. Letter to Editor. *Washington Post*.

Harley-Davidson. Advertisement. *USA Today*.

Hax, Caroline. "Tell Me about It." *Washington Post*.

Hayward, Steven F. "Bill and Ron." Rev. of *The Ron I Knew* by William F. Buckley. *National Review*: 42–43.

Heintz, Jim. "U.S. Soldier Killed in Baghdad's Sadr City." washingtonpost.com.

Hertzberg, Hendrik. "The Talk of the Town: Comment: Appointments." *New Yorker*: 41.

Hesse, Monica. "We Just Couldn't Look Away: The Viral Videos of '08." *Washington Post*.

Hill, Catey. "Expert Predicts Longest Advertising Spending

Decline since Great Depression; Retail, Auto Lead Pack."
nydailynews.com.

Holley, Joe, and Martin Weil. Obituary. "Political Scientist
Samuel P. Huntington." *Washington Post*.

Holt, Jim. "No. 56: Because New York Has Become a World
Capital of Philosophy." *New York*: 72.

"Hot Hollywood: Kate Walsh Sudden Split!" *US*: 9.

"Hot Stuff: Kate and Owen, Friends with Benefits." *Us*: 37.

Hussain, Zahid, and Matthew Rosenberg. "Suicide Bombing
Kills at Least 36 in Northwest Pakistan." *Wall Street Journal*.

Hwang, Heemyung. Letter to Editor. *USA Today*.

"In Our Pages 100, 75 & 50 Years Ago: '1908: Earthquake
Devastates Italy.'" *International Herald Tribune*.

"Intelligencer: Old School." *New York*: 20.

"The Interview: Person of the Year Barack Obama." *Time*: 66–
70.

"Iraq Bomber Targets Gaza Airstrike Protest." *International
Herald Tribune*.

"Israeli Hospital Moves into Bomb Shelter due to Missile
Strike Fears."nydailynews.com.

"Israel's Gaza Defense." Unsigned editorial. *Wall Street Journal*.

"Israel Strikes Gaza in 2nd Day of Attacks." nydailynews.com.

Itzkoff, Dave. "Speed the Rehearsals as Actor Zips into a Lead."
New York Times.

Rev. of *I've Loved You So Long*. "Movies: Now Playing." *New
York*: 111.

Jersey Joe 1 [pseud.]. Comments on "The Blue Screen" by Ralph
Vacchiano. nydailynews.com.

Jones, Del. "CBS Executive Asks: How Do You Want to Be Remembered?" *USA Today*.

"The Kaizen Kraze." *Trentonian*.

Kay, Jane. "Drillers Eye Oil Reserves off California Coast." sf gate.com.

Kelly, John. "The High Quality of Care at Children's Is No Accident." *Washington Post*.

Kings County Doc [pseud.]. Web comments. nydailynews .com.

Kondracke, Morton. "Left's Witch Hunt Should Be Halted." *Trentonian*.

Kristol, William. "George, Abe, Rick & Barack." *New York Times*.

Lahr, John. "The Theater: More about Me: Two Solipsists Onstage." *New Yorker*: 84–85.

"Lawyers' Bills Pile High, Driving Up Health Care Costs." Editorial. *USA Today*.

Lazo, Alejandro. "Herndon-Based Volkswagen Executive Says He Understood Bailout Rationale." *Washington Post*.

Leibowitz, Zach. "Hotlanta." washingtonpost.com.

Leinwand, Donna. "Bogus Money Goes Mainstream." *USA Today*.

Leitch, Will. "No. 26: Because Not Even the Dolans Can Take the Fun out of Watching These Knicks." *New York*: 54.

Lipton, Eric, and David D. Kirkpatrick, "Veterans of '90s Bank Bailout See Opportunity in Current One." *New York Times*.

"'Little Michael's' Mom Found in Suitcase." *Trentonian*.

Loge, Peter, and Zoe Beckerman. Letter to the Editor. *Washington Post*.

Rev. of *London Cries. New Yorker*: 18.

"Loose Talk: What the Stars Said This Week." *Us*: 12.

Lowenstein, Henry A. Letter to the Editor. *New York Times*.

Lowry, Richard. "'The Freedom Speech' in Retrospect." *National Review*: 20–21.

Lynch, David J. "Formerly Soaring Trade Stomps on the Brakes." *USA Today*.

Marciano, John Bemelmans. "A Deadly Wave, a Lucky Star." *International Herald Tribune*.

Marshall, Steve (with wire reports). "On Deadline: What Others Are Reporting: 'The Passing of the Polaroid.'" *USA Today*.

———. "Navy, Environmentalists Reach Deal over Sonar." *USA Today*.

Maslin, Janet. "Innocent? No One in Town Fits Profile." *New York Times*.

McDonald, Mark. "Hundreds Are Feared Dead in Bay of Bengal." *New York Times*.

McKinley, Jesse, and Malia Wollan. "Skaters Jump in as Foreclosures Drain the Pool." *New York Times*.

Medcalf, Rory. "Securing the Sea-Lanes: China's Gunboat Diplomacy." *International Herald Tribune*.

Rev. of Michelangelo Exhibition at Palitz Gallery, "Michelangelo: The Man and the Myth." *New Yorker*: 24.

Montaner, Carlos Alberto. "Barack Obama Can Crack Cuba

Open—but Only after Fidel Castro Dies." nydailynews .com.

"Mr. Kaine's Budget." *Washington Post*.

Myers, Steven Lee, and Cooper, Helene. "Gaza Crisis Is Another Challenge for Obama, Who Defers to Bush for Now." *New York Times*.

"My 3 Dead Kids Are the Reason." *Trentonian*.

Newman, Tony. Letter to Editor. *USA Today*.

Nordlinger, Jay. "Music: Centenarian of the Hour." *National Review*: 47–48.

Nussbaum, Emily. "No 40: Because Our Pregnant Women Kick Ass." *New York*: 62.

O'Gorman, Joe. "Gang Green Goes Down." *Trentonian*.

———. "In Battle of QBs, Pennington Has Last Laugh." *Trentonian*.

O'Harrow, Robert, Jr., and Brady Dennis. "The Beautiful Machine." *Washington Post*.

O'Leary, Kevin. "The Ring Is Off!" *Us*: 42–47.

Oren, Michael B., and Yossi Klein Helevi. "Palestinians Need Israel to Win." *Wall Street Journal*.

"Orszag's Health Warning." Editorial. *Wall Street Journal*.

Osborn, Andrew. "As If Things Weren't Bad Enough, Russian Professor Predicts End of U.S." *Wall Street Journal*.

O'Sullivan, John. "The Politics of Everyman." *National Review*: 18–20.

Oxfeld, Jesse. "No 36: Because Even Our Hot Dogs Are Political. *New York*: 59.

Paley, Amit R. "For Kurdish Girls, a Painful Ancient Ritual." *Washington Post.*

Peaple, Andrew. "Deregulating Insurance, China-Style." *Wall Street Journal.*

Pearson, Erica, Kerry Burke, and Alison Gendar. "Police Nab Cop-Impersonating, Home-Invading Grinches." nydaily news.com.

Perry, Tony. "Navy, Environmental Groups, Settle Suit." *Washington Post.*

Petrecca, Laura. "Which Ads Rose Above Bad Times in '08?" *USA Today.*

Picow, Maurice. Letter to Editor. "A Threat to Jordan." *International Herald Tribune.*

Pinckney, Darryl. "The Book of Lists: Susan Sontag's Early Journals." Rev. of *Reborn: Journals and Notebooks, 1947– 1963. New Yorker*: 104–8.

Polansek, Tom. "Black Sea Region Wheat Exports Surge." *Wall Street Journal.*

Pressler, Jessica. "No 16: . . . But Other Times They Do." *New York*: 45.

Prothero, Stephen. "A Look Back, a Step Forward." *USA Today.*

Raghavan, Sudarsan, and Islam Abdel Kareem. "Food and Medical Supplies Grow Scarce on Besieged Gaza Strip." *Washington Post.*

Raisfeld, Robin, and Rob Patronite. "Pub Grub with Aplomb." *New York*: 84–85.

"Reasons to Love New York, 2008." *New York*: 5.

Reich, Holly. "Clean Air Buses in the City: Eco-Friendly Hybrid and Natural Gas Vehicles Make Up Alot of Fleet." ny dailynews.com.

Rich, Motoko, and Joseph Berger. "False Memoir of Holocaust Is Canceled by Publisher." *New York Times*.

Rev. of Richard Avedon exhibition at PaceWildenstein. *New Yorker*: 24.

Ritter, Malcolm. "Brain May Contribute to Hearing Loss with Age." seattlepi.com.

Robinson, Craig. "B-Ball with Barack." *Time*: 76.

Rosenbaum, Thane. "The War on Terror Has Not Gone Away." *Wall Street Journal*.

Rosenberg, Anita K. "Acrophobia: Soar Subject, New Perspective." *Washington Post*.

Ross, Alex. "Critic's Notebook: Daniel and Noah." *New Yorker*: 18.

Rowling, Megan. "Agriculture Experts Urge More Aid for Women Who Farm." *International Herald Tribune*.

Rucker, Philip. "Obama's Tax Cuts Likely Soon: Senior Advisor Says Middle Class Needs 'Some Relief Now.'" *Washington Post*.

St. George, Donna, and Petula Dvorak. "Child Neglect Cases Multiply as Economic Woes Spread." *Washington Post*.

Sandys, Toni L. "Having to Put a Senior Season on Hold." *Washington Post*.

Saul, Michael. "Caroline Kennedy No Whiz with Words." ny dailynews.com.

"Savvy Shoppers Eschewed Gift Cards." *USA Today*.

Schjeldahl, Peter. "Unpretty Pictures: A Marlene Dumas Retrospective." *New Yorker*: 112–13.

Schmid, Joseph. "For Small Champagne Houses, a Very Good Year." *International Herald Tribune*.

Schone, Mark. "Often Critical of Hamas, Obama Hedges His Bets." suntimes.com.

Sengupta, Somini. "No Easy Indian Response to Pakistan's Troop Shift." *New York Times*.

Shales, Tom. "'Decider': Eight Years of Dubious Reasoning." *Washington Post*.

Shapira, Ian. "Get-Rich Offers Swell on Facebook." *Washington Post*.

Shell, Adam. "Will '09 Be OK? Watch January." *USA Today*.

Silverman, Erica, Matthew Kalman, and Helen Kennedy. "Israel Strikes Gaza in 2nd Day of Attacks, Troops Mass at Palestinian Border." nydailynews.com.

Slater, Joanna. "Weaker Dollar Worries Japan, Germany." *Wall Street Journal*.

Smith, Kevin M. "Rick Warren Is an Unfortunate Choice." latimes.com.

Smith, R. Jeffrey. "Under Bush, OSHA Mired in Inaction." *Washington Post*.

"Spaniards in Huge Rally Emphasize the Family." *International Herald Tribune*.

Spencer, John. "Ford Fusion Hybrid Is a Real Gas Sipper." Comment. latimes.com.

"Sportsline." "Johnson Ready for Fresh Start in 2009." *USA Today*.

starburd [pseud.]. latimes.com.

Stein, Rob. "Premarital Abstinence Pledges Ineffective, Study Finds." *Washington Post*.

Steinberg, Neil. "Israel's Had Enough." suntimes.com.

Steveack2004 [pseud.]. "Voice of the People for December 29, 2008." nydailynews.com.

Steyn, Mark. "Happy Warrior." *National Review*: 52.

———. "Vision, Honor, Action: The Right Man Was in the White House on September 11." *National Review*: 29–31.

Straziuso, Jason, and Amir Shah. "Explosives-Laden SUV Kills 14 Afghan Schoolchildren." *Washington Post*.

"Study: Obesity Surgery Reverses Diabetes in Teens." *Trentonian*.

Sudarsky, Noah Marcel. "Art: The Matchmaker Vik Muniz on Guest-Curating His MOMA Show." *New York*: 98.

Surowiecki, James. "The Financial Page: News You Can Lose." *New Yorker*: 48.

Tavernise, Sabrina. "Tajiks Bleed in a Xenophobic Russia." *International Herald Tribune*.

Taylor, Phil. "Getting Ahead by Staying in Place." *Sports Illustrated*: 88.

Thomsen, Ian. "Inside the NBA: Help Wanted." *Sports Illustrated*: 82.

"Time to Break Out the Big Guns." *USA Today*.

Twain, Mark [Samuel Clemens]. "The Privilege of the Grave." *New Yorker*: 50–51.

"2008 Memories: Infamous Moments from the Meltdown." latimes.com.

"2008: The Year in Review." *Trentonian*.

Vinciguerra, Thomas. "Parting Gift from 2008: An Extra Second." *International Herald Tribune*.

"The Week." *National Review*: 4–16.

Weisbrod, Les. "Focus on Medical Mistakes." *USA Today*.

"Wet, Wind-Whipped Midwest Still on Alert." *USA Today*.

Williams, Stephen. "It's the Laptop, by a Nose." nytimes.com.

Winston, Clifford. "'Stimulus' Doesn't Have to Mean Pork." *Wall Street Journal*.

Wiseman, Paul. "Boom in Australia Goes Bust in Record Time as Global Slowdown Hits." *USA Today*.

Wolf, Richard, and Andrea Stone. "Amid Gaza Violence, a New Task for Obama." *USA Today*.

Wong, Edward. "Romance, and Slow Recovery, in a Quake-Devastated Chinese County." *New York Times*.

"World Watch: Afghanistan. Suicide Bomber Kills 14 Grade-School Students." *Wall Street Journal*.

Worthen, Ben, and Jessica E. Vascellaro. "Discounts Not Enough to Revive Online Retail Sales." *Wall Street Journal*.

Yap, Diana Michèle. "A Failure of Nerve, and a New Beginning." *New York Times*.

Yeshua [pseud.]. Comment. nydailynews.com.

Index

KIRKWOOD

5/11/2015

428.2 CIOFFI
Cioffi, Frank L.,
One day in the life of the English language :
R2002730683 KIRKWD

Atlanta-Fulton Public Library